Appeal to Pity

SUNY Series in Logic and Language
John T. Kearns, Editor

Appeal to Pity

Argumentum ad Misericordiam

Douglas Walton

State University of New York Press

Published by
State University of New York Press, Albany

© 1997 State University of New York

For information, address State University of New York
Press, State University Plaza, Albany, N.Y., 12246

Production by E. Moore
Marketing by Fran Keneston

Library of Congress Cataloging-in-Publication Data

Walton, Douglas N.
    Appeal to pity = Argumentum ad misericordiam / Douglas Walton.
        p.   cm. — (SUNY series in logic and language)
    Includes bibliographical references and index.
    ISBN 0-7914-3461-3 (hard : alk. paper). — ISBN 0-7914-3462-1
(pbk. : alk. paper)
    1. Appeal to pity (Logical fallacy) I. Title. II. Series.
BC175.W32 1997
160—dc20   96-35821
                                                                  CIP

10 9 8 7 6 5 4 3 2 1

For Karen, with love.

Contents

Acknowledgments

I would like to thank the Social Sciences and Humanities Research Council of Canada for support in the form of a research grant, and to specifically thank the following individuals for their help:

- Amy Merrett, for word processing the text and figures of the manuscript.
- Victor Wilkes, for helping to collect materials that were used in the research.
- Alan Brinton and Erik Krabbe, for discussions that provoked thoughts and suggested some of the subjects and ideas pursued in the book.

I would like to thank the editors of *Argumentation* for permission to reprint (in slightly altered form) my paper, "Appeal to Pity: A Case Study of the *Argumentum ad Misericordiam*," *Argumentation*, 9, 1995, 769–84. As a Research Associate at the University of Western Australia in 1996, I had access to facilities that were necessary for the final stages of producing this book. I would like to thank Michael Levine and the other members of the philosophy department at UWA for their support and encouragement during my stay in Perth.

Introduction

The *argumentum ad misericordiam,* or (literally) argument to pity, usually translated as "appeal to pity," has, for the last century or so, been treated by the logic textbooks as a fallacy. However, this rather one-sided view of arguments based on appeal to pity has recently been challenged in the literature on argumentation. Here it has been contended that such arguments can, in some instances, be reasonably used to shift a burden of proof in a balance-of-considerations situation (Walton, *Place Emot.* 1992). There are some cases, like charitable appeals—for example, requests for funding for medical research to aid or relieve the distress of afflicted children—where the *ad misericordiam* type of argument is used in a reasonable, or at least nonfallacious way. The problem then is to set out criteria that can be used to help a rational critic judge when an *ad misericordiam* argument is reasonable or not, in a given case.

There is no shortage of everyday case study materials on this type of argument. In fact, it would be difficult not to encounter familiar cases that appear everywhere in modern life that illustrate very graphically how powerful the *ad misericordiam* is as a tool of persuasion. Especially in the 1990s, people accept appeals to pity in all kinds of cases—in trials, immigration hearings, parole cases, charitable appeals for aid, public relation campaigns on behalf of causes like animal rights, and all sorts of other causes—and act to comply with the requests made on the basis of these appeals. As a professor for twenty-five years, I have been told many tearful tales of pitiable circumstances in pleas to grant extensions for assignment deadlines. In one of the more dramatic pleas of this kind, the student claimed that he would be deported and shot if he did not get a passing grade.

A number of televised high-profile trials in the 1990s have illustrated how important the appeal to pity has become, as part of the trial process. The focus of a trial seems to be shifting away from considering the evidence on the issue of whether the defendant committed the crime, and more on to excuses that, in televised trials, take the form of emotional performances by the defendant to gain the sympathy of the television audience. Leo (1994, p. 17) calls *the culture of feelings* the attitude that feeling is more important than thinking. He cites the case of the televised Menendez trial, where two brothers were tried for killing their parents with shotguns. The brothers were emotionally portrayed by their attorney, Leslie Abramson, as victims of child abuse. Although the evidence was overwhelming that the brothers had murdered their parents, the successful use of the appeal to pity by Abramson, enacted dramatically and widely televised, suggested that even parricide may now be excusable. The trial ended in 1994 in a hung jury, but eventually, two years later, the brothers were convicted of murder.

The problem with *ad misericordiam* arguments exploiting the cult of feelings (as shown in this book) is that attention is focused on the short-term consequences. The satisfaction of responding with a warm emotional glow to an appeal to pity replaces harder practical questions of whether one's action might, in a long-term perspective, be doing more harm than good. The warmness of the response in responding to an *ad misericordiam* plea seems to be the end of the issue, as far as the cult of feelings is concerned. But the real issue, in many cases, should be whether the action taken really accomplishes the goal of helping someone, and whether the appeal to feelings fits into the broader picture of the evidence in a given case. Critical questions may need to be asked, if the *argumentum ad misericordiam* is to be evaluated in a balanced, comprehensive and rational way. *Appeal to Pity* offers criteria for judging particular cases of *ad misericordiam* arguments by first identifying the structure of the argument, and second placing that structure in a context of use, so that it can be evaluated in relation to the evidence supplied by the context. The book shows how and why in some cases an *ad misericordiam* can be used in a reasonable way to make a point. In other cases the *ad misericordiam* argument should be critically questioned as falling short, or even rejected as fallacious.

This book reveals the underlying structure of how appeals to pity, compassion, sympathy, and mercy can correctly be used as species of practical reasoning in a type of argumentation called *argu-*

ment from need for help. The book then develops a method for helping the reader to distinguish, on a case by case basis, between the fallacious and nonfallacious uses of this argument.

The earliest known origins of the *argumentum ad misericordiam* as a logical fallacy are traced to periodicals in the nineteenth century. From there it is traced to its appearance as a standard fallacy in early twentieth-century logic textbooks. However, recognition of appeal to pity as an important and powerful type of argumentation is traced back to ancient times. Several interesting cases from Greek and Roman trials are related where appeal to pity was used with powerful effect on juries. The book goes on to outline the views of some of the leading schools of thought in ancient times on the merits and demerits of this type of argument, to outline the Christian view of appeal to pity as expressed by the leading theologians in medieval times, and to survey early modern views of sympathy as an ethical concept that are of interest.

The main theme of the book is to use a case study method to examine examples of uses of appeals to pity and compassion in real arguments, to classify, analyze, and evaluate the types of arguments used in these appeals. One case studied is that of the Jerry Lewis Telethon for Muscular Dystrophy. It was much criticized by activists for the rights of the disabled on the grounds that Lewis exploited pity by televising pathetic images of the "tortured bodies" of disabled children to raise money. Another case concerned a story that babies were being pulled from incubators by Iraqi troops occupying Kuwait. This was tearfully told by a young Kuwaiti woman in a moving appeal before a U.S. senate subcommittee that was widely broadcast by the U.S. media. This appeal was instrumental in the senate deliberations that led to the invasion of Kuwait by U.S. forces. Later, it was found that the young woman was the daughter of the Kuwaiti ambassador, and that her appeal was part of a public relations campaign financed mostly by the Kuwaiti government. In another case, pictures of cuddly baby seals being attacked with baseball bats by seal hunters were featured by animal rights activists as part of a highly successful public relations campaign to get the Canadian government to ban seal hunting.

Before going on to study these more substantial cases, the book begins with a survey of how the appeal to pity has been standardly treated by the logic textbooks. This survey is the necessary point of departure for any study of the appeal to pity as a type of argument.

The Textbook Treatment

The *argumentum ad misericordiam*, or appeal to pity, is standardly listed as one of the fallacies in twentieth-century logic textbooks.[1] The following two textbook accounts of the fallacy, each of which covers about half a page, are highly typical of the entries one finds.[2]

Kaminsky and Kaminsky (1974, p. 46) define the appeal to pity (*argumentum ad misericordiam*) as the type of argument that "makes an unwarranted appeal to obtain sympathy for the cause or demands of an individual or a group." They give the following example (p. 46):

> *Case* 1.1: We must give the engineering position to Henry Jones. After all, he has six children to feed and clothe.

Conceding that sometimes the appeal to pity is viewed as warranted on humanitarian grounds, Kaminsky and Kaminsky add that logical considerations in this case suggest that if Mr. Jones is not qualified, and the job requires a qualified engineer, then Jones should not get the job. Hence the appeal to pity in case 1.1 is fallacious.

Crossley and Wilson (1979, p. 40) characterize appeal to pity, or "playing on your feelings" as "a technique for bypassing one's thinking abilities." They give the example of the following speech, given by a senior citizen to a group of city councilors (p. 40):

> *Case* 1.2: How could anyone consider the unreasonable increase
> in the price of senior citizen bus passes from $10 to
> $20 a year? Are you not aware, my dear friends, that

you are deliberately penalizing that small and helpless group of older people who built this city of ours?
There are many of us who scrimp and save on our
meager incomes just to make ends meet—and you
want to impose another heavy burden on us at a time
when we can hardly afford to keep ourselves alive. I
plead with you to reconsider this proposal. If you
won't do it for me, then do it for an older loved one
who needs your support.

The fallacy in this case, as Crossley and Wilson see it (p. 40), is the
speaker's use of "highly emotive terminology" to "play upon the
hearer's feelings" to gain acceptance of his conclusion. They warn
the reader to try to avoid "irrelevant considerations and illegitimate
appeals" (p. 40).

In this case, it is not so clear that the appeal to pity is alto-
gether irrelevant or illegitimate. But even though much depends on
the context, it is not too hard to see what Crossley and Wilson are
driving at.

1. IRRELEVANCE

In the modern textbooks where *ad misericordiam* is recognized
as a distinctive fallacy in its own right under that name, in fact the
leading characterization of it as a fallacy is as a failure of relevance.
Relevance is not defined in these textbooks, in any general way. But
most of them take their cue from Aristotle's fallacy of *ignoratio
elenchi*, defining the fallacy as a failure to prove the conclusion an
arguer is supposed to prove.[3] Although Aristotle did not include
appeal to pity in his list of fallacies—see chapter 2, he did define
the fallacy of *ignoratio elenchi*, in *On Sophistical Refutations*, as
the failure to refute the proposition you are supposed to refute, in a
dialectical exchange.[4] The problem is that this is broad failure that
could include all kinds of fallacies. But at least it gives us a specific
clue why *argumenta ad misericordiam* might be thought generally
to be fallacious.

Joseph (1916, pp. 590–91) classifies the *argumentum ad misericordiam* under the heading of *ignoratio elenchi* or irrelevance—
"proving another conclusion than what is wanted." Thus Joseph
sees the *argumentum ad misericordiam* as an inherently fallacious
type of argument. He illustrates it using the classic case of Socrates'
refusal to use this kind of argument, as described in the *Apology*:

Subterfuges of that kind are however so frequent a resource of the orator, that it is hardly necessary to illustrate them. Every reader of Plato's *Apology* will remember how Socrates refused to appeal to his judges with tears and entreaties, or to bring his wife and children into court to excite their commiseration; for his part was to persuade them, if he could do it, of his innocence and not of his sufferings.

Such appeals as Socrates declined to make are sometimes called *argumenta ad misericordiam*, arguments addressed to show that a man is unfortunate and deserves pity, when it ought to be shown that he is innocent, or has the law on his side.

Subsequent textbooks that also cite the case of Socrates' refusal to appeal to pity in the *Apology* include Copi (1961, p. 59), Carney and Scheer (1964, p. 24), and Frye and Levi (1969, p. 221). I will comment further on this passage from the *Apology* in the historical considerations on appeal to pity in chapter 2.

Joseph and a later text, Castell (1935), share a similar account of *ad misericordiam* as a fallacy of irrelevance. But there are some differences in how they define the *argumentum ad misericordiam*. Both define it as appeal to pity, but Castell also describes it as an appeal to sympathy.

Castell (1935, p. 31) defines the *argumentum ad misericordiam* as an inherently fallacious type of argument where "appeal is made to one's sense of pity." Castell (p. 31) sees the fallacy as a failure of relevance—more specifically, a failure to produce relevant evidence, accompanied by an attempt to cover up the failure rousing (irrelevant) feelings of pity:

> To show that some proposition should be believed, one should produce evidence in the light of which the said proposition is more probable than any other one. Such a procedure may be inconvenient, difficult, or impossible. Under such circumstances attention may be drawn to some otherwise irrelevant facts which rouse one's feelings of pity in such a manner that one is prepared to agree to the truth of the proposition being argued for, despite the lack of relevant evidence. One is thereby convinced by an Argumentum ad Misericordiam.

Interestingly, Castell adds (p. 31) that a lawyer who "convinces a jury that the accused is not guilty, by playing on their sympathy" also commits the *ad misericordiam* fallacy. This wording seems to suggest that in the *ad misericordiam* argument, there may be little or no difference between pity and sympathy, or at any rate, that one can be used as a fallacious irrelevant appeal, just as much as the other, an assumption we will later question.

Little, Wilson, and Moore (1955, p. 38) define the *argumentum ad misericordiam* in such a way that it can be either an appeal to pity or an appeal to sympathy:

> If a person uses an appeal to sympathy or pity instead of pre-senting relevant evidence, he is committing the fallacy called *argumentum ad misericordiam*. This kind of argument is fre-quently heard in courtroom trials, when an attorney for the defense may ignore the relevant facts and try to get favorable consideration for his client by playing upon the sympathy of the jury.

Although they explicitly state that sympathy is "a noble human emotion" that should "motivate many of our actions," they see the fallacy of *ad misericordiam* as occurring where appeal to sympathy replaces or obscures "relevant facts" (p. 39).

This account too appeals to the concept of relevance as an explanation of why the *argumentum ad misericordiam* is fallacious. But it also brings in an additional dimension of suppressing or ignor-ing facts, suggesting appeal to sympathy is not "factual evidence."

Another textbook defines *ad misericordiam* as appeal to com-passion or sympathy, instead of pity. Toulmin, Rieke, and Janik (1979, p. 175) cite a fallacy called *appeal to compassion*, which they see as "not necessarily fallacious," but is so in cases where "human sympathy" is used or played on, to obscure an issue. They give the following example (p. 175). The idea of obscuring an issue suggests irrelevance as being the basis of the fallacy:

> *Case* 1.3: Defense lawyers in criminal cases will often resort to this tactic, if not to convince the jury that their clients are innocent, at least to lessen their sen-tences. Thus, in defending a young car thief, a lawyer may underline the facts that his client came from a home where he was insecure and continually lonely; that his parents abused him, and he ran away from home to avoid this; that he fell prey to the influence of hardened criminals, who were the first persons to

treat him with any appearance of kindness—and ask the court to take all these facts into consideration before pronouncing too heavy a sentence.

This case is an interesting one, rightly suggesting that appeals to sympathy are widely used in courtroom argumentation. But one aspect of it is puzzling.

While sympathy, compassion, and mercy may be appropriate at the sentencing stage of a trial, where leniency may be argued for explicitly and appropriately, the same kind of plea for compassion might be quite inappropriate at the earlier stage, where evidence is supposed to be used to decide whether the charge is justified.

One question about the *ad misericordiam* is whether it is only a fallacy because of a failure of relevance, or whether there could be other explanations for its being a fallacy as well. Frye and Levi (1969, p. 221) opt for the former account of the fallacy. They describe appeal to pity (*argumentum ad misericordiam*) as an "address to pity or sympathy." They write, "This case of irrelevant conclusion is distinctive merely for naming a specific emotion" (p. 221). According to this account of the *ad misericordiam*, it is only fallacious because of irrelevance, and comes entirely under the wider fallacy of irrelevant conclusion, except that a specific emotion (pity or sympathy) is aroused in order to avoid discussing the merits of a case.

2. APPEAL TO PITY AS INHERENTLY FALLACIOUS

Other textbooks portray appeal to pity as fallacious on the grounds that such an appeal to mere emotion is a failure to give (actual, factual) evidence. Some of these textbooks are pretty hard on the *ad misericordiam* argument, stating or implying that appeals to pity (compassion, sympathy, and the like) are inherently fallacious. The idea seems to be that emotions or feelings are worthless as evidence. This approach suggests a tendency, often prominent in Western thought since Plato, to condemn the emotions as inherently misleading or untrustworthy.[5] The general approach presumed here is one of driving a sharp wedge between emotion and reason, as reminiscent of the Stoic view of emotions found, for example, in Seneca (see chapter 2).

Several textbooks define the *argumentum ad misericordiam* in a way that presumes that argumentation of this type is inherently fallacious. This approach seems to obviate the need to even give any explanation or justification for evaluating specific instances of the *ad misericordiam* as fallacious.

Copi (1961, p. 58) defines the *argumentum ad misericordiam*, which he translates into English as "appeal to pity," as "the fallacy committed when pity is appealed to for the sake of getting a conclusion accepted." This way of defining it makes the *argumentum ad misericordiam* inherently fallacious as a type of argument. For so defined, every argument that appeals to pity "for the sake of getting a conclusion accepted" is fallacious.

Another textbook that treats the *ad misericordiam* as a fallacy of relevance is Engel (1982). According to Engel (p. 181) the *fallacy of appeal to pity* exploits the emotion of sympathy "to win people over" by "playing on their emotions." Engel (p. 181) explains the Latin name of the fallacy, *argumentum ad misericordiam*, as meaning "literally, an argument addressed to our sense of mercy." The reason such arguments are fallacious, according to Engel (p. 182) is that "however moving they may be, they may be irrelevant to the issues, in which case they should carry no weight with us." Engel's account is a good example of a textbook treatment that cites only irrelevance as the factor that makes an appeal to pity fallacious. That is, he does not consider the possibility that an appeal to pity could be relevant, but still be fallacious, in some cases. Neither does Engel include or consider cases where an appeal to pity is nonfallacious.

Clark and Welsh (1962, p. 141) also describe the *argumentum ad misericordiam* as a fallacious appeal to pity that appeals to emotion instead of offering proof of a thesis:

> The *argumentum ad misericordiam* (roughly: appeal to pity) appeals to the emotions of the hearer instead of offering proof of its thesis. A lawyer, for example, would commit this fallacy were he to show that a man is unfortunate or had bad luck or deserves sympathy when he should be showing that he was innocent or illegally charged; or if he shows that a man had served his country well when what is needed is proof that he is innocent of tax evasion.

The example given seems to evoke irrelevance as the basis of the failure of the argument. But it also presumes or suggests that any appeal to emotions, like pity, is a failure to offer proof of a thesis.

Hurley (1991, p. 112) is an instance of a recent textbook that still continues to characterize the *argumentum ad misericordiam* or appeal to pity as being a fallacy, implying that it is always wrong to appeal to pity in an argument:

> The fallacy of appeal to pity occurs whenever an arguer poses a conclusion and then attempts to evoke pity from the reader or listener in an effort to get him or her to accept the conclusion.

However, a difference between Hurley's treatment and that of some other textbooks that also treat appeals to pity as inherently fallacious is the following point. These other textbooks define the type of argument equated with *ad misericordiam* or appeal to pity as being irrelevant appeals, attempts to cover up for lack of relevant evidence, and the like. Hurley does not build the inherent fallaciousness into the definition of the type of argument categorized by the name *argumentum ad misericordiam*. Instead he defines it as evocation of pity to try to get a respondent to accept a conclusion, presuming that this type of tactic in argumentation is generally or inherently fallacious.

The Clark and Welsh definition leaves more room for the appeal to pity to be used nonfallaciously. It seems to leave open the possibility that an appeal to pity might be all right logically if it appealed to emotion, but did not do so in place of offering proof for a thesis. According to the Hurley definition, however, any evoking of pity to get a listener to accept a conclusion is fallacious.

Soccio and Barry (1992, p. 134) define *the fallacy of pity* as "an argument that arouses compassion to advance a conclusion." Like the accounts of Copi and Hurley, this definition of the *ad misericordiam* is dismissive, in the sense that it builds a blanket rejection of appeals to pity into the definition itself as fallacious. It obviates the need to deal with appeals to pity on a case by case basis, or to consider the possibility that such appeals could be legitimate evidence, or good reasons for drawing a conclusion, or choosing a course of action, in some instances.

3. NOT ALL CASES FALLACIOUS?

Many of the more recent textbooks have become more sophisticated and less dismissive in their treatments of the *ad misericordiam*. In varying degrees, they have become more receptive to leaving open the possibility that *ad misericordiam* arguments could be nonfallacious in some cases.

Harrison (1992, p. 493) defines the appeal to pity as a fallacy that "occurs to the extent that, instead of giving evidence to support a conclusion, an arguer appeals merely to the pity of the receiver to accept the conclusion." The idea is that the fallacy occurs because there has been an appeal to pity made in place of giving evidence to support a conclusion. This suggests that an appeal to pity could never, in itself, be a kind of evidence, even of a weak sort, to support a conclusion—a dismissive kind of approach.

However, Harrison does not claim that all appeals to pity are fallacious, and cites a case (p. 494) where an appeal to pity is put forward as an excuse on reasonable grounds, as part of a moral argument.

When, then, are such appeals fallacious? Harrison judges them so (p. 493) when they are irrelevant to support the conclusion that is supposed to be at issue in a case. Thus Harrison's treatment combines irrelevance with lack of evidence as a basis for judging *ad misericordiam* arguments fallacious, but in a way that leaves some room for nonfallacious cases.

Damer (1980, p. 87) defines the fallacy of appeal to pity as "attempting to persuade others of one's point of view by appealing to their sympathy instead of presenting evidence." This seems to imply that the type of argument described is inherently fallacious. However, Damer explicitly denies this, claiming that "there may be some situations" where appeal to pity is relevant (p. 87), especially in moral reasoning (p. 88). In such cases, however, Damer contends that the arguer who appeals to pity should make clear why the appeal is relevant.

This seems to be a burden of proof kind of approach. That is, Damer appears to suggest that there should be a general presumption in place that appeals to pity are, or tend to be, irrelevant in argumentation. However, this rule or warning is not absolutely true, without qualifications. Hence if an appeal to pity is made in a given case, arguers who made it should be prepared to answer the objection that it is irrelevant, and should even answer this objection in advance, at the same time they put the appeal to pity forward as an argument.

Some of the more recent textbooks distinguish between appeal to pity and appeal to mercy, as subspecies of the *argumentum ad misericordiam*. Moreover, some of these texts do not make the claim that all such *ad misericordiam* arguments are fallacious. Barker (1965, p. 193) claims that a distinction can be made between the fallacious and nonfallacious uses of the *ad misericordiam* by citing several contrasting types of cases:

> An appeal to pity or a plea for mercy is not a fallacy unless it is claimed to be a logical reason for believing some conclusion.

The *ad misericordiam* fallacy is committed by the employee who argues "Please, Boss, you can see that my work is worth higher wages; I've got many hungry wives and children to feed." And a criminal would be committing this fallacy if he tried to offer evidence about his unhappy childhood as a reason why the court should believe that he did not perform the killings of which he stands accused. (However, it would be no fallacy for him to offer evidence about his unhappy childhood in trying to show that he deserves to be treated leniently.)

This approach is a big step forward from so many of the earlier texts, where any appeal to pity or *argumentum ad misericordiam* is described or even defined as being inherently fallacious.

Vernon and Nissen (1968, p. 150) take this a step further by redescribing and qualifying the fallacy as "illicit appeal to pity," implying that appealing to pity can be nonfallacious in some instances. They give two contrasting cases to support this claim (p. 150).

This long-familiar fallacy is sometimes referred to by a Latin name, *ad misericordiam*, or "(appeal) to pity." The name we have used is less misleading, however, since not all appeals to pity in an argument are illicit, or irrelevant. In the course of an argument for euthanasia, for example, it would not be irrelevant to call attention to the suffering of a person in the last stages of an incurable cancer. However, such appeals are often used irrelevantly. An example is the student who tries to persuade his instructor to change his grade from a *D* to a *C* on the ground that, if he receives a *D*, his parents will cut off his allowance, or he will be ineligible for a fraternity membership. Such considerations, however moving, are of course quite irrelevant to the student's grade, which is nothing more or less than an indication of academic performance.

Here a fallacious case (see section five below) is contrasted with the case of an argument for euthanasia, where appeal to pity (or compassion, or sympathy, even more plausibly) could be relevant. It is not hard to imagine that there must be some cases of arguments where appeals to feelings like sympathy could be quite appropriate, and relevant to the conversation or issue being discussed.

Yanal (1988, p. 392) has a generic category of fallacies called *appeals to feeling*, which he sees as generally being bad arguments.

However, he does claim that some appeals to feeling are nonfallacious. The example he gives is a charitable appeal that would be classified as an *ad misericordiam* by most textbooks that include this fallacy:

> There are cases in which some sort of appeal to feeling produces an acceptable argument: *There are thousands of undernourished, diseased babies in Ethiopia. So it is urgent that you donate to the Red Cross.* This is a kind of appeal to feeling. It summons up images of starving, dying children, hence feelings of pity and (the arguer hopes) the desire to help them. It makes the listener disposed to accept the conclusion. Yet the argument does provide a reason to donate to the Red Cross: There are thousands of undernourished, diseased babies in Ethiopia. In other words, this argument is not a fallacious appeal to feeling, even though feelings may well be aroused in the course of considering the argument.

This makes a good deal of sense, and as we will see below (section seven), a consideration of charitable appeals does not take long to establish that such appeals to feelings can be a legitimate and appropriate part of the sequence of argumentation.

Of course, once this possibility is admitted, the job of evaluating specific cases of the *ad misericordiam* becomes nontrivial. One text, in particular, acknowledges the problem.

Munson (1976, p. 269) stresses that identifying the *ad misericordiam* can be difficult in some cases. He presents an example (p. 269) to show that some appeals to sympathy can be relevant arguments:

> The *ad misericordiam* is a particularly tough fallacy to identify in some cases. Not all mention of factors which appeal to our sympathies is irrelevant, and the trick is to distinguish legitimate appeals from spurious ones. Suppose someone argued, for example, that our system of welfare payments ought to be changed because it produces much misery and suffering. As evidence, he describes cases in which people on welfare are harshly and unfairly treated. The situation he presents is a moving one, but is he guilty of using an *ad misericordiam* argument? Not necessarily. One of the standards by which social policies and institutions are judged is the extent to which they alleviate human suffering. Accordingly, the fact that people are

made miserable by a system not only elicits our pity; it counts as a reason for altering the system. It would be quite relevant in an argument demanding a change in welfare policies and practices.

Even a brief consideration of such a case suggests that appealing to pity could be a relevant argument in some cases.

And once you start to consider even some of the standard cases given in the logic textbooks to illustrate, in more depth, the *ad misericordiam* fallacy, the idea of this type of argumentation as being inherently fallacious starts to crumble.

This suggests that what we need to do is to survey and examine some of these key cases in greater detail and depth, to try to sort out between the fallacious and nonfallacious aspects of the *argumentum ad misericordiam* in each case. Munson's surprising remark that appeal to pity can be quite relevant as an argument in some cases puts the problem in a new perspective. If we can no longer be dismissive with critically evaluating appeals to pity as arguments, a deeper analysis of them is called for.

4. LEGAL CASES

One of the most plentiful types of cases of *ad misericordiam* cited in the textbooks are the legal cases, where typically the defendant in a murder trial appeals to pity in an emotional way. As we will see in chapter 2, this tactic has been well known and used in the courts since ancient times. The modern textbooks, however, have generally presumed that the *ad misericordiam* argument can be generally categorized as a fallacy in legal argumentation, on the grounds that it is not relevant evidence in a court of law.

Copi (1961, p. 58) gives as an example of the *argumentum ad misericordiam* the address of Clarence Darrow to the jury, in defense of Thomas Kidd, an officer of the Amalgamated Woodworkers Union, who was indicted on a charge of criminal conspiracy:

> *Case* 1.4: I appeal to you not for Thomas Kidd, but I appeal to you for the long line—the long, long line reaching back through the ages and forward to the years to come—the long line of despoiled and downtrodden people of the earth. I appeal to you for those men who rise in the morning before daylight comes and who go home at night when the light has faded from

the sky and give their life, their strength, their toil to make others rich and great. I appeal to you in the name of those women who are offering up their lives to this modern god of gold, and I appeal to you in the name of those little children, the living and the unborn.

This argument could be described as a kind of dual appeal to pity and sympathy. To the audience of those who see themselves as being in the downtrodden working person class cited, the appeal would be to sympathy with their fellow workers. To those who do not perceive themselves as being in this class, the appeal would be pity for these poor souls. Either way, the argument finds a receptive audience whose feelings it would appeal to compellingly.

This same case was previously cited by Werkmeister (1948, p. 59), who described the *argumentum ad misericordiam* as an appeal to both emotions of pity and sympathy.

Another example (Little, Wilson, and Moore, 1955, p. 39) suggests consequences being appealed to as an instance of the *ad misericordiam* fallacy:

> *Case* 1.5: The attorney for the defense may, for example, bring into the courtroom the poorly-dressed wife of the defendant, surrounded by pathetic children in rags, and thus say in effect to the jury, "If you send my client to the electric chair, you make a widow of this poor woman and orphans of these innocent children. What have they done to deserve this?"

This very same type of case is also cited by Blyth (1957, p. 37), who describes it as an *argumentum ad misericordiam* because pity is "substituted for relevant evidence." Because of the common use of argument from consequences, this case seems similar to the *ad misericordiam* in the student's plea case. But there is a difference. In this case, the trial is supposed to determine guilt or innocence, and the appeal to pity does not seem relevant to this legal finding, one way or the other. As Blyth puts it, it is not "relevant evidence."

The case cited by Copi is somewhat different. It is more of a flowery appeal using emotional language and a kind of rhetoric of belonging and sympathy. Yet the problem in both cases seems to be one of questionable relevance.

Manicas and Kruger (1968, p. 346) define the *argumentum ad misericordiam* disjunctively as "the appeal to sympathy or pity."

They cite as an example "the appeal that the lawyer uses when he introduces the accused's wife and children." They see such an appeal as irrelevant in one sense, yet relevant in another (p. 346):

> The fact that the accused has a wife and many children, however, is irrelevant to whether or not he is guilty, though it might have a bearing on the punishment to be meted out *if* the relevant facts show that he is guilty.

An argument that is relevant at one stage of a trial may not be relevant at another stage. This suggests that relevance is best seen as contextual—that is, as depending on the context of dialogue or conversation, and in particular, on the stage a dialogue exchange has reached.

The problem indicated here is that appeal to pity could be relevant as an argument, at the appropriate stage of the development of a dialogue exchange. So it should not be dismissed, at least automatically, as fallacious on grounds of irrelevance.

Fearnside (1980) describes the *argumentum ad misericordiam* as an "appeal to pathetic circumstances" or "crybaby" argument. He is careful to indicate that this type of appeal is not always inappropriate in legal argumentation. He cites the difference in a criminal trial, between the stage of determining guilt and the latter stage of sentencing. At the one stage, the appeal to pathetic circumstances might be quite irrelevant, while at the later stage, it could be appropriate:

> *Case* 1.6: Take the criminal prosecution in which conviction will mean great hardship for the accused and his family. The jurors have sworn to make a finding of "guilty" if and only if guilt is shown by evidence beyond reasonable doubt; otherwise they are to find "not guilty." Appeals to pathetic circumstances are not a proper way to influence the jury's determination of guilt, and some of the rules of evidence are framed to limit their use. Since a trial at law is often closer to a dogfight than a search for truth, one may expect to find counsel for the defense busy making appeals to sympathy wherever possible. And the jury, unfortunately and despite all oaths, may well be swayed by these considerations irrelevant to the question "Did the accused do the act charged?"

> Incidentally, where a defendant is found guilty and
> special hardships are involved, these are proper mat-
> ters for the judge to take into account when choosing
> between the alternatives of fine, imprisonment, or
> suspended sentence. The law provides counsel with
> opportunity to bring out mitigating circumstances
> *after* the question of guilt is decided.

This makes the good point that an *ad misericordiam* argument in a
legal type of case could be relevant at one stage of the proceedings,
yet the same appeal could be irrelevant at another stage. If so, the
textbooks seem to be on shaky ground in their tendency to dismiss
ad misericordiam arguments as irrelevant and fallacious generally in
legal argumentation.

One textbook, however (Harrison, 1992, p. 493), seems to take
the line that even after an admission of guilt, a plea for mercy in
sentencing should be judged as a fallacious appeal to pity. Harrison
cites the following case where a lawyer "all but weeping" pleads for
his client:

> *Case* 1.7: My client did in fact murder Carlos Cervera in an
> attempted robbery. And you have justly found him
> guilty of that crime. No matter what you do now,
> Mr. Cervera cannot be returned from the dead. Yet
> my client has young children. Think of your own
> children when you vote on whether to sentence my
> client to be executed or not. Therefore, I beg you
> not to sentence my client to death.

Evaluating the plea for mercy in this case, Harrison (p. 493) comments:

> Touching as this scene might be, merely appealing to the pity of
> the jury is irrelevant to support the conclusion of the defense
> lawyer. Whether the defendant ought to be executed or not is a
> matter of applying the law in a consistent way to a particular
> situation. Of course, in a particular case there might be legiti-
> mate considerations mitigating against imposing the death
> penalty. But merely feeling pity for that individual is not one.

This evaluation seems to go against the general presumption in law
that pleas for clemency or leniency in sentencing are, in many cases,
given some consideration, once the charge has been determined and
the person found guilty. However, Harrison does admit that, in some

cases, mitigating circumstances might be legitimate considerations. Perhaps he does not think that this case is one of these cases. Or perhaps he thinks that "merely feeling pity" should not be the basis of such an appeal. At any rate, there appears to be some uncertainty in the textbooks on when appeal to pity is appropriate or not as an argument in a legal context.

5. THE STUDENT'S PLEA CASE

Castell (1935, p. 31) cites the case of a student's appeal to pity to try to save himself from failure, classifying it as a fallacious *argumentum ad misericordiam*:

> *Case* 1.8: A student who tries to save himself from a failure by reminding his instructor how disastrous such an event would be, is trying an Ad Misericordiam. The unfortunate consequences entailed by any fact do not render it any less a fact. The failure to see this is the essence of the Ad Misericordiam fallacy.

Although that is all Castell has to say about the case, it is interesting to see that he sees the fallacy as utilizing a species of argumentation from consequences. Castell classifies the *ad misericordiam* fallacy as a species of failure of relevance, or failure to present relevant evidence to prove a point at issue. Hence the failure in this case turns on the irrelevance of the unfortunate consequences to the student. As Castell puts it, the consequences do not render the fact of the student's poor showing on his assignments "any less a fact."

What is quite remarkable in Castell's brief treatment of this case of appeal to pity is that he clearly identifies it as a kind of argument from cited consequences. This comes to be of some importance, as shown in section eight below.

Little, Wilson, and Moore (1955, p. 39) state their version of the student's plea case as follows:

> *Case* 1.9: A student's mother says to a faculty member, "How can you fail my boy, Professor Flunkmore? You have always been a good friend of the family, and you know the financial difficulties we are having in sending him to college."

This time the student's mother is doing the pleading. In addition to citing financial difficulties, however, she also tries to appeal to the professor's relationship as a friend of the family. This is perhaps a somewhat different type of appeal from the *ad misericordiam*, and would nowadays be definitely seen as a breach of ethics. On many campuses, there are now rules prohibiting direct personal relationships, like those of family ties, between professors and students.

However, the financial difficulties aspect is definitely a use of appeal to pity. It is similar to Castell's case in that it involves citing of adverse consequences.

An even more detailed account of this type of case is given by Blyth (1957, p. 38). Blyth also sees it clearly as a kind of argument from consequences:

> *Case* 1.10: There is probably no person or group charged with the enforcement of a set of rules or laws that has not been exposed to the pressure of an appeal to pity. Suppose, for example, that a student has violated an explicit rule of an honor system under which examinations are administered. Even though there is no dispute over the facts of the case and the rules clearly prescribe the penalty to be imposed, there will almost certainly be an appeal to pity. The guilty party will point out all the dire consequences of an adverse decision even though the penalty be relatively mild. Suppose, for instance, that the penalty is that of receiving a failure in a course. This would have several consequences. The student would receive no credit for what he had done. He would have to repeat the course or take another. This might involve additional financial strain. He would always have a black mark on his record which might interfere with his future career. Through such an appeal it is hoped that the decision of the honor court may be affected. [p. 38]

Blyth's description of some of the context of this kind of case as an event that occurs in an institutional framework of rules and established procedures is revealing. The professor has the job of grading assignments on the basis of merit of performance, and is supposed to do so in a fair way that does not give special treatment to one and not to others. To assure this, rules are in place that are supposed to apply equally to all students. Blyth (p. 38) articulates the generality of the institutional situation very well, commenting that penalties for violation of a rule or law, by their nature, have bad consequences for the offender. Thus citing these bad consequences after having violated the rule is irrelevant, if the claim is that the rule was not really violated. This is just not the right sort of evidence to back up the claim.

Evidently there is more to this story, however, for as Blyth (p. 39) notes, the law does describe some discretion in determining the severity of a penalty. Thus it may be relevant, in a legal case, for example to recommend or to plead for mercy due to undue hardship.

Here we seem to have a possible distinction between appeal to mercy and appeal to pity. In law, mercy appeals may be appropriate at the later, sentencing stage of the case, even if appeals to pity may be irrelevant during the earlier stages of the trial, where determination of the charge is the issue.

However, in the cases of *ad misericordiam* typically cited in the textbooks, while the excuses given could be classified, at least partly perhaps, as appeals to mercy, they tend to be very weak appeals, made in a context where they would not seem to be appropriate at all.

For example, Rescher (1964, p. 79) defines the *argumentum ad misericordiam* as an argument where the premises make an appeal to pity "in order to secure acceptance" of the conclusion. Rescher sees the fallacy of misuse of this argument as a failure of relevance, illustrated by the following case (p. 79):

> *Case* 1.11: Surely my paper is a better job than that D grade indicates, Mr. Instructor. I'm working to support myself at school and don't have as much time for reference-work as other students do. And my uncle who is contributing to my support will be very upset with me if I don't get at least a C in this course.

These are pretty weak excuses, and would not be appropriate in making a plea for a better grade just as a paper with a D grade is being returned to the student. Certainly, it is not too hard, at least, to imagine circumstances in which such an appeal to pity would be inappropriate as an argument for getting a better grade on a paper.

A different variation on the same case is given by Frye and Levi (1969, p. 221). They describe the *argumentum ad misericordiam* as an address to pity or sympathy using emotions to argue for an irrelevant conclusion:

Case 1.12: It has happened that a student anxious to receive a certain grade in a course enters into a discussion with his instructor, avoiding the question of what grade he has earned, and devoting himself to a sorrowful story of what will happen to him and his parents and the neighbors if he receives a lower grade.

Here the case is described, so that the appeal to pity or sympathy is fallacious, on the grounds that the student avoids the question of what grade he has earned—that is, there is a failure of relevance.

Michalos (1969, p. 370) offers a few other variations on the same theme:

Case 1.13: A student who missed practically every class and did nothing outside of class to master the material notified me that if he failed the course he would probably be drafted into the army. Others have been faced with losing their parents' support, being thrown out of school, losing their girls or their fraternity membership, etc. Even *after* the appeal to *pity* is explained to them, they come up with these howlers! But, of course, the question at issue in such cases is not what happens if the student fails, but whether or not he deserves to fail. The appeals to one's compassion are stimulating but irrelevant.

As anyone knows, who has had much experience in teaching logic, it is remarkable how some students will persist with this kind of appeal to compassion line of argumentation, even after the *ad misericordiam* has been explained to them as a fallacious kind of argument.

Munson's version of the case is this (Munson 1976, p. 268):

Case 1.14: If I don't pass this course, I won't be able to graduate in the Spring, and I don't have enough money to go to summer school. Really, Professor Ruston, you just *have* to give me a C.

This version has the student putting more pressure on the professor by concluding, "you just *have* to give me a C." Like the last three cases, the appeal is pretty weak, and it would not be too difficult to get students in a logic class to accept the classification of these cases as fallacious appeals to pity.

A subtlety of the student's plea type of case is that the appeal to pathetic circumstances may be relevant to the argument. This aspect is noted by Manicas and Kruger (1968, p. 346) in their version:

> *Case* 1.15: [This is] the appeal that students use when they ask to be excused from an assignment or to be given a passing grade because of some personal misfortune. [In this case], the draft plight of the failing student is not relevant to the grade he *earned* in the course—if grades we must have—though his plight is very relevant to the *need* he has for the passing grade.

In one sense, the student's citing of his plight is relevant—it is relevant to his *need* of the passing grade. In the context of a plea for help to attain some need or goal, the appeal to pitiable circumstances does have a kind of practical relevance. Moreover, the plea could be relevant in various other ways. Perhaps the personal misfortune could involve a legitimate excuse—for example, to be given a deferred exam, on the grounds of some medical disability, or legitimate kind of exceptional situation recognized in the university calendar. So failure of relevance, at any rate, does not seem to be the whole story of what makes this type of plea a fallacious argument.

Using a somewhat different type of case, Runkle (1978, p. 292) argues that the *argumentum ad misericordiam* can be relevant and reasonable as one factor to be taken into account:

> *Case* 1.16: There are times, of course, when appeals to sad circumstances are not entirely irrelevant. One may argue against a proposed tuition increase by citing poverty-stricken students who just barely get by at the *present* rate. That there are some students who could not pay more or could do so only at great hardship is relevant to the issue whether tuition should be raised. The appeal to their plight becomes fallacious in the ad misericordiam manner only if it is presented as the *only* relevant fact and in such a way as to generate a lot of emotion. When pity is aroused in order to produce some kind of passionate oversimplification, a fallacy is present.

What this type of case suggests is that an appeal to pity can be relevant in some cases, but it could still be a fallacy, due to other factors. These other factors relate to how the argument is presented. If it is presented as the only relevant argument, this would be a fallacy of oversimplification of the issue. The problem in this kind of case is not one of irrelevance, but one of giving due weight to an argument that is only one factor among many that ought to be taken into account.

It is not hard to see how the student's plea type of case came to be cited by so many of the textbooks. The textbook writers, as teachers in the universities, are constantly confronted with all kinds of subtle, and sometimes ingenious and fantastic variations on this appeal to pity argument. They are forever being put in the position of having to judge these excuses, and make rulings, according to university regulations.

But if you think of it, anyone in any kind of position of authority, who has to make rulings or implement them, will be familiar with this kind of problem of dealing with appeals to pity, sympathy, and compassion. It seems to be a nontrivial type of decision or judgment, and one that can only be made on a case-by-case basis.

6. EXCUSES AS ARGUMENTS

Excuses have had a longstanding place as legitimate appeals, in the right circumstances, in both ethics and the law. Standard lists of legal excuses often include items like the following: ignorance, immaturity, insanity, automatism, duress, necessity, coercion, compulsion, mistake, and accident (H. M. Smith, 1992, p. 345).

In law, excuses have long been recognized as a way of reducing or absolving guilt for an alleged crime. For example, even if a defendant in a murder case admits that he killed the victim, he can claim to be not guilty of murder on grounds of insanity. In effect, insanity, often defined in law as not knowing the nature and quality of the act, functions as a kind of excuse that lessens or absolves responsibility for an action.

The presentation of an excuse as a type of argument, in such a case involves a shifting of the burden of proof. For example, in law when a charge of murder is made, the proponent who brought the charge forward has the burden or proving it (beyond a reasonable doubt). But the burden shifts, if the defendant brings forward an insanity defense. Then the defendant has the burden of proving that he or she was insane, at the time the crime was committed. And this is the way excuses work generally. They provide a defense, often in the form of being a claim to be an exception to a rule, which requires the pleader to make a case by providing some sort of justification or backing of his or her claim to be excused.

In the student's plea type of case, there is some rule regarding the conduct of grading of assignments and courses that will be stated in the academic calendar for the given institution. However, it will be generally recognized that certain classes of exceptions and appeals can be made. A student can appeal a grade if there is some question of not enough marks being given on a test because an answer was overlooked. Or the student can ask to hand an assignment in late, or have a test rescheduled if there is some clearly legitimate excuse for not having written it—for example, a medical reason. However, in some cases, these excuses can be borderline, and a professor has to use discretion and judgment in deciding fairly (to the others in the class), but with due regard to the special circumstances of a case. Some of the would-be excuses one is presented with are quite colorful, and would make interesting cases for discussion of the subject of excuses in ethics.

Such decisions are by no means trivial, however. And it would be implausible to propose that any appeal to pity used as an excuse, in the context of the student's plea type of case, must be a fallacious *ad misericordiam*. It could be that, in some cases, such a pitiable appeal could be judged to be a reasonable excuse, in the circumstances. And as such, one would have to conclude, it seems, that the appeal to pity or *ad misericordiam* argument would not be fallacious.

At least one textbook has put the student's plea type of case into a broader context, indicating that sometimes excuses based on an *ad misericordiam* appeal can be nonfallacious. This suggests that the place of *ad misericordiam* arguments in the context of pleas and excuses of various kinds needs to be much more carefully studied.

Harrison (1992, p. 493) gives a good case to support the contention that not all appeals to pity of the student's plea type are fallacious. In his version of the case, a student approaches an instructor who has a strong policy of "no make-up" on a test, and presents the following argument:

> *Case* 1.17: I missed your test last week because I recently discovered my parents are divorcing. This was when I had to go home to see my brother who was just in a car crash. Otherwise I would have been prepared for your test and would have taken it. I know you have a "no make-up" policy. But I really couldn't help what has happened to my parents and

brother. It is only fair to permit me to make up a
missed quiz. One ought to do what is fair. So, you
ought to allow me to take the test.

In this case, there is an appeal for compassion, but presumably the
instructor should not just dismiss the argument out of hand as a
fallacious appeal to pity. He should consider the plea on its merits,
and consider making an exception to his rule, on the basis of his
judgment about the excuse offered.

As Harrison puts it (p. 493), the instructor should go into the
facts, and find out things, like how seriously the brother was hurt,
and so forth. There is an appeal to pity, but it is part of a larger moral
appeal in which a plea for an excuse is made. Whatever the outcome, the student's argument should not be rejected in advance as
fallacious.

Excuses often involve making exceptions to a general rule that
is not absolute. Hence they come under the heading of defeasible
reasoning in logic, and require special treatment under this heading.

7. CHARITABLE APPEALS

Cases of charitable appeals for funds have occasionally been
included in logic textbooks under the heading of the *ad misericordiam* fallacy. Little, Wilson, and Moore (1955, p. 39) give the following examples of this fallacy:

Case 1.18: The beggar on the street emphasizes his appeal for
money by prominently displaying his blind eyes or
twisted limbs to the pity of the passers-by.

Case 1.19: An advertisement in a newspaper reads: "Veteran
with sick infant pleads for Chicago apartment."

Little, Wilson, and Moore simply dismiss these cases as instances of
the fallacious *argumentum ad misericordiam*. But there are questions about whether such appeals to compassion or pity to solicit
funds for charitable reasons are fallacious arguments *per se*, just
because they appeal to these feelings. There seems to be more that
needs to be said about these kinds of cases.

Fearnside (1980, p. 21) calls the fallacy "appeal to pathetic
circumstances." He defines it as the "attempt to substitute feelings
of sympathy and mercy for a cold weighing of the merits." However,

he concedes that some charitable appeals might be appeals to human sympathy and decency that are not necessarily fallacious. To accommodate this possibility, Fearnside takes a more subtle approach of describing the fallacy in this as certain cases where the appeal to sympathy is abused (p. 21):

> *Case* 1.20: The fallacy lies in *taking advantage* of pathetic circumstances. The beggar wears rags and the brochure of a charitable foundation exhibits the picture of an emaciated child. If these are typical and not prearranged for show, then they are legitimate evidence of the need for aid which is the heart of the problem, but when such evidence is overdrawn or fabricated, then there is an attempt to take advantage of our emotions. If the beggar or the charity seek to stir sympathy, at least the situation is one in which human considerations are relevant. On other occasions, however, it is simply improper to take account of pathetic circumstances.

In cases of charitable appeals for funds for help for starving children, medical research to find cures for children's diseases, and so forth, as Fearnside rightly notes, "evidence of the need for aid" is the "heart of the problem." Here then, it would seem, the appeal to pity, sympathy, or compassion is relevant, and is not a fallacious line of argument. "Human considerations," as Fearnside puts it, "are relevant."

Weddle (1978, p. 35) agrees that, in the case of a charitable appeal that arouses sympathy for the plight of someone in need of help, appeal to pity could be a relevant argument:

> *Case* 1.21: If an agency which proposes to lessen child starvation heightens its pleas for funds with photos showing a starving child in all his wretchedness, this maneuver will surely arouse emotional responses. Well and good. Part of moral persuasion, after all, does involve thrusting others' moral lapses into their faces. The children's wretchedness *is* the issue; the funds elicited are to eliminate that wretchedness. Therefore the emotional appeal is at least relevant. (Whether sufficient, or strong, is another matter.)

In this type of case, the pathetic situation of the children is part of the legitimate issue that is being addressed by the argument. Hence an appeal to sympathy or pity is relevant, even if it arouses an emotional response in the reader. It seems to be relevant in the context of an argument that conveys a plea for help, appealing to the respondent to help alleviate a situation where somebody is in a wretched situation and needs our help.

If this is the case then it is not justified to dismiss appeals to pity outright, as irrelevant and fallacious arguments. As Hamblin (1970, p. 43) put it, "where action is concerned, it is not so clear that pity and other emotions are irrelevant."

How then are we to judge when an *ad misericordiam* argument is fallacious and when not? Fearnside advises that such appeals are fallacious when "overdrawn or fabricated," when not typical of the circumstances, or when "prearranged for show." Weddle (1978, p. 35) suggests that such an appeal is fallacious when it "milks the issue." Weddle (p. 35) proposes the following principle: an argument that arouses sympathy must be "presented with a force proportional to the issue's claim to consideration." And to be sure, it is easy to appreciate how appeals to pity are in fact "milked" or blown out of proportion in argumentation.

Soccio and Barry (1992, p. 135) mention a kind of appeal to pity frequently used in advertising and promotion of causes. This type of appeal to pity uses visual displays in the form of photographs, films, or artwork:

> Case 1.22: Controversy has surrounded appeals to pity in ads and films used by some anti-abortion and animal rights groups. One group mails out graphic photographs of baby harp seals being killed for their fur. One especially disturbing photo shows a cute little baby seal, its large dark eyes staring lifelessly out of its bloodied white face. The contrast of the blood against the white fur is effective. This flyer counts as an example of an appeal to pity because the picture is the first thing the reader encounters. The feeling is raised before any argument is encountered. An anti-abortion campaign in a major midwestern city consisted of large, white billboards with a small bloody handprint and the word "please," in dripping, blood red in the lower right-hand corner.

The problem with this type of case is that the visual appeal to pity tends to be extremely powerful in influencing public opinion. There may be very little or no supplementary discussion of the issue, or the facts or circumstances of the case, presented along with the picture. Thus the impact of the appeal is overwhelming.

The problem may be that appeals to pity and sympathy tend to be partial or peripheral arguments that support or detract from an argumentation within a much larger body of relevant supporting evidence and facts of a case. By itself, however, in some cases, a moving appeal to pity may be blown out of proportion, and have an emotional impact far greater than its weight as evidence should merit.

The bottom line seems to be that appeals to pity or compassion in argumentation need to be judged in a broader context of evidence in a given case, so that the circumstances of each case are weighed on its merits. Thus the appeal to pity may need to be evaluated in relation to matters like what is relevant evidence in a given case, depending on the type of dialogue (like a legal proceeding), and the other evidence already given in the case, along with the appeal to pity.

Thus in the charitable appeal type of case, much may depend on what the money, or other form of help or contribution, is supposed to be used for, and whether in fact, evidence has been given that such a contribution will indeed contribute to the goal cited. These seem to be questions of practical reasoning that need to be judged in relation to the circumstances of particular cases.

The suggestions of the textbooks are that charitable appeals to pity are fallacious when they are irrelevant, or when they are blown out of proportion and substitute, or cover up for, a lack of (other) evidence needed to support a conclusion. These appear to be good suggestions, as routes to explore. But the problem is that, generally, in many commonplace instances of charitable appeals for funds, appeals to pity can be relevant. And, in some cases, appealing to pity does, at least arguably, provide actual evidence giving some support to a conclusion, for taking some proposed action.

More deeply, the problem is that appeal to pity often does seem to provide some relevant evidence in a case, but it is generally a weak or inconclusive sort of evidence that needs to be weighed in a larger picture where other more factual or objective evidence may also play a large, legitimate part in justifying a conclusion. And even more deeply, the worth of appeal to pity as an argument seems to vary, depending on the type of conversation (dialogue) the arguers are engaged in, and what stage the dialogue is in.

It seems that we need a more subtle approach to the question of evaluating arguments that appeal to pity, one that recognizes that such appeals can frequently be relevant in persuading someone to take on a commitment to a course of action. Some of the more recent textbooks have in fact taken steps in this direction.

8. ARGUMENT FROM CONSEQUENCES

Cederblom and Paulsen (1982, p. 100) define appeal to pity as a type of argument differently than most of the other textbooks: "When a person gets you to agree to something because *he will be hurt* if you don't agree, this is an appeal to pity." This way of defining appeal to pity makes it seem like a species of argumentation from consequences. And in fact Cederblom and Paulsen (p. 102) explicitly make the claim that appeal to pity is a "particular instance" of a "more general fallacy" they call *appeal to consequences*, where "you adopt a certain belief about certain consequences—avoiding harm to yourself or others."

This way of characterizing the fallacy of appeal to pity is interesting, because it brings out an aspect of the student's plea case already recognized by Castell (1935) and Blyth (1957), as noted above. Both Castell and Blyth saw the appeal to pity in the student's plea case as a species of argument from consequences.

Bonevac (1990, p. 75) brings out this aspect of the argument in the student's plea case very clearly in his presentation of his version of it:

> *Case* 1.23: A classic example, close to college professors' hearts, is an argument used by a student seeking a higher grade. "I'm pre-med. I really want to go to medical school and become a doctor. But my grades, so far, are just borderline. If this C stays on my record, I'll never make it. All these years of hard work will be wasted."

Bonevac even sketches out the form of the underlying type of argument he sees as the attempt to "play on our altruism" by appealing to pity (p. 76), where A and B are individuals, and X and Y are actions:

(F1) A's doing X will harm B.
∴ A shouldn't do X.

(F2) A's doing Y will help B.
∴ A should do Y.

Bonevac sees these forms of argument as having instances that could be good arguments in some cases:

> Some arguments succeed. If doing Y will help someone, and there's no reason not to do it, then you probably should do Y. If, by giving to charity, you can help save lives without producing any harm to yourself or others, then you should.

But clearly these arguments, when they are good (successful, reasonable) are not deductively valid. Instead, they seem to be based on a balance of considerations. Bonevac, above, uses the adverb *probably* to qualify them. But what he seems to have in mind is not probability (of the kind identified with statistical reasoning), but defeasible reasoning, appropriate where a balance of consequences needs to be judged.

Bonevac (p. 76) brings out this important aspect of the student's plea case very clearly when he notes that judging the argument's reasonableness should be seen as relative to an "all being equal" clause:

> But the condition "there's no reason not to do it" is very important. The rule "Help others" holds only when other things are equal. Suppose that giving the pre-med student a C really will harm that student. Before concluding anything about the grade, it's necessary to consider the effect on others of raising the grade, as well as any general principles of fairness involved. If changing the grade to a B would help the student get into a medical school, the change would help that particular student but would cost some other student a place. So, the consequences are not unambiguously positive; one student would benefit, another would suffer. Further, another C student performing as well as or perhaps even better than the pre-med student would receive a lower grade.

These insights are very interesting, because they suggest that the type of appeal to pity typified by the student's plea case could contain a legitimate (reasonable, correct) type of argument modelled by (F1) and (F2) which could be called *appeal for help* or the *argument from supplication*, or some such name. As a subspecies of argument from consequences, the appeal for help could be seen as, within constraints, a reasonable type of argument to be used in a conversational exchange between two parties.

The appeal to help could be seen as the type of argument involved in the cases of charitable appeals studied above, where a request for help in the form of a plea for funds to assist in a charitable effort is put forth. To the extent that such arguments can be reasonable, even though they do appeal to pity, compassion or sympathy for someone who is in need of help, they could be based on this underlying form of the appeal for help.

But the big problem posed by these considerations could be expressed in the following question. If (F1) and (F2) are in some sense *valid* (correct, reasonable, good, successful) arguments, what theory or structure of argument can we use in which to prove or justify these positive evaluations? Clearly, as noted above, these arguments are not deductive in nature. And they do not seem to be inductive arguments of any known or familiar sort—that is, based on sampling, or statistical evidence.

Hence two required steps in the project of giving a logical basis for judging cases of appeal to pity (sympathy, compassion, and the like) as fallacious or nonfallacious arguments, in a given case, are (a) to clearly define the structure of the type of argument involved, as some sort of identifiable type of inference from premises to a conclusion, and (b) to give some sort of broader structure or theory in which this form of argument can be judged successful (correct, reasonable, nonfallacious, and the like). Given recent developments in argumentation theory, this task may not be as difficult as it seems. The problem is that the traditional structures and methods of deductive and inductive logic do not appeal to provide resources. Nor do these methods appear to be particularly appropriate or useful for the job.

A third step is the task of determining which particular instances of this type of argument are so badly wrong, or exhibit the right kind of misuse, that they should be called fallacious. This, in itself, is a distinct task, because not all incorrect or unsuccessful arguments merit the label of fallacious.

9. JUDGING FALLACIOUS CASES

The majority of the textbooks see the *ad misericordiam* fallacy as one of irrelevance. This is a good beginning point, for it is true that in some cases, the appeal to pity is used as a distraction from the task of fulfilling a burden of proof in argumentation by furnishing other (relevant) evidence. But relevance, as we saw in the student's plea case, for example, is not the whole answer. In some cases, appeals to pity or sympathy are relevant to the case, but are nevertheless fallacious arguments. Thus it seems we need to take other factors into account, to give a full analysis of the *ad misericordiam* fallacy. Some of the more subtle analyses of the textbooks take steps in this direction.

Freeman (1988, p. 74) defines *appeal to pity* as the fallacy that occurs where an arguer "presents a most pathetic, tear-jerking story to obtain agreement—not because any good reason has been given but because the hearer feels sorry." However, Freeman stresses (p. 74) that not all arguments that appeal to pity are fallacious. What is fallacious "is the arousing of pity without any reasons why it should be aroused" (p. 74).

However, Freeman's account is more complex than this, for he also invokes both the concept of relevance and the concept of "being able to decide for ourselves" whether an emotion is appropriate to a situation" (p. 75):

> An argument involves the fallacy of appeal to pity when
> 1. it arouses pity in the course of making its case and
> 2. that emotion is out of place or questionable because only factual considerations are relevant or we may be unable to decide for ourselves whether the emotion is appropriate to the situation.

The second clause is violated in the type of case where an arguer is "trying to manipulate our emotions" instead of letting us "react properly to the situation" (p. 74). This suggests that relevance is not the whole story. An appeal to pity can also be used fallaciously where it is blown out of proportion to the extent that we are unable to leave room for other considerations that may also be relevant.

Weddle (1978, p. 35) also proposes a more subtle way of evaluating appeals to pity as arguments. He proposes that two questions need to be asked: (1) Is the appeal relevant? (2) How much weight should be given to it? Thus, according to Weddle, it is possible to have a case of appeal to pity that is relevant, but is fallacious because it makes an inflated claim as a factor in the case. So appeals to pity can be fallacious for either of two reasons—irrelevance or the degree (weight) of the appeal. Weddle gives the following case to illustrate this (pp. 35–36):

> *Case* 1.24: A firm hiring crane operators for urban renewal may sympathize with an otherwise qualified applicant

> who has become subject to fainting fits, but his plea
> that he should be hired because he has been unable
> to get work in order to support his children, though
> it may touch the hearts of his prospective employ-
> ers, fails to touch the real issue, the question of
> whether the operator ought to be one of those hired.

It's not that the circumstances of the man's children and personal situation are wholly irrelevant. The fallacy is committed where this is
blown out of proportion in being weighed alongside other relevant
considerations.[6]

This account of what makes an *ad misericordiam* argument
fallacious is supported by the one given by Bonevac. He stresses that
there may be all kinds of relevant arguments or factors that need to
be weighed up together in the larger picture of evidence in a given
case.

This seems to be the best account of the *ad misericordiam* fallacy furnished by the textbook treatments so far, then. It is a fallacy of relevance, but also a fallacy of "blowing up" the element of
pity so that it is out of proportion in the total evidence picture for a
case.

However, there are some other aspects of the fallacy to be
considered as well. Two kinds of cases require additional consideration. Both of these examples, from the same textbook (Kreyche
1970), raise interesting questions about why an appeal to pity should
be considered a fallacious argument that seems to go beyond the
kind of account given by Weddle and Bonevac.

One curious type of case used by several of the textbooks[7] could
be called the *orphan case*. The variant below is quoted from Kreyche
(1970, p. 33):

> *Case* 1.25: A young man is on trial for slaying both of his par-
> ents. The defense lawyer addresses himself to the
> jury: "How can you possibly pronounce sentence
> on this young man? For one thing, he didn't know
> what he was doing. But more: if you convict him,
> the consequences will be too horrible to contem-
> plate. Can you imagine what it would be like to
> send a poor orphan to prison?"

Kreyche (p. 33) diagnoses the fault as "the attempt to substitute pity
for more suitable rational persuasion." But more specifically, what
seems to be at the basis of the problem with this case is the fact

that the young man committed the act himself that put him in the situation of being an orphan. This violates a general requirement that determines when appeals to pity are appropriate or not in given circumstances. It is appropriate to feel pity for someone in pathetic circumstances only if the individual in question did not himself create those circumstances (freely, by his own action).

Kreyche (1970, p. 34) cites a subfallacy of the *argumentum ad misericordiam* he calls the *sentimentalist fallacy*. It consists in the feigning of a distress that is not real, in order to achieve some end. Defining this fallacy as "feigning pity where none actually exists" (p. 34), Kreyche cites the following example:

> *Case* 1.26: Very often people "weep crocodile tears" in a situation where motives for weeping are unrelated to the actual weeping itself, as when a child sometimes weeps loudly and mournfully in order to get some new toy that he does not actually need.

In this kind of case, the appeal to pity is an intentional deception to try to persuade somebody to act in a particular way. So it is easy to appreciate why one is tempted to classify it as an instance of the *ad misericordiam* fallacy. But the basic problem is that the individual is lying. That is, the argument from appeal to pity seems to be based on a false premise. But a fallacy is not just an argument with a false premise, is it? Hence there is a problem in knowing how to deal with this kind of case.

10. SUMMARY

Even before we get around to the task of evaluating *ad misericordiam* arguments as strong, weak, fallacious, there is a preliminary problem of no small magnitude. As we have seen, there are considerable disagreements and uncertainties in the textbook treatments on how to define or clearly identify *ad misericordiam* as a distinctive type of argument. Is it appeal to pity, sympathy, compassion, mercy, or what? These differences of definition make a big difference when it comes to evaluating the argument as fallacious or not, because *pity* has a much more negative connotation than either *sympathy* or *compassion*, making it much easier to dismiss as a fallacious kind of appeal in argumentation.

Of course, most of the textbooks define the type of argument in terms of appeal to pity. So certainly the notion of pity should be seen as centrally important, from a pedagogical point of view.

The majority of the textbooks translate *argumentum ad misericordiam* as appeal to pity. These include Joseph (1906; 1916), Castell (1935), Copi (1961), Clark and Welsh (1962), Vernon and Nissen (1968), Weddle (1978), Runkle (1978), Crossley and Wilson (1979), Cederblom and Paulsen (1982), Freeman (1988), Hurley (1991), and Harrison (1992). But several define *argumentum ad misericordiam* disjunctively, as appeal to pity or sympathy. These include Little, Wilson, and Moore (1955), Manicas and Kruger (1968), and Frye and Levi (1969). One textbook, Werkmeister (1948), defines *argumentum ad misericordiam* conjunctively, as appeal to pity and sympathy. Another one, Toulmin, Rieke, and Janik (1979), defines it disjunctively as appeal to compassion or sympathy.

Several others characterize *argumentum ad misericordiam* as appeal to pity, but mention sympathy. These include Damer (1980) and Engel (1982). Damer characterizes the type of argument as appeal to pity, but mentions sympathy in the definition of this type of argument.

Bonevac (1990, pp. 75–76) doesn't mention the Latin expression *argumentum ad misericordiam*, but uses the phrase *appeal to pity*. He defines (p. 75) it as:

> *Definition* An argument *appeals to pity* if and only if it tries to justify an action by arousing sympathy or pity in the audience.

Weddle (1978) doesn't mention the Latin expression either, simply using *appeal to pity* as his designated phrase for the type of argument. But he sticks consistently to the word *pity* instead of using *sympathy* or *compassion* as descriptors.

Kaminsky and Kaminsky (1974) define appeal to pity (*argumentum ad misericordiam*) as an "unwarranted appeal to obtain sympathy" for a cause or demand. Michalos (1970, p. 51) characterizes the fallacy as (irrelevant) appeal to pity, but then defines what this is by means of a disjunction between sympathy and compassion:

> The fallacy of introducing an irrelevant appeal to *pity* (*argumentum ad misericordiam*) is committed when one tries to persuade someone to accept a particular view by arousing his sympathy or compassion.

This way of defining *ad misericordiam* seems to be very broad, for practical purposes, since it allows any or all of three different things that can be appealed to—pity, sympathy, or compassion.

Kreyche (1970) characterizes the argument as appeal to pity, but mentions compassion. Soccio and Barry (1992) also call the argument appeal to pity, but use the term *compassion* in defining it.

Barker (1965) defines the type of argument as appeal to pity or mercy. Fearnside (1980) calls it appeal to pathetic circumstances, but mentions both sympathy and mercy. Yanal (1988) calls it appeal to feeling. The ninth edition of Copi and Cohen (1994, p. 129) defines the appeal to pity, or argument *ad misericordiam*, as "a special case of the appeal to emotion, in which the altruism and mercy of the audience are the special emotions appealed to."

Thus the predominant designation of the argument is as appeal to pity. But as you can see, there is considerable variation, with *sympathy* and *compassion* being featured prominently in many of the accounts, and even in some cases, being used as the leading designation of the argument type.

How the textbooks treat the *argumentum ad misericordiam* as fallacious or not falls into three categories. Those that treat it as inherently or generally fallacious are Castell (1935), Clark and Welsh (1962), Engel (1982), and Hurley (1991). Michalos defines the fallacy as an irrelevant appeal to pity, but leaves open the possibility of nonfallacious appeals to pity. Those that say it can be fallacious or not, but stress the fallacious aspect, include Little, Wilson, and Moore (1955), Toulmin, Rieke, and Janik (1979), Damer (1980), Yanal (1988), and Harrison (1992). Those that take a more balanced approach of emphasizing the nonfallacious as well as the fallacious uses of the argument include Barker (1965), Vernon and Nissen (1968), and Freeman (1988).

Several of the textbook treatments indicated that the *argumentum ad misericordiam* is often a species of argumentation from consequences. These include Castell (1935), Blyth (1957), Cederblom and Paulsen (1982), and Bonevac (1990).

These treatments could be generally summed up as follows. The *ad misericordiam* argument is most often identified as appeal to pity, but a significant proportion of the textbook accounts identify it as appeal to sympathy or appeal to compassion. Virtually no attention is given to attempting to define what pity is, or to distinguishing between pity and sympathy, or pity and compassion. Indeed, many of the textbooks seem to presume that these three concepts can be treated interchangeably, as far as the *argumentum ad misericordiam* is concerned. They don't appear to think the differences are significant, or worth commenting on. In fairness, this may be due to the short space allotted to the *argumentum ad misericordiam* in the textbooks.

There is a general presumption that the *argumentum ad misericordiam* is fallacious, especially in the earlier textbooks. But this seems to be changing, in at least a fair number of the textbooks, where it now often tends to be acknowledged explicitly that this type of argument can be nonfallacious in some cases.

2

Historical Background

The *argumentum ad misericordiam* did not begin to appear in logic textbooks, or other writings in the field of logic, until the twentieth century. Its first known occurrence using the phrase *ad misericordiam* is in an article on the repeal of the corn laws in the *Edinburgh Review* in 1824.[1]

However, the use of appeal to pity as an effective tactic of argumentation for influencing a judge or jury in court has long been known to lawyers. And in fact there is good evidence that the appeal to pity was well known to ancient rhetoricians and philosophers as a type of argument.

Among the sophists and rhetoricians mentioned in Aristotle's *Rhetoric* (see the introduction to the English translation by Freese 1937, p. xvii) was Thrasymachus of Chalcedon (circa 457–400 B.C.), who wrote so-called Compassion Speeches (*Eleoi*), that were intended to excite the emotions of the hearers—see *Rhetoric* (III. 1.7–8). Thrasymachus is said (Freese, xviii) to have attached great importance to this method of persuasion.

1. ORIGINS IN THE MODERN TEXTBOOKS

It is not known how the *argumentum ad misericordiam* originally came to be featured as a fallacy in logic textbooks, or recognized as a distinctive type of argument in logic. It was not included as a fallacy in Aristotle's list of sophistical refutations in *On Sophistical Refutations*. Nor was it included in the list of *ad* fallacies introduced by Locke in his *Essay*—see Hamblin (1970, pp.

159–60). Hamblin gives us no clue where it might have originated.

Despite a fairly thorough search of the usual sources where a fallacy of this type might have originated, including Schopenhauer, Whately, Watts, Bentham, Arnauld, DeMorgan, and Mill, no mention of it was found. The earliest occurrence of it found in a logic textbook was that of Joseph (1906, p. 550; 1916, p. 590).

In Whately's influential textbook *Elements of Logic* (1870; first published 1826), the *ad hominem*, *ad verecundiam*, and *ad ignorantiam* fallacies are treated, but no explicit mention is made of the *ad misericordiam*. As noted in case 2.2 below, Whately did use an example that could perhaps be classified as an appeal to pity of a sort, but he classified it as an *ignoratio elenchi* fallacy. This suggests that although the *ad misericordiam* fallacy was known in popular usage during the nineteenth century, and certainly the *ad misericordiam* argument was known to lawyers, it did not get into the logic textbooks (at least explicitly, by this name) until the later nineteenth or early twentieth century. This is as much as we can narrow down its origin, on the basis of present data.

As Hamblin showed, Locke, in his *Essay Concerning Human Understanding* (1690) introduced the *ad hominem*, *ad verecundiam*, and *ad ignorantiam* arguments, as distinctive assent-producing devices that can be used as fallacies.[2] And the logic textbooks subsequently began to incorporate treatments of these types of argumentation into their sections on fallacies, adding them to the Aristotelian list. Curiously however, *ad misericordiam* does not appear in the early logic textbooks, alongside these other three.

Hamblin (1970, pp. 164–65) quotes a classification of fallacies in Watts's *Logick* (1725, pp. 465–66), almost the only logic book written in the eighteenth century. The last item is called by Watts *argumentum ad passiones*, and includes *ad populum* as a variant (p. 164):

> I add finally, when an Argument is borrowed from any Topics which are suited to engage the Inclinations and Passions of the Hearers on the Side of the Speaker, rather than to convince the Judgment, this is *Argumentum ad Passiones*, an Address to the Passions: or if it be made publickly, 'tis called an *Appeal to the People*.

Ad misericordiam, although not mentioned by name, could easily fit in here as a subfallacy of, or even as equivalent to, *argumentum ad passiones*.[3]

In some of the later textbooks, we do find examples of what are in fact *ad misericordiam* arguments. They would have been familiar to Quintilian or Cicero, but are treated as fallacies under other headings.

Clarke (1921) uses an example (p. 448) under the heading of *ignoratio elenchi* or evading the question. It would fit the usual text-book classification of the *ad misericordiam* perfectly:

> *Case* 2.1: The skillful barrister will often seek to draw off the attention of the jury from the real point at issue, viz., the guilt or innocence of the prisoner, by a pathetic description of the havoc that will be wrought in his home if he is convicted, or by seeking to create an unfair prejudice against prosecutor or witnesses.

But Clarke makes no mention of *ad misericordiam* at all, and does not classify this case specifically as an appeal to pity or compassion.

Creighton (1929, p. 185) does mention the *argumentum ad misericordiam* by name, but classifies it as a special case of the *argumentum ad populum* (pp. 185–86):

> The *argumentum ad populum* is an argument addressed to the feelings, passions, and prejudices of people rather than an unbiased discussion addressed to the intellect. The use of question-begging epithets frequently accompanies this fallacy. The *argumentum ad misericordiam* seems to be only a special case of this fallacy, when an appeal is made to the pity or sympathy which people may be made to feel for a person accused of crime. Or sometimes it may be attempted to recommend some party or cause by arousing such feelings for its adherents, or a law, by dwelling on the plight of those whom it would perhaps relieve.

This is all he has to say about the *ad misericordiam*.

Under the heading of *ignoratio elenchi* (irrelevance, or proving the wrong conclusion), Whately (1870) cites an example of "improper appeal to the passions." He feels Aristotle would classify it under the heading of "extraneous to the matter at hand" (p. 140). However, Whately does not classify this example (p. 141) as an *argumentum ad misericordiam*.

> *Case* 2.2: Instead of proving that "the poor ought to be relieved in this way rather than in that," you prove that "the poor *ought to be relieved*."

Although Whately does mention the other *ad* fallacies by name, he does not use the term *argumentum ad misericordiam* as a distinct species of fallacy. And even Whately's example (case 2.2), although it involves a charitable appeal, does not seem to be meant as a case where the fallacy turns essentially on appeal to pity. It seems more like a case where the arguer has proved the wrong conclusion, a case of what we would now call irrelevance or red herring. Only if the arguer went on to give lamentable details of the suffering of the poor, and so forth, would the case be clearly an *argumentum ad misericordiam*, in the sense in which this phrase has now come to stand for a distinctive type of fallacy in the modern logic textbooks.

On the basis of this negative evidence, the best conjecture seems to be that the *ad misericordiam* was a late addition to the logic textbooks. Before the twentieth century, it had not been treated as a specific fallacy. Instead, this type of appeal had been included under the broader Aristotelian category of the *ignoratio elenchi* fallacy. However, there is evidence of some prior occurrence of the expression *argumentum ad misericordiam*, outside the field of logic.

2. EARLIEST KNOWN ORIGINS OF *AD MISERICORDIAM*

Some clues to early uses of the term *ad misericordiam* are given in the *Oxford English Dictionary* entry (Simpson and Weiner 1989, p. 166):

> *ad misericordiam* (æd mizɛri'koːdiəm). [L.] Of an appeal, argument, etc.: to mercy, to pity.
> *1824 Edin. Rev.* XLI.55 The fallacy of those arguments *ad misericordiam* on which the agriculturists now principally rest their claims to protect. *1863* THACKERAY *Round. Papers* 73 No day passes but that argument *ad misericordiam* is used. *1885 Manchester Exam.* 27 Feb. 5/3 He now made an *ad misericordiam* appeal for an extension of that time, on the ground of his ignorance of the practice. *1929* E. MARJORIBANKS *Marshall Hall* x. 359 Later, in his final speech, he was making an appeal *ad misericordiam* for his client.

The earliest mention of *ad misericordiam* is in the *Edinburgh Review* in an article published in 1824, where it is specifically called a fallacy. This is a thirty-page article by one W. Whitmore, M.P., on the abolition of the corn laws. The author writes of "showing the fallacy of those arguments *ad misericordiam* on which the agriculturists now principally rest their claims to protection" (p. 55). But other than that, nothing in the article throws light on or further mentions *ad misericordiam*.

The reference in *The Life of Sir Edward Marshall Hall* (Marjoribanks 1929, p. 359) suggests that appeal to pity was acceptable as a legal argument, but one that required evidence to back it up. During a trial, Hall apparently used an argument explicitly called *ad misericordiam*, to defend a client against the prosecuting attorney, Mr. Milward:

> Later, in his final speech, he was making an appeal *ad misericordiam* for his client, and was saying that he had been ruined by the scandal of this case, having been compelled to sell his business. Strictly, in order to use this plea he should have called evidence as to these facts, and Mr. Milward said so. Marshall Hall offered to do so.
>
> "Well," said Milward, "if you do, do you know I shall have the last word?"
>
> Now the old lion was thoroughly roused. "Do you think I am afraid of your last word?" he retorted. "I don't care if you talk from now till Doomsday. I'm not afraid of that. I know I shall not be here to listen to it. You can make as many speeches as you think fit."

Here, the *ad misericordiam* is not classified as a fallacy, and nothing further is mentioned about it.

The Thackeray reference to *ad misericordiam* originally occurred in a letter to the editor reprinted by Thackeray, in his essay *Thorns in the Cushion*, printed in *The Cornhill Magazine* in 1860. Thackeray had begun to find editing the magazine tiresome and described his various problems in the job as "thorns in the cushion." As one example, he cites a letter to the editor he received (p. 126). Enclosed with the letter was "a little poem or two":

> Camberwell, June 4.
>
> *Case* 2.3: Sir,-May I hope, may I entreat, that you will favour me by perusing the enclosed lines, and that they may be found worthy of insertion in the *Cornhill Magazine*. We have known better days, sir. I have a sick and widowed mother to maintain, and little

brothers and sisters who look to me. I do my utmost as a governess to support them. I toil at night when they are at rest, and my own hand and brain are alike tired. If I could add but a *little* to our means by my pen, many of my poor invalid's wants might be supplied, and I could procure for her comforts to which she is now a stranger. Heaven knows it is not for want of *will* or for want of *energy* on my part, that she is now in ill-health, and our little household almost without bread. Do—cast a kind glance over my poem, and if you can help us, the widow, the orphans will bless you! I remain, sir, in anxious expectancy.

Your faithful servant,
"S. S. S."

Thackeray calls this letter a "thorn," and offers the following comment on what he calls its "logic":

"I am poor; I am good; I am ill; I work hard; I have a sick mother and hungry brothers and sisters dependent on me. You can help us if you will." And then I look at the paper, with the thousandth part of a faint hope that it may be suitable, and I find it won't do: and I knew it wouldn't do: and why is this poor lady to appeal to my pity and bring her poor little ones kneeling to my bedside, and calling for bread which I can give them if I choose? No day passes but that argument *ad misericordiam* is used. Day and night that sad voice is crying out for help. Thrice it appealed to me yesterday. Twice this morning it cried to me: and I have no doubt when I go to get my hat, I shall find it with its piteous face and its pale family about it, waiting for me in the hall.

Thackeray does not specifically call the *ad misericordiam* a fallacy. But he does use the word *logic* when he characterizes this type of argument as "I am poor; I am good, etc. You can help us if you will." This use of the word *logic*, and his characterization of the form of argument as a type of appeal for help, does suggest that he sees the *ad misericordiam* as a type of argument that should be condemned or criticized, in the case in point, on logical grounds. What Thackeray is suggesting is that such an appeal is inappropriate, because the issue of whether the poem should be included in the magazine should be decided by the editor on the basis of the perceived merit of the poem itself, not on the basis of the pitiable circumstances of the poet.

Of these three references, the Thackeray one is by far the most interesting. In fact, the case Thackeray describes, which in key respects seems very similar to the student's plea type of case featured in chapter 1, offers a good deal of insight into how the *ad misericordiam* functions, both as an argument and a fallacy. The basic argument relies on a plea for help, which, in principle, could be legitimate as a type of argumentation.[4] It is very powerful, and very difficult to resist. And in fact, as Thackeray notes, it seems to put him in a difficult situation where he seems almost compelled to give in. The basic fallacy seems to lie in the twisting of this powerful argument around, or misusing of it, so that it is applied to a situation where it is not appropriate, and even an obstruction to making a good decision.[5]

3. ANCIENT USE AS A COURTROOM TACTIC

In trials in ancient Greece, it was very common at the peroration (concluding) stage of the defense speech to bring in an explicit use of appeal to pity. It was a common, and even expected practice for defendants to "parade their distraught friends and relatives before the court to appeal to the jurors' compassion" (Lewis 1993, p. 107). According to Lofberg (1976, p. 15), "Direct requests for pity were so common that failure to beg for the jurors' compassion was regarded as a sign of antagonism towards the popular courts and their methods." In the *Rhetorica ad Alexandrum* (36. 1444b–1445a), we are told that the purpose of the peroration is to recapitulate the speech, and make the jurors favorably disposed towards the pleader, and that this can be done by "making ourselves pitiful in their sight" (Cooper 1994, p. 2).

In Roman times, the appeal to the emotion of pity was also well known as a type of argumentation in trials. Cicero (*Brutus* xxii 88–xxxii 123) tells the story of Galba, an orator who "was fired by a kind of innate emotion, which produced a style of speaking earnest, passionate, and vehement" (xxiv 93; Hendrickson, p. 85). Galba was acquitted of the charge, and "won the approbation of everyone present" when he used "many moving appeals to the mercy of the court" to plead his case forcibly and impressively (xxii 88; Hendrickson, p. 81). This suggests an acceptance of appeal to pity as a legitimate tactic used in Roman trials.

Cicero also tells us that on another occasion of his being charged with massacring surrendered prisoners, Galba used an "impressive appeal to the emotions of the listener" (xxii 88; Hendrickson, p. 83). When this charge was pressed against Galba, he responded by throwing himself on the mercy of the court, with an emotional appeal:

> *Case* 2.4: Thereupon Galba, asking no favour for himself, but appealing to the loyalty of the Roman people, with tears in his eyes commended to their protection his own children as well as the young son of Gaius Gallus. The presence of this orphan and his childish weeping excited great compassion because of the memory still fresh of his illustrious father. Thus Galba by stirring the pity of the populace for little children snatched himself from the flames. [*Brutus* xxiii 90–91; Hendrickson, p. 83]

The charge against Galba was dropped. This was a surprising outcome, given the seriousness of the charge, according to the commentary in *John Rainold's Oxford Lectures on Aristotle's Rhetoric* (1578, p. 129):

> After Servius Sulpitius Galba broke his word and murdered thirty thousand Lusitanians, he was vehemently and harshly accused before the Roman people by M. Cato. Galba was convicted of an infamous crime, and just when he was sinking under the most righteous hatred of the judges, and just when he was about to receive the extreme penalty, he brought his small sons into the public assembly, and, with the orphan son of his kinsman Gallus high on his shoulders, he stirred the people to such pity, that, although convicted of the most atrocious crimes, he still was pardoned. Cato recorded this in his writings, saying that if Galba had not used boys and tears he would have been given his due.

This account suggests that the appeal to pity proved to be a very powerful type of argument indeed, in Roman courtroom argumentation.

Cicero himself showed an impressive grasp of the appeal to pity as a courtroom tactic when, in defense of Lucius Flaccus, he introduced Flaccus's son to arouse the sympathy of the jury:

Case 2.5: To this poor lad, a suppliant to you and your children, you will give, gentlemen, by this trial a rule of life. If you acquit his father, you will show him what sort of citizen he should himself be. But if you take his father from him, you will show that you are offering no regard for a plan of life that is upright, steadfast, and honourable. He now begs you not to increase his grief by his father's tears, nor his father's sorrow by his weeping; for he is of an age to suffer for his father's grief but not to help his father. See, he turns to me, he looks at me appealingly and, in a way, he weeping calls on my honour, and asks for that place of distinction which I promised formerly to his father for saving our native land. Have pity, gentlemen, on the family, have pity on this most courageous father, have pity on the son; for the sake of the family, for the sake of its ancient lineage, for the sake of the man himself, preserve for the state a most illustrious and glorious name. [*Pro Flacco* xiii 105–107; Lord, pp. 475–77]

This argument is a kind of one-two attack that appeals to *ethos*, the honorable character of Flaccus, as a good person, and to *pathos*, using the son as "innocent victim." There was also a strong visual appeal to the crying face of the son, something that would still have a strong impact today—for example, in a photograph or on television.

Cicero lays it on so thick here that the appeal would seem obviously heavy-handed to a modern audience. But even so, it is not hard to see how, put in a modern, or more up-to-date context, this same type of staged lachrymose appeal could still be highly effective in moving a jury.

The ancient rhetoricians were very well aware of the appeal to pity as a device of persuasion in oratory generally. It is often referred to a common tactic of argumentation in writings on rhetoric. According to Cooper (1994, p. 3), "supplicating the jury" by an appeal to pity had become recognized and categorized by Greek rhetoricians, even as early as the later fifth century and early fourth century B.C., as a standard rhetorical device to arouse pity in the pleader's closing remarks before a jury. Closely connected to this supplicating ritual was the practice of imploring of mercy on behalf of the pleader's family. Quintilian, for example, specifically describes and advocates appeal to pity as a persuasive type of argument.

According to Quintilian, in the *exordium*, or opening part of a speech, which prepares the audience to be receptive to the speech's argument, it is important to secure the good will of the audience for the person of the pleader (*Institutio Oratoria* IV. 1. 5–7). Quintilian states that, in his opinion, "whatever concerns the pleader is relevant to the case" (IV. 1. 12). As part of this stage of an argument, Quintilian specifically includes appeal to pity, where appropriate:

> The character of our client himself may, too, be treated in various ways: we may emphasize his worth or we may commend his weakness to the protection of the court. Sometimes it is desirable to set forth his merits, when the speaker will be less hampered by modesty than if he were praising his own. Sex, age and situation are also important considerations, as for instance when women, old men or wards are pleading in the character of wives, parents, or children. For pity alone may move even a strict judge. [*Institutio Oratoria*, IV. 1 13]

Interestingly, however, Quintilian adds that such points "should only be lightly touched upon," and not "run to death" (IV. 1 14). The general impression here is that the appeal to pity was generally recognized as a powerfully effective rhetorical type of argument by rhetoricians of the time. And the remark that "pity alone may move even a strict judge" suggests an awareness that appeal to pity can, in some cases, be used in a courtroom, where it might even offset the need to provide actual evidence relevant to a defendant's guilt or innocence of a charge.

Quintilian is not, however, in the business of identifying fallacies as faulty arguments, from a critical or logical perspective. His point of view on the appeal to pity as a type of argument is that it is a useful and effective tactic of persuasion in an advocacy legal setting. In a trial, the character of the client is a legitimate subject for argumentation, which, as Quintilian says, "can be treated in various ways." One of those ways he identified is to exploit the perceived weakness of the client, appealing to the "protection of the court." In this context, then, Quintilian is suggesting that appeal to pity can be a good line of argument for moving "even a strict judge." From a rhetorical point of view, he is advocating this tactic, not condemning it as fallacious. However, the implication is there that such a powerful tactic could even be used where you do not really have much of the right kind of evidence that would properly be needed to persuade the judge that your client is not guilty.

However, as we will see below, there were some mixed feelings about these practices of appealing to pity in argumentation. Some orators used it, but tended to treat it as a lowbrow crowd-pleaser that would not be a very respectable kind of argument to use to reasonably convince a serious audience of one's equals. Other rhetorical handbooks, according to Stevens (1944, p. 5) even advised the orator to proactively counter the appeal to pity by reminding the audience that a person does not deserve pity if he did not show pity himself when he committed his crime.

Counterbalancing the appeal to pity as an argument was the ancient rhetorical form of argument called the *banishment of pity (ekbole eleon)*, the argument to the effect that this person, who claims our mercy, does not deserve it, because he himself did not show mercy in similar circumstances (Stevens 1944, p. 9). The idea behind this counter-argument is logical in nature. If a killer who showed no mercy to his victim then asks for mercy, or appeals to pity when tried for the crime, his appeal is pragmatically inconsistent or illogical in the sense that his argument is inconsistent with his own actions. Since he gave no mercy, it is inappropriate for him to plead for it now. He does not deserve it.

An ancient example of the argument from banishment of pity is given in Antiphon's oration, *Against the Stepmother* (Stevens 1944, p. 9). In the epilogue, the orator seeks to forestall the effects of the stepmother's appeal to pity by demanding that the jury "deal as pitilessly with her as she had dealt with her husband." According to Stevens, both the appeal to pity and the banishment of pity were well known to writers of rhetorical handbooks in ancient times, and were widely used both in public and legal argumentation. In the speech that Thucydides attributes to Cleon in his speech asking the Athenian assembly to reconsider its decree condemning the adult population of Mytilene to death (427 B.C.), Stevens (p. 1) finds not only the form of argument called the appeal to pity, but also the countervailing form of argument called the banishment of pity.

4. SOCRATES' REJECTION OF APPEAL TO PITY

Socrates' famous speech in the *Apology*, where he refuses to use appeal to pity in his courtroom defense, illustrates that this type of defense was so common that the jury expected it to be used. It is also interesting to note, however, that in the speech, Socrates rejects the appeal to pity as a disreputable method of argumentation that he finds personally disgraceful. It is so bad it brings shame on any city that tolerates its use. This is shown by the part of the speech in the *Apology* (34c–35c), near the end of his defense, where he gives his reasons for refusing to use this tactic (trans. Grube, 1975, pp. 36–37):

> *Case* 2.6: Very well, gentlemen of the jury. This, and maybe other similar things, is what I have to say in my defence. Perhaps one of you might be angry as he recalls that when he himself stood trial on a less dangerous charge, he begged and implored the jury with many tears, that he brought his children and many of his friends and family into court to arouse as much pity as he could, but that I do none of these things, even though I may seem to be running the ultimate risk. Thinking of this, he might feel resentful and angry and cast his vote in anger. If there is such a one among you—I do not deem there is, but if there is—I think it would be right to say in reply: "My good sir, I too have a household and, in Homer's phrase, I am not born from oak or rock but from men, so that I have a family, indeed three sons, gentlemen of the jury, of whom one is an adolescent while two are children. Nevertheless, I will not beg you to acquit me by bringing them here. Why do I do none of these things? Not through arrogance, gentlemen, nor through lack of respect for you. Whether I am brave in the face of death is another matter, but with regard to my reputation and yours and that of the whole city, it does not seem right to me to do these things, especially at my age and with my reputation. For it is generally believed, whether it be true or false, that in certain respects Socrates is superior to the majority of men. Now if those of you who are considered superior, be it in wisdom or courage or whatever other virtue makes them so, are seen behaving like that, it would be a disgrace. Yet I have often seen them do this sort of thing when standing trial, men who are thought to be somebody, doing amazing things as if they thought it a terrible thing to die, and as if they were to be immortal if you did not execute them. I think these men bring shame upon the city so that a stranger, too, would assume that those who are outstanding in

virtue among the Athenians, whom they themselves select from themselves to fill offices of state and receive other honours, are in no way better than women. You should not act like that, gentlemen of the jury, those of you who have any reputation at all, and if we do, you should not allow it. You should make it very clear that you will more readily convict a man who performs these pitiful dramatics in court and so makes the city a laughingstock, than a man who keeps quiet.

This speech acknowledges that "pitiful dramatics" can be used as a very successful argument in front of a jury. But at the same time, it denigrates such an appeal, as beneath good standards of argumentation appropriate for a man like Socrates in court. Socrates is supposed to be a wise man, and it is suggested that it would be beneath his dignity to use his family to engage in a dramatic appeal to pity— "it would be a disgrace."

Plato has Socrates say that he has often seen defendants use appeal to pity when standing for trial, suggesting that it was a common practice. But Socrates thinks that Athenians who make such a plea, or those who accept it, "bring shame upon the city." These remarks suggest that the use of appeal to pity, as practiced in pleading in the courts, was viewed by some as being beneath the standard of good reasoning appropriate for a philosopher and wise man, like Socrates, to use as an argument.

In a way, however, the speech has an ironic aspect. Even in running down appeal to pity as an argument, Socrates is, to some extent, engaging in it himself, by reminding the jury that he does in fact have a family.

Perhaps this is not exactly irony, however, but a rhetorical strategy of *omission*—by saying he is not going to appeal to pity, Socrates is actually (in effect) bringing the subject of pity up, reminding the audience of it, and thereby having the rhetorical effect of putting the subject of pity (implicitly) into the argument. As Rossetti (1989, p. 231) emphasizes, it is a feature of Socrates' rhetoric that he leaves much unspoken—his silence leaves open suggestions that enables his interlocutor to "decode the covert message." Applying Rossetti's analysis of Socrates' rhetorical technique to the speech in the *Apology*, it is possible to interpret Socrates' speech as using an appeal to pity.

This is in fact the interpretation proposed by Lewis (1993) who argues that in his speech in the *Apology*, Socrates is engaging in a kind of rhetoric of deception: "he is disguising his appeal to pity so well that he can use the appeal and he can also claim credit for not using the appeal" (p. 107).

Lewis shows how Socrates' speech is similar to a peroration in the *Palamedes*, an example of the rhetoric of the day, written by Gorgias. Palamedes' jury also expected him to appeal to pity, but he declines, saying that appeal to pity may be helpful when the trial takes place "before a crowd," but is not proper when addressed to "men of good repute" who are "first among the Greeks" (Seeskin 1987, p. 160).[6] This part of the speech is very similar in its condemnation of appeal to pity to Socrates' refusal to use appeal to pity in the *Apology*, except that Socrates' disavowal is more subtle.

Socrates' speech is very revealing about ancient attitudes toward appeal to pity as a type of argument used in court. It shows that this type of defense tactic was widely used, but it shows also that there must have been wide popular cynicism about it as well. The suggestion is that appeal to pity is a lowbrow crowd-pleaser that is effective enough before a not very intelligent audience, but would be regarded with derision as "pitiful dramatics" by more discerning observers. The attitude revealed then, is one of some conflict regarding the worth of appeal to pity as a type of argumentation, and some questioning of its respectability.

5. ARISTOTLE ON APPEAL TO PITY (*ELEOS*)

In his book on fallacies, *On Sophistical Refutations*, Aristotle does not mention *argumentum ad misericordiam* as a distinctive type of fallacy, although he does consider irrelevance (*ignoratio elenchi*, "ignorance of refutation" or failing to prove the right conclusion), as a fallacy.[7] Even so, Aristotle does write quite a bit about pity (*eleos*) in his other works, and particularly in the *Rhetoric*, showing that he is well aware of the use of appeal to pity as a tactic of argumentation for rhetorical purposes.

Aristotle writes in the *Rhetoric* (1378 a 1–7) that, in order to convince his hearers, the orator needs to appeal to emotions. Among such emotions he includes pity, specifically (1378 a 8–9):

> The emotions are all those affections which cause men to change their opinion in regard to their judgments, and are accompanied by pleasure and pain; such are anger, pity, fear, and all similar emotions and their contraries.

Aristotle even goes on in the *Rhetoric* (1385 b 2–1386 a 12) to define *pity* with care, and to outline what excites it as an emotion that can be invoked. Although he is occasionally negative about appeals to emotion as arguments used—in court, for example—he does not classify them as being fallacious, or as committing any distinctive type of fallacy. And on the contrary he even states that appeals to pity and other emotions can be appropriate arguments, good arguments for an orator to use, at certain stages of a speech. For example, he writes in the *Rhetoric* (1419 b 2) once the proof has been established in making a case, "the natural thing is to amplify or depreciate." And this can be done by appeal to emotions, including pity (1419 b 3–4):

> Next, when the nature and importance of the facts are clear, one should rouse the hearer to certain emotions—pity, indignation, anger, hate, jealousy, emulation, and quarrelsomeness.

This certainly shows that Aristotle would not have condemned use of appeal to pity as inherently fallacious in argumentation. And it may partly explain why he did not cite *argumentum ad misericordiam* as a specific fallacy in his list of fallacies.

On the other hand, it is quite consistent with seeing appeal to pity as a tactic of argumentation that could be abused, and the ancients, as noted above, were quite familiar with this type of abuse of appeal to pity. Indeed, right at the beginning of the *Rhetoric* (354 a 4–7), Aristotle complains that the rhetoricians chiefly devote their attention to "the arousing of prejudice, compassion, anger, and similar emotions" that have no connection to the matter of a discussion, but are directed only to the judge or jury who decide the outcome of a trial. Aristotle adds (354 a 6) that it is wrong to warp the judge's feelings by arousing emotions like anger, jealousy, or compassion, which would "be like making the rule crooked which one intended to use." These remarks certainly indicate an awareness for the potential for misuse of the tactic of appeal to pity to warp or prejudice an audience or judge toward accepting your views by "crooked logic."

However, generally in his ethical views, Aristotle was not against pity as being an inherently irrational emotion, or obstruction to clear thinking, in the way that the Stoics were. He tended to see pity as a normal human response that was not inherently good or bad in itself, even though it could lead to good or bad ends, or it could be bad if given into excessively or thoughtlessly.

Aristotle (*Rhetoric* 1385 b 2–3; Freese, p. 225) defines *pity* (*eleos*) in terms of the state of mind of those who feel it, and in terms of the persons or things that arouse it, or are the objects of it:

> Pity [is] a kind of pain excited by the sight of evil, deadly or painful, which befalls one who does not deserve it; an evil which one might expect to come upon himself or one of his friends, and when it seems near. For it is evident that one who is likely to feel pity must be such as to think that he, or one of his friends, is liable to suffer some evil, and such an evil as has been stated in the definition, or one similar, or nearly similar.

Pity is based on a mental attitude related closely to empathy, because it requires that the pitying party be able to see himself (or one of his friends) in the same kind of distressing situation as the pitied party. Of the things that arouse pity, Aristotle (*Rhetoric* 1386 a 10) lists painful, distressing, and destructive things like injuries, ill-treatment, old age, disease, and lack of food.

Aristotle clearly sees pity as a relation between two parties—a pitier and the person pitied. And he defines pity in terms of the attitude or state of mind of the first party, and the characteristics or situation of the second party. He adds (*Rhetoric* 1386 a 15) that the two parties must have a close proximity to each other, where the "evil appears close at hand."

The Greek words usually translated as pity are *eleos* and *oiktos*. Aristotle always uses the term *eleos*, the less emphatic of the two (Alford 1993, p. 263). The Greek concept of pity may be different, in certain respects from the Latin-based Christian concept that we know as *pity* today (based on *misericordia*), according to Alford (p. 265):

> The Greek concept of pity is pre-Christian. Not the disposition to mercy and compassion, but the felt connection to the suffering of others like oneself, is key. *Suggnome*, a term that Nussbaum (1990: 375) renders as "fellow-thought-and-feeling" captures the experience upon which pity depends, and it is this experience of connection in pity that I emphasize. Or as Stanford (1983: 24) puts it, in *eleos* and *oiktos*, "there is no question here of the pitier being separate from another's agony. You respond to it in the depths of your being, as a harp-string responds by sympathetic resonance to a note from another source."[8]

The Greek terms *eleos* and *oiktos* seem to avoid one of the most objectionable features of pity that were articulated above—namely, the "us-them" bifurcation of the two parties, the pitier and the pitied, being separate and exclusive of each other. The Greek concept seems more like what we would call *empathy* or *sympathy* than *pity*.[9]

Seneca *On Mercy* (II. IV. 4) defined *pity* as "the sorrow of the mind brought about by the sight of the distress of others which it believes come undeservedly" (Basore 1928, pp. 441–42). This definition appears to be quite comparable with Aristotle's. However, there is a contrast in that Seneca's analysis of the implications of pity as an ethical concept are much more negative than Aristotle's. No doubt much of this is simply due to the Stoic point of view, which, as we will see below, was one of suspicion toward the emotions generally.

But there is also a linguistic difference here. Seneca wrote in Latin, in which the term generally used to refer to pity is *misericordia*. This term may have generally had more negative connotations than the Greek term *eleos*.

This negative aspect is brought out even more explicitly when you consider that the adjective *miser* has a strongly negative meaning, well brought out in *A Latin Dictionary* (Lewis and Short 1907, p. 1150):

> *mĭser, ĕra, ĕrum, adj.* [prob. Sanscr. root mi-; cf. minuo; akin to Gr. μῑσοδ; Lat. maestus, maereo], *wretched, unfortunate, miserable, pitiable, lamentable,* etc. (cf.: infelix, calamitosus).

Among other meanings of *miser* listed by Lewis and Short (p. 1150) are "bad, vile, poor, worthless," "sick, ill, indisposed," and "afflicting, sad, wretched, melancholy."

6. THE STOIC CONDEMNATION OF PITY

The school of thought that was most emphatically negative in its views on pity in ancient times was Stoicism. This viewpoint on pity is consistent with the Stoic attitude of suspicion toward emotions generally. The Stoics rejected the Platonic and Aristotelian viewpoint that reason and emotion are two different parts of the soul that can each represent a way of thinking or deliberating to guide virtuous conduct. According to the Stoic viewpoint, the wise person or *sage* is guided by reason alone, in a state of peace of mind of serenity (*ataraxia*). According to the general account of Stoicism given in Striker (1992, p. 1211) the Stoic sage rises above "the passions that trouble ordinary people," maintaining an attitude of detachment from passions like grief or pity. Thus for the Stoics, emotional reactions like pity, fear, or distress, are inherently erroneous, or contrary to the kind of reasoning used in wise deliberation.

Contrary to a somewhat oversimplified account of the Stoic view that seems to be popular, the Stoics did not absolutely condemn all the emotions as irrational. According to Kraye (1988, p. 364), who cites Diogenes Laertius, the Stoics believed that the emotions of joy, precaution, and wishfulness were rational, and therefore good (*eupatheiai*): "But all others, which they categorized under the four general headings of pleasure, distress, fear and desire, were designated as passions (*pathe*) and were by definition wrong and vicious." According to Zeller (1901, p. 246), this reduction of passions or "irrational impulses" to these four cardinal passions is due to Zeno. Presumably, pity would come under the heading of distress. Or, at any rate, it would be condemned by the Stoics insofar as it is a species of distress. The wise man, in the Stoic view, had to overcome these irrational impulses, and even eradicate them, if they became habitual (Zeller 1901, p. 246).

According to Striker (1992, p. 1211) the sage only assents to true "impressions" (propositions or rational thoughts), and is therefore not guided by emotions. To be guided by an emotion, like pity, would be the mark of foolish or erroneous reasoning (p. 1211):

> By contrast, people who are not wise—"fools," as the Stoics called them—are likely to be misled by passion or emotions. These "affections of the soul" were declared by the Stoics to be impulses caused by or consisting in erroneous assent, given to propositions to the effect that some object other than virtue or rationality is good or bad.

In the Stoic view, being guided by a passionate response like distress or pity is a kind of thinking that is based on erroneous assent, and is therefore seen as inherently defective or fallacious reasoning.

Usually the Platonic view is taken to be pretty hard on reasoning based on emotional reactions. For emotion, as a guide to conduct, is seen by Plato as "unruly"—as requiring control or regulation by reason, and as generally being inferior to reason as a guide to conduct. However, the Stoic view is even more sharply dismissive of emotion as a basis for reasoning. Passions, for the Stoic, are inherently misleading, or erroneous, as a basis for reasoning in deliberation, and wise persons will not be influenced by them at all in their thinking.

According to Inwood (1985, p. 125) the term *pathos*, or "passion" is a "term of art" for the Stoics. They treated *pathe* as "wrong by definition" (Inwood, p. 125), so using the term "emotion" to translate *pathos* is misleading, for its Stoic use. Inwood (1985) emphasizes that for the early Stoics, "passions are by definition wrong and vicious" (p. 130), and so Zeller is right to translate *pathe* as "irrational impulses." They were wrong for the Stoics in the sense that following them as impulses violated the Stoic theory of rational action. The wise man is guided in his conduct only by rational impulses, so that being guided by a passion or irrational impulse is characteristically the conduct of the fool.

The later (Roman) Stoic philosopher, Lucius Annaeus Seneca (circa 5 B.C.–65 A.D.), also emphasized that emotions tend to disrupt the tranquility of mind necessary for clear thinking. In his essay *On Anger (De Ira)*, Seneca portrays anger as a kind of disruption or obstruction to reason, in arguing out an issue (I. XVIII. 1–2; Basore 1918, p. 153):

> Reason grants a hearing to both sides, then seeks to postpone action, even its own, in order that it may gain time to sift out the truth; but anger is precipitate. Reason wishes the decision that it gives to be just; anger wishes to have the decision which it has given seem the just decision. Reason considers nothing except the question at issue; anger is moved by trifling things that lie outside the case.

Seneca pinpoints an appeal to emotion like anger as fallacious for two connected reasons: (1) it is moved by irrelevant concerns that "lie outside the case," and (2) it is moved by "trifling things," things that should (according to reason) carry only a small weight as evidence, but that, in a given instance, may "in the heat of the moment" carry quite a large weight in deciding an issue.

In his essay *On Mercy (De Clementia, A.D. 55 or 56)*, Seneca is also quite negative about pity. He writes (II. IV. 4) that although many commend pity (*misericordia*) as a virtue, he thinks it is a "mental defect," an extreme that we ought to avoid, in our thinking (Basore 1918, p. 439). Seneca writes that the good man will display mercy (*clementia*) and gentleness, but will avoid pity. He calls it "a failing of a weak nature that succumbs to the sight of others' ills," an error of reasoning "seen in the poorest types of persons" who are "moved by the tears of the worst criminals" (II. IV. 3). Generally, Seneca sees appeal to pity as a disruption of the wise man's use of reason in argumentation. Although he does not label the *argumentum ad misericordiam* specifically as a fallacy or sophistical refutation,[10] he is consistently negative about it as a type of reasoning, or a way of arriving at a reasoned decision.

7. THE CHRISTIAN VIEW OF PITY

The idea that pity is not a virtue, or that it could even be the failing of a weak and gullible person who succumbs to faulty reasoning, would certainly seem to be a problem for Christian ethics. For Christ is portrayed in the Bible as being very sympathetic and compassionate to people who are sick, poor, or otherwise in desperate circumstances. Not only that, but Christ often appears to advocate a highly compassionate and empathetic attitude. He forgives sinners, heals the sick, blind, and lame, and generally advocates the virtue of helping those in need of assistance.

In the parable of the good Samaritan (*Luke* 10, 29–37), he commends the Samaritan who, when he encountered a man wounded by robbers along the roadside, was moved by pity to bind up the man's wounds and take him to an inn. In *Luke* 18 (22–23), he tells people to sell everything they have, and give the money to the poor. In *Luke* 18 (31–48) a blind man asks Jesus to have pity on him, and Jesus restores his sight. All this suggests strongly that from a Christian point of view, there is nothing wrong with appealing to pity.

However, the problem for Christian theologians is that they are aware of the Stoic objections to the wise man being moved by passion, and therefore have a need to deal with questions raised by appeals to pity as a basis for reasoned action.

In *Question 59* of the *Summa Contra Gentiles* (Book III), Aquinas states that passions are not in themselves good or evil (Pegis 1945, p. 449). His reason is that passion is just "a movement of the sensitive appetite," whereas human "good and evil is in terms of the reason" (p. 449). Aquinas's definition of moral virtue is expressed in Aristotelian terms of "the mean" between extremes and "the prudent man": "a habit of choosing the mean appointed by reason as a prudent man would appoint it" (p. 450). Pity is described as a virtue, then, just to the extent that it is commensurate with reason (*Reply Obj. 3*, p. 450):

Reply Obj. 3. Pity is said to be a virtue, *i.e.,* an act of virtue, in so far as *that movement of the soul is obedient to reason; viz., when pity is bestowed without violating justice, as when the poor are relieved, or the penitent forgiven,* as Augustine says. But if by pity we understand a habit perfecting man so that he bestows pity reasonably, nothing hinders pity, in this sense, from being a virtue. The same applies to similar passions.

Aquinas is very well aware of the problem posed by feelings like pity as a possible interference in prudent reasoning. He quotes previous philosophers who have remarked on passions destroying the judgment of prudence or making it not easy for the mind to grasp the truth (p. 451). He even cites the Stoics (p. 451), who held the passions to be "inordinate affections" that are "incompatible with virtue" (p. 452).

In *Article 3*, Aquinas asks whether sorrow is compatible with moral virtue (p. 452). He notes (p. 452) that the Stoics "denied that anything corresponding to sorrow could be in the soul of the wise man." However, Aquinas indicates his disagreement with the Stoic view:

> *On the contrary,* Christ was perfect in virtue. But there was sorrow in Him, for He said (*Matt.* xxvi. 38): *My soul is sorrowful even unto death.* Therefore sorrow is compatible with virtue. [p. 452]

Aquinas concludes, after a careful evaluation of the Stoic viewpoint, that only immoderate sorrow is bad, for praiseworthy sorrow for another's sin is, or for one's own sin, can be a contributing step toward salvation (p. 453). So (p. 454), a virtuous person will have sorrow for acts that are against moral virtue.

Aquinas sees that the problem of how to handle appeal to pity as a kind of argument depends on how you define *pity*. If pity is defined as a passion or emotion, it follows that appeal to pity is neither against reason nor in support of it. But if we understand pity as something that is bestowed reasonably, in a way that contributes to, rather than hinders prudent deliberations, then nothing prevents pity from being seen as a virtue.

Although elements of Stoic ethics had been adopted by early Christian writers, the Stoic view that the emotions should be eradicated was troubling (Kraye 1988, p. 367) to some of the church fathers. Thus there was a need for Christian theologians to deal with the conflict between the Stoic view and the sympathy and compassion displayed by Christ, which was a model of virtue for the Christian. This conflict was a source of concern to many Christian thinkers in the renaissance period documented by Kraye (pp. 368–69):

> Salutati at first questioned whether any man, except Christ, could achieve the emotionless virtue demanded by the Stoics. Later he concluded that not even Christ had attained this state, for he had wept and bellowed at the death of Lazarus. So, in Salutati's view, the Stoic doctrine of apathy was in conflict not only with nature but also with the example set by Christ himself. Christ's anger at the scribes and Pharisees was used in similar fashion against the Stoics by Clichtove, who corroborated the point by citing Augustine's view that those emotions which followed right reason were neither diseased nor vicious. Calvin rejected the views of those contemporary followers of Stoicism who considered not only weeping and moaning but even feeling sadness and concern to be vices. Christ had wept and moaned at his own misfortunes and those of others; and he had taught his disciples to do likewise. Vermigli thought that the Aristotelian acceptance of the emotion was closer to Christianity than the Stoic repudiation of them: "Christ wept; the prophets and saints wept. And we are told to feel compassion for the suffering." Melanchthon complained that the Stoics wanted to eradicate all emotions, good and bad alike; whereas the good ones, such as fear of God, trust and love for one's wife and children, were actually required by divine law.

Clearly then from a Christian point of view, there is much to be said for the emotion of compassion for the suffering as a basis for good acts of charity.

From this point of view, the Stoic position is too inflexible to accommodate compassion as a virtue, and the Aristotelian ethic of virtue as a mean is a much more compatible approach, one that can admit appeals to feeling, in moderation. It seems then that from the Christian point of view, there is a presumption generally in favor of pity and compassion as good qualities. However, there is also a clear awareness, well articulated by Aquinas, of the danger of immoderate or uncritical appeals to pity that could be in conflict with the reasoning of a prudent person.

8. SYMPATHY AS AN ETHICAL CONCEPT

In the history of ethics, there have been a few major thinkers—especially in the eighteenth century—who have given sympathy a place of prominence in their ethical theories. These notably include David Hume, Adam Smith, and Arthur Schopenhauer.

It is noteworthy that these thinkers prefer the word *sympathy* as their chosen term for this quality they designate as a special virtue, and not the word *pity*. In general, the way they think of sympathy is probably closer to what we would nowadays call *empathy*.

David Hume (1711–1776) is most well known among the ethical theorists who have based their theories on the concept of sympathy. Sympathy had a central place in Hume's ethics. He defined it (1888; 1965, p. 317) on the basis of our idea or impression of self, which he described as "lively" and "vivid." But since other people closely resemble ourselves, we can "enter into" the sentiments or passions of others (p. 318). Thus sympathy is a kind of "second-hand" sentiment (our term, not Hume's)—that is, the sentiment of the other is converted into one's own sentiment of sympathy (p. 319) by means of an association between the idea of another person "and that of our own" (p. 322). As Hume put it, in the form of an analogy, "the minds of men are mirrors to one another."

What Hume stressed in this account of sympathy is the ability of one person to "identify" with the feeling he presumes another to have, by the kind of transference process he describes. What Hume called sympathy, then, would probably be called empathy nowadays, a term derived from the social sciences—see chapter 3. Empathy is precisely this "capacity to understand what another person is experiencing from within the other person's frame of reference " (Bellet and Maloney 1991, p. 1831).

In fact, according to the account of Hume's concept of sympathy given by Lindgren (1992, p. 1162), Hume's notion of sympathy is often called empathy:

> The function of sympathy is to reconcile a disparity between action and spectator. The perspectives taken by the actor and the spectator are separated by a gulf which must be bridged if judgment is to take place. Sympathy, imagining oneself in the situation of the other, bridges that gulf. Hume was content with sympathy of this kind, often called empathy.

Chismar (1988, p. 259) calls this a "minimalist" definition of sympathy, and suggests that it was perhaps the need to refer to it by a distinctive word that led to the coining of the term *empathy* in the twentieth century (see chapter 3).

Adam Smith (1723–1790) had a somewhat more robust concept of sympathy that took into account the kind of case where the interests of the actor and spectator may be different, so that an "affective gulf" between the two must be bridged. According to Lindgren (1992, p. 1162), Adam Smith's concept of sympathy requires the two parties to come close together in a kind of affective concord:

> [According to Smith's account], sympathy is required to bridge the gulf, although sympathy of a different sort. Here what is required is that both actor and spectator attune the interest they take in the actor's situation until the two are in sufficient concord to permit them to sustain one another's company. The process by which that concord of sentiment is negotiated among the parties resembles the bargaining of a marketplace.

Despite this additional dimension, Smith's account of sympathy still seems "mimimalist," and is so described by Chismar (1988, p. 259), putting it also in the category of empathy.

Another philosopher who gave the concept of a leading role in his ethical theory was Arthur Schopenhauer (1788–1860). Schopenhauer praised sympathy as the highest of the moral virtues, and defined it as the "will to live . . . breaking through the separateness that divides one person from another" (Mooney 1992, p. 1223).

Schopenhauer (1818; 1961, p. 386) described sympathy as a kind of participation one person can have in the feelings of another—and not always just the negative feelings of grief, sorrow, or pain of the other. He also saw it as a positive kind of emotion that could take the form of participating in another's joy: "sympathy shows itself in the sincere participation in [another person's] joy and grief, and the disinterested sacrifices made in respect of the latter" (386). This quite robust view of sympathy seems to go beyond empathy, and to take into account participation and sacrifice in the other party's interests and emotions.

Within these accounts of sympathy, there seem to be different opinions and shades of emphasis on how sympathy should be defined. Is it more like empathy—a kind of disinterested or minimalistic entering into another party's point of view or frame of reference without being active or positive in supporting that point of view—or siding with it? Or should sympathy be seen as more than mere empathy? Should sympathy be seen as empathy plus more positive support or participation in the other's joy or grief, as Schopenhauer defined it?

Mercer (1972, p. 21) criticizes Hume's account of sympathy by alleging that he fails to include practical concern with the other, an essential part of *sympathy*. See also Ardal (1966, chapter 3), however, and Baier (1991, 146–51) for further discussion. Another curious aspect of Hume's account is that sympathy is emphatically *not* seen as an emotion or passion (in his sense), but as a transference of emotion or "emotional infection" (Mercer 1972, p. 21). Hence our description of it as being equivalent to what we would now call empathy. However, Hume did clearly distinguish between sympathy and pity. Although sympathy was a positive basis for his ethical viewpoint, he had some negative things to say about pity.

9. EARLY MODERN VIEWS OF PITY

The concept of pity posed a problem for Hume. Although pity, for Hume, is based on and presupposes sympathy, it seems to contain two different directions of sympathy that are at odds with each other. The way Capaldi (1992, p. 182) explains Hume's concept of pity, it almost seems to be a concept that contains a tension or contradiction:

> Pity is problematic because it gives rise to a sympathetic hatred as well as a sympathetic love. From one point of view, the observer feels hatred because of the poverty and meanness of the victim. From another point of view, the observer feels love and a secondary sensation resembling benevolence (*Treatise*, p. 385). The problem is one of accounting for the presence of anything but benevolence or "why does sympathy in uneasiness ever produce any passion beside goodwill and kindness?" [*Treatise*, p. 385]

Hume's solution to this problem is to distinguish between weak and strong sympathy. Weak sympathy is limited to the present moment, whereas strong sympathy includes the broader circumstances of a person's situation "whether past, present or future; possible, probable or certain" (*Treatise*, p. 386). Using this distinction, Hume is able to give a solution to the problem of pity (*Treatise*, p. 385):

Now I assert, that when a sympathy with uneasiness is weak, it produces hatred or contempt by the former cause; when strong, it produces love or tenderness by the latter. This is the solution of the foregoing difficulty, which seems so urgent.

Hume solves the problem by arguing that in the same case where one party pities another, the pitying party could be affected by both a strong and a weak sympathy, at the same time. Hence contempt can be felt, mixed in with the strong sympathy of love or tenderness.

Other ethical theorists have also brought out some negative implications in the concept of pity. Adam Smith (1759; 1964), defined *pity* (or *compassion*) as "the emotion which we feel for the misery of others, when we either see it, or are made to conceive it in a very lively manner." By this definition, pity has a negative implication that sympathy does not seem to have. For to be in *misery* is to be in a bad situation, and, as Hume remarked, that means that the observer feels a certain kind of *hatred* or negative reaction to the situation, or even the person of the *victim*.

Spinoza was even harder on pity as an ethical concept than Adam Smith. He gave some additional reasons why it should be regarded as bad. In *Ethics* (book 4, p. 224), Spinoza wrote that pity is "in itself evil" and is for "a man who lives according to the guidance of reason" something that is "in itself bad and unprofitable." Spinoza seemed to object to pity on grounds that are at least partly logical in nature—he portrayed it as an emotion that is useless for the guidance of reason, because it can too easily mislead or deceive this guidance of reason (*Ethics*, book 4, p. 225):

> We must add also that a man who is easily touched by the emotion of pity, and is moved by the misery or tears of another, often does something of which he afterward repents, both because from an emotion we do nothing which we certainly know to be good and also because we are so easily deceived by false tears.

Spinoza is against pity on two counts. Not only is it bad or inappropriate as an ethical response in itself, but it is also a source of deception and bad reasoning.

This is a surprisingly strong view of pity. It seems very reminiscent of the Stoic view, especially in seeing pity as an "irrational impulse" or harmful emotion that disturbs and goes against clear-minded reasoning. Spinoza sees "false tears" as deceptive, implying that in rationally responding to appeals to pity, there is great danger of committing a fallacy or mistake in reasoning.

Nietzsche was also highly negative on the concept of pity, and presented arguments against it. He associated pity with the negative reactions of slave morality to an aristocratic master morality. This response is a resentment of the power of the master morality, and there is a direct connection between pity and this resentment, or *ressentiment*, according to Green (1992, p. 63):

> *Ressentiment* is the suppression of a desire for revenge against those stronger or more accomplished than oneself and the psychological concomitants of such suppression. Those suffering from *ressentiment* often look for indirect means of revenge against the strong. The advocation of pity is an example of such indirect revenge. The weak advocate pity in an attempt to restrain and to weaken the strong by instilling in them a value that inhibits the expression of strength. In addition, imaginary punishment of the strong, through God's intervention, is part of many moralities of pity, most notably Christianity.

From this account, it is clear that Nietzsche saw pity in a negative light, and he even argued that pity, based as it is on resentment, involves an inconsistency as an attitude. Green (1992, p. 65) cites the example of someone who rejects the value of winning, because he feels pity, and says "If only everyone could win!" But this is logically absurd, because in such a case "there would be no winners or losers at all" (p. 66). Thus from Nietzsche's viewpoint, the attitude of pity has an inherent contradictoriness built into it.

Of course, this is an ethical viewpoint that cannot be directly applied to appeal to pity as a kind of argument used in logic. But it does suggest that, by being so negative about pity generally as an attitude, someone who adopted the Nietzschean viewpoint would be inclined to think of appeal to pity as very suspicious, as a logical type of argument.

10. TERMINOLOGICAL QUESTIONS

A central problem now revealed is the ambiguity of the term *misericordia* posing a great gulf. The ethical thinkers are ready to defend and to value sympathy or compassion, but the verdict on

pity is much more mixed. Not only are many of them highly negative about pity, but some, like Hume and Nietzsche, even find contradictory elements in the notion.

The logic textbooks use the Latin phrase *argumentum ad
misericordiam*, suggesting perhaps a technical term with more pre-
cision than the English word *pity*. Does *misericordia* really mean
pity, or does it refer to something else, like mercy or compassion,
that might not have the negative implications of pity outlined above?

Looking at the definitions given by some standard Latin dictio-
naries, *misericordia* seems to be pretty close to pity, and appears to
have the same kinds of negative connotations.[11] However, these dictionary entries also appear to allow considerable room for ambiguities.

The *Oxford Latin Dictionary* (Glare, 1982, p. 1118), gives two
meanings for the noun *misericordia*:

> *misericordia* ~ae. *f.* [MISERICORS + -IA]
> *1* Tender-heartedness, pity, compassion.
> *2* Appeal to compassion, pathos.

Both meanings contain the item *compassion*, but only one of them
contains the item *pity*. However, the word *pathos* (the root of
pathetic) may contain the same negative implications that are sometimes found objectionable in the word *pity*. The adjective *miseri-
cors* is given a similar two-tiered meaning in the *OLD* (p. 1118),
except that the word *pitiful* occurs explicitly in the second meaning:

> *misericors* ~rdis, *a compar.* ~rdior. [MISER + COR]
> *1* Tender-hearted, merciful, compassionate.
> *2* Calculated to excite compassion, pitiful.
> assidua pro fratre ac ~rs deprecatio RUT.LUP. I.20.

It seems fair to conclude, judging by this account, that *misericordia*
is ambiguous, even though the two meanings overlap somewhat,
and are not that far apart. It also seems that one of the meanings, the
one that seems to fit the usage of the *argumentum ad misericordiam* as a type of argument characterized in the logic textbooks
(meaning 2, above, in both entries) has a stronger negative implication than the other. Indeed, you might say that meaning 1 does not
have the negative implications of *pity*, while meaning 2 does have
such implications.

The *Oxford English Dictionary* (Simpson and Weiner 1989, p.
864) gives the primary meaning of *misericord* as "compassion, pity,

mercy." Three more specialized senses are also given (p. 864). One is the monastic meaning of a special apartment where certain relaxations of the rules of the monastery were permitted. Another is a shelving projection under a hinged seat in a choir stall that gave support to someone standing in the stall—for example, an aged monk who needed special support to stand during church services. A third meaning refers to a special type of dagger used to give the coup de grâce to a wounded knight who is suffering.

Of course, we are not bound to retaining the original or old meaning of the Latin phrase *argumentum ad misericordiam* as a technical term for a certain type of argument in logic. And we are also free to retain the Latin phrase, but give it a new, or more precise, meaning as a term of art. But what should we take it to mean—appeal to pity or compassion (or mercy or sympathy, or something else, or some combination of the above)? As shown in the next chapter, it will make a big difference which option is selected, when it comes to identifying, analyzing, and evaluating this type of argument from a logical point of view.

3

Identifying the *Ad Misericordiam* As a Type of Argument

Before we can get to the main problem of judging *ad miseri-cordiam* arguments as fallacious or nonfallacious, there is a prior problem of defining the type of argument involved. For, as chapter 1 abundantly indicated, there is considerable disagreement, even to the point of confusion, within the textbook treatments, on how to define the *ad misericordiam* as a clearly identifiable species of argumentation. Is it appeal to pity, or appeal to sympathy? Or perhaps both combined? Or does it include appeal to compassion or mercy? And what are pity and sympathy anyway? What are compassion and mercy? Can all of these terms be defined in a clear enough way so that we can tell, in some practically useful way, whether the argument we have in a given case really is an appeal to pity (or sympathy, or compassion, or mercy)? And what exactly is the difference between pity and sympathy anyway? Is there a significant difference, and if so, does it mean that the one type of appeal is fallacious while the other is not? These are the prior questions that need to be addressed before *ad misericordiam* arguments can be evaluated.

One important difference between pity and sympathy has already come out clearly. While sympathy is generally conceived as good or virtuous, from an ethical point of view, pity is often seen as containing negative connotations of condescension and even contempt. This perceived negative aspect of pity is a good place to begin.

1. THE JERRY LEWIS TELETHON
FOR MUSCULAR DYSTROPHY

Muscular dystrophy is a group of inherited diseases that cause degeneration of muscle fibres. The most common form, Duchenne dystrophy, starts in the preschool years. Walking difficulties usually require the use of a wheelchair for these children, but muscle wasting continues, often resulting in death before age twenty.[1]

The Muscular Dystrophy Association (MDA), founded in the 1950s by patients, physicians, and parents of children with muscular dystrophy, supports research centers and services to patients and their families. Since 1965 the Muscular Dystrophy Association's annual telethon, hosted by Jerry Lewis, has been a familiar televised plea for funds featuring Jerry's kids, children with muscular dystrophy, and popular celebrities. A Labor Day tradition, the Jerry Lewis Telethon attracts audiences of a size that competes with the Super Bowl and Academy Awards every year. In 1991 it raised over forty-five million dollars, and by 1992 it had raised a total of over one billion dollars. About 24 percent of the proceeds goes to administrative expenses (Del Valle 1992, p. 36).[2] Lewis himself receives no money for the telethon (Associated Press 1978, p. 69).

In 1977 Lewis was nominated for the Nobel Peace Prize in honor of work for the Muscular Dystrophy Association. In 1978 he was honored by the American Institute for Public Service for the "greatest public service for the disadvantaged" (*Special to the New York Times*, June 28, 1978, A16).

But starting in 1981, a number of individuals with muscular dystrophy, including some who had formerly appeared on the telethon as children, began to criticize Lewis for using pity to make money. Evan Kemp, Jr., chairman of the Equal Opportunity Commission in the Bush administration, who has a form of muscular dystrophy, accused Lewis of using a "pity" approach that reinforces a "stigma" or "stereotype" of disabled people by emphasizing their helplessness (Kemp 1981, A19):

> With its emphasis on "poster children" and "Jerry's kids," the telethon focuses primarily on children. The innocence of children makes them ideal for use in a pity appeal. But by celebrating disabled children and ignoring disabled adults, it seems to proclaim that the only socially acceptable status for disabled people is their early childhood. The handicapped child is

appealing and huggable—the adolescent or mature adult is a cripple to be avoided.

Treating all disabled people as children is tragic both to the child and to society. Playing to pity may raise money, but it also raises walls of fear between the public and us.

Instead of portraying disabled people as working and raising families, Kemp concluded, the telethon portrayed them as "sick" people who should let others take care of them until a cure is found.

During subsequent telethons, demonstrations were put on in various cities by persons with muscular dystrophy, including former "poster children" who had earlier taken part in the telethon campaigns. They said that Lewis had "portrayed them as objects of pity instead of capable people worthy of respect" (*New York Times National* 1992, p. 39). Disability activists accused the fund raisers for charities of using demeaning and insulting tactics (Johnson 1992, p. 232):

> They accuse the charities of treating disabled people as objects of pity and say they paint a picture of disability as a fate worse than death, and of disabled people as desperately waiting for a cure, without which their lives are worthless. They particularly hate Lewis, who insists on calling adults with muscular dystrophy "Jerry's kids." They say that viewing disabled people as eternal children, sexless and incapable of handling their affairs, is a real cause of disability discrimination in this country.
>
> In 1990, just weeks after the signing of the Americans with Disabilities Act, when most activists were still buoyant about their civil rights win, *Parade* magazine ran a particularly noxious piece by Lewis as the celebrity's annual Labor Day appeal article. In "If I Had Muscular Dystrophy," Lewis wrote, "So I decided, after 41 years of battling this curse that attacks children of all ages . . . I would put myself in that chair . . . that steel imprisonment that long has been deemed the dystrophic child's plight. . . . I just have to learn to try to be good at being half a person."

The objection made by Johnson (1992, p. 233) to the Jerry Lewis Telethon is that the fund-raising appeal rests on the underlying concept that "we," the healthy people, are on a "superior perch," and need to give money to those "failed normals" to save them. The objection is to the condescension that the appeal to pity is based on.[3] Another critic put it by saying that Lewis treats people with muscular dystrophy "as though he's in an ivory tower handing something down" (Del Valle 1992, p. 36).

Lewis replied that his critics are "a small minority" who "confuse compassion for pity" (Shapiro 1992, p. 39). But one of the critics, citing the *Parade* article, replied, "pity is exactly what Lewis appeals to" (Shapiro, p. 39). The implication accepted by both sides in this dispute seems to be that it is appealing to pity, which is specifically the basis for objection, and that appealing to compassion, by contrast, is not objectionable.

The controversy continues. In 1991, MDA spent twenty-one million dollars on medical research, and fifty-one million dollars on treatment, equipment, and counseling—76.7 percent of its income on program services (Shapiro, p. 40). Against criticisms that all telethons are inherently bad because they portray the disabled as pitiable, defenders of the telethon claim that they no longer use a "pity approach" (Shapiro, p. 40):

> Lewis and telethon supporters counter that MDA, the world's largest private sponsor of neuromuscular-disease research, needs to tug on heartstrings in order to raise money for good works. But James Williams Jr., head of the National Easter Seal Society, says his group's telethon actually started making more money—from $23 million in 1985 to $42 million this year [1992]—once it listened to complaints from disabled people and shunned a "pity approach." MDA did respond, too. Last year, 58 percent of its profiles were of adults.

This reply has evidently not satisfied the protesters, however. They even see the new research breakthroughs in identifying the causes of some common forms of muscular dystrophy as a misplaced emphasis on a cure of something negative, instead of seeing the issue in more positive terms of rights and empowerment.

The protesters' point of view can perhaps be explained, to some extent, by the competition for allocation of funds for cure and medical research, on the one hand, and for improving things like access to employment and transportation, on the other hand. The Americans with Disabilities Act (ADA), passed by the U.S. House of Representatives on May 22, 1990, which went into effect on January 26, 1991, extended protection against discrimination against people with physical or mental disabilities.[4] This bill required every retail establishment to be made accessible, including lifts and wheelchair ramps where necessary. It also made it illegal to refuse to hire a qualified applicant just because of the person's disability. It is revealing to note that the ADA was the subject of much public discussion right around the time the protests to the Jerry Lewis Telethon began to be made.

More recently, the objections of the protesters have been even more fully and forcefully articulated. A book (Shapiro 1993) argues for the thesis that there should be no pity or tragedy in disability, and that it is society's stereotypes who make being disabled difficult. A British group of protesters, called Block Telethon, adopting the slogan "piss on pity," argued that telethons perpetuate a "pathetic and dependent victim image" (Fletcher 1992, p. 22). Another protester wrote (Milam 1993, pp. 23–24) that he saw the Jerry Lewis Telethon as a kind of "blackmail tactic," a "bold use of pity to extract money" that deeply offended him:

> Jerry's Kids, the sweet smiles and clean faces used to whip us up—and to whip us—for contributions. The palsied bodies, the tears, the raw sentiment (this could happen to you!), all with the purpose of extracting millions of dollars from a willing audience. It is a highly programmed, highly organized blackmail, utilizing every device, every tool.

The argument expressed here is that the appeal to pity conveyed by the orchestrated television appearance of Jerry's kids is a deliberate public relations tactic of deceptive whipping up of emotions for the calculated purpose of raising money.

To some extent, the negative reaction of protesters is based on reasons similar to the Stoic rejection of appeal to pity—pity is portrayed as a sentiment or passion that is being exploited as a rhetorical device, an "irrational impulse" that is substituted for and interferes with rational thinking. But the objection of the protesters to pity goes deeper than that. Their objection is ethical in nature. Their objection is to the concept of pity itself, which for them has highly negative connotations of condescension toward the pitied party as a "pathetic and dependent victim." The basis of their objection is that pitying the children who have muscular dystrophy is portraying them in a negative way, by projecting an image that is depriving them of their civil rights.

What has been made apparent generally from these reactions to the Jerry Lewis Telethon is the feeling of a very strong negative reaction to the use of appeal to pity, and to pity generally as an attitude. The basis of it is that it divides the pitier and the pitied in an us-them relationship where the subject is seen as superior and the object (the pitied person) as inferior. This relationship, according to the protesters, denies dignity and respect to the object of pity.

Surprisingly perhaps, this negative attitude toward pity is very much evident in the treatments of some recent philosophers who have addressed themselves to defining and analyzing pity as an emotion with negative moral implications.

2. NEGATIVE ATTITUDES TOWARD PITY

Ben-Ze'ev (1993, p. 3) defines *pity* as "sympathetic sorrow over substantial misfortune of someone who is considered inferior in some aspect and whose situation will not be significantly changed by the subject." This definition explicitly makes pity highly negative in two respects. First, the pitied party is "considered inferior." Second, the pitying party cannot change the situation of the pitied party (significantly). Ben-Ze'ev (p. 4) goes so far as to characterize pity as not only requiring that the subject have sympathy for the object (as he calls the pitied party), but also a "contempt of the object." He sees both pity and envy as "based on a perception of inferiority in a comparison between the subject and the object of the emotion" (p. 5). This is a strikingly negative definition of pity as an ethical concept, one that makes the negative implications of it quite explicit.

However, as we saw in chapter 2, section 7, there does seem to be a broadly Christian presumption that pity is a good quality or virtue, which can be a motivation for charitable deeds. Hence there does seem to be a conflict inherent in traditional Western attitudes toward pity. Although pity has been seen as generally good, or a basis for good by some, others have viewed it in a very negative way, seeing it, in some instances, as inherently bad.

The conflict of attitudes in Western ethical traditions is well brought out by the entry on pity in the *Dictionary of Philosophy* (Runes 1984, p. 236). Although there is a biblical tradition in support of pity as a virtue, there is also evident in philosophical writings a sharply negative feeling about pity as an ethical concept:

> *Pity:* A more or less condescending feeling for other living beings in their suffering or lowly condition, condoned by those who hold to the inevitability of class differences, but con-

demned by those who believe in melioration or the establishment of more equitable relations and therefore substitute sympathy (q.v.). Synonymous with "having mercy" or "to spare" in
the Old Testament (the Lord is "of many bowels"), Christians
also are exhorted to be pitiful (e.g., 1 Pet. 3.8). Spinoza yet
equates it with commiseration, but since this involves pain in
addition to some good if alleviating action follows, it is to be
overcome in a life dictated by reason. Except for moral theories
which do not recognize feeling for other creatures as a fundamental urge pushing into action, such as utilitarianism in some
of its aspects and Hinduism which adheres to the doctrine of
karma (q.v.), however far apart the two are, pity may be
regarded a prime ethical impulse but, due to its coldness and
the possibility of calculation entering, is no longer counte-
nanced as an essentially ethical principle in modern moral
thinking.—K.F.L.[5]

The negative aspects brought out here include not only condescension but also "coldness" and "calculation." This account makes pity
seem mainly negative, from an ethical point of view, even going so
far as to conclude that it has no place in modern moral thinking as
an ethical principle. This rejection of pity seems to be on grounds
similar to those given by the Stoics.

Lucius Annaeus Seneca, as we noted in chapter 2, section 6,
was very specific in his condemnation of pity as an emotion. Seneca
definitely did not see pity as a virtue. He pointed out certain specific
faults with pity, as a basis for his objections to it. In *On Mercy* (II. v.
3)[6] he wrote "no sorrow befalls the wise man," who stays above
emotions like pity. For pity would blunt the power of the wise man's
power of clear thinking and foresight. Hence, according to Seneca
(*On Mercy*, II. v. 3) this wise man will not pity but will give help,
"will succor, will benefit" (Basore, pp. 441–43). Seneca generally saw
pity (II. VI. 1) as "a weakness of the mind that is much over-per-
turbed by suffering" (Basore, p. 443). This is a typical Stoic doctrine
to the effect that excessive emotions like pity are bad, because they
disturb the tranquility of thinking that the wise man must culti-
vate.

Seneca writes (*On Mercy*, II. IV. 4; Basore, p. 437) that "many
commend [pity] as a virtue, and call a pitiful man good," but this is
an error. According to Seneca (Basore, p. 439), this error is often seen
in the poorest types of persons, "who are moved by the tears of the
worst criminals who, if they could, would break open their prison."

Here pity is portrayed as a weak emotional response to which the worst type of person is most susceptible.

And as was shown in chapter 2, the ancients were well aware of the danger of emotional appeals, like the arousing of pity or anger, used to distract a judge or jury away from the matters they should be paying attention to in an argument. Aristotle, in the *Rhetoric* (1354a) complained that the rhetorical handbooks in use at the time devote too much attention to such appeals.[7]

What seems to be identified as bad by these ancient writers, however, is not so much pity, in itself, as an ethical concept, but the appeal to pity as a type of argument that can be irrelevant, or a distraction from clear reasoning or good judgment.

However, even in the ancient world, as shown by Seneca's remarks above, by Roman times there did seem to be emerging more of a negative ethical attitude toward pity as something that should not be classified as a virtue. But the basis for this rejection seems to be different from that voiced by the protesters in the Jerry Lewis case. In Seneca's rejection of pity as a virtue, the problem is that pitiers are exhibiting an irrational response that shows that they are "weak" and too easily manipulated by, say, a hardened criminal who sheds tears. The protesters' rejection is on a different basis. They object that pitiers are putting themselves on a higher level than the pitied, treating them like a "helpless victim" and thereby robbing them of their human dignity as a person. It is this ethical basis for rejecting pity that we find supported in the modern commentators.

According to Ben-Ze'ev (p. 9) pity is an emotional interaction between a subject and an object, and each party has characteristic attitudes. The subject has an attitude of sympathetic sorrow, and this is an inherently negative attitude. Hence the objects of pity are not happy about this state—"people do not like to be pitied" (p. 9). Here then is one important ethical basis of the negative reaction of the protesters. The "object" is treated as inferior or wretched, implying the subject is in a superior position, or "on a pedestal" to cite a phrase used by the protesters.

These negative reactions are further articulated by Mercer (1972, p. 18):

> The use of the word "pity" in a particular context seems to imply that the speaker is in some way better off than the person who is pitied. The king pities the subject; the judge pities the prisoner; the sane man pities the idiot; mankind pities the beasts. We implore others "to have pity on us" in much the

same way as we implore them "to have mercy on us." "I pity you" is more often than not equivalent to "I despise you." It does not even appear that "pity" entails an attitude of concern towards the other creature—although, of course, it is often used as an explanation for helping.

In particular, the implication of "I despise you" from "I pity you" is notable as a common connotation. This description of the connotations of the word *pity* as used in conversational language articulates many of the feelings expressed by the protesters to the Jerry Lewis Telethon very well.

But how does this negative implication arise? It seems that the answer is that, by the definition of *pity*, the party being pitied must be in some kind of severe distress, or very bad situation, that the pitying party sees as highly unfortunate—one that she or he would not want to be in.[8] Hence, inevitably, in this type of relationship, the one party is better off than the other, and feels "sorry" for the other.

Snow (1991, p. 196) agrees that when we feel pity, we are "sorry" for the person we pity, and hence we feel "superior" to them:

> When we pity another, we feel sorry for that person, whose negative condition we believe we would not experience, or would not experience in the same way as the one whom we pity. Pity includes a stance of superiority toward the object of emotion that is often expressed in condescension.

The suggestion here is that we feel superior because we (the onlookers) feel we would be able to handle the situation better than the person we pity. Somehow the pitied person is being looked down upon as not being able to handle the situation very well. This is a kind of negative judgment toward the person pitied, implying that the onlooker, or pitying person, is superior, in the sense of being more capable of dealing with a bad situation.

To pursue this question further by pinning down exactly how this negative aspect is essential to the concept of pity, it is necessary to give a clear, analytical definition of pity. The textbook accounts of the *argumentum ad misericordiam*, as noted in chapter 1, too often carelessly translate *misericordia* as sympathy, compassion, mercy, or pity. Now this failure becomes highly significant because the words *compassion* and *sympathy* may not be as objectionable as the term *pity*, which seems to be singled out as the focus of the protester's objections.

As noted in section 1, the reply given by Lewis was that the protesters were confusing compassion and pity. Presumably then, there is an important distinction to be made here. And presumably, *compassion* does not have the negative implications attributed to *pity*.

To work toward a beginning of understanding the basis of this reply, let us begin by attempting a preliminary analytical definition of the term *pity*.

3. A DEFINITION OF *PITY*

In chapter 2, section 5, Aristotle's definition of *pity* from the *Rhetoric* (1385 b 2–3) was quoted. He defined pity (*eleos*) as a kind of "pain excited by the sight of evil, deadly or painful, which befalls one who does not deserve it." Pity, as Aristotle defined it, is a kind of relationship—a mental attitude that one person has toward another.

Aristotle's definition does not look negative, or as though it was meant to be inherently negative. But the negative aspect of it is clearly stated—the pitied party is suffering from an evil, "deadly or painful." The one who feels pity presumably does not suffer from this evil personally—the key requirement being that he or she must think that they are liable to suffer from it.

It is not clear, on Aristotle's account, whether the person who feels pity can do anything to relieve the suffering of the person who is pitied. Possibly he can't if the evil is "deadly," as Aristotle writes. But no explicit ruling on this seems to be made.

Aristotle's way of defining *pity* suggests a kind of framework that can be used to give a more precise analysis of the concept of pity, as follows. According to this analysis, there are eleven distinctive adequacy requirements needed to identify something as an instance of pity:

1. There are two parties x and y, who exist in a relationship to each other; x is the pitier, or subject, and y is the pitied party, or object of pity.
2. x can identify with y—that is, x and y are enough alike, or have enough in common, so that x can relate to y as another person.
3. y is in a situation, or set of circumstances C, as far as x knows (or at least x thinks this to be the case).
4. x does in fact put himself mentally into the situation C of y, so that he can appreciate how y feels about it.

5. C is a bad or catastrophic situation for y (an event or set of circumstances that would be generally judged as particularly unfortunate).
6. y thinks that C is bad, his attitude toward it is one of pain or suffering, at least to some extent, and generally it would be judged as a situation where feeling pain and suffering would be normal and appropriate.
7. y does not deserve being in this set of circumstances.
8. x does not have this same or a comparable bad situation (C) in his personal circumstances.
9. x is liable to suffer from this same type of bad situation (C), meaning that it is possible, and a risk for x.
10. x knows that proposition 8 is true, or thinks it is true with justification.
11. x cannot do much directly to mitigate y's suffering, or to make the evil disappear.

So characterized, pity is a kind of attitude, a relation between two parties where the one party has a characteristic attitude toward the particular situation of the other party. The eleven clauses express necessary conditions for pity to exist in a given case. And presumably, the eleven requirements, taken together, also provide a set of conditions sufficient to determine a case of pity.

This definitional framework is a good basis for analysis and discussion in what follows, but there are several aspects of it that are very controversial. In particular, clause 11 is a source of much controversy.

First, it is debatable whether clause 11 is really necessary. In the Jerry Lewis Telethon case, some of those involved felt that scientific research could help to deal with muscular dystrophy, or even provide a cure, and there was evidence that this was true. However, the protesters seemed to oppose this point of view, or to feel it didn't address their problem.

Generally, those who see pity as a morally negative concept may see clause 11 as the basis of the problem. Seneca, as noted above, thought pity negative because one should "succor" or give help, instead of pitying someone. Citing clause 11 then, one could object that pity is a kind of "helpless" or counterproductive attitude that does not address the problem or misfortune in a constructive way.

But is clause 11 really essential to the concept of pity? Aristotle does not require it, and some might argue that it should be dropped, as a mandatory requirement. Here might be the basis of a distinction between compassion and pity, perhaps, as discussed in the next section, below.

But several other bases can be found for evaluating pity negatively from a moral point of view: x and y are separate parties, the "subject" and "object." Does not this "objectify" the situation of y, making y into a nonhuman object? This relation creates the us-them characteristic of pity—or so goes the objection. But in reply to the objection, the word *object* here is not necessarily meant in a derogatory or dehumanizing sense. It merely means that in a relation between two parties of this type the attitude of one *(x)* concerns the situation of the other *(y)*.

Moreover, as clause 2 makes clear, the two parties must be "close" (in some sense) for a relation of pity to exist, so that the one party can put himself into the situation of the other, feeling empathy for the other person's situation. This seems to go against the dehumanizing or objectifying aspect of pity that is objected to those who see pity as negative.

However, judging from the Jerry Lewis Telethon case, it is probably clauses 5, 6, and 8, taken together, that provide the deepest basis for the negative evaluation of pity. Taken together, these clauses seem to suggest that the subject of pity is better than the object—or that he or she is "on the pedestal," looking down on the unfortunate and miserable object, who is in an "evil" situation. It is primarily this aspect of pity that the protesters object to. It makes pity seem so morally negative as a concept.

However, some would question this implication. Evil and misfortune really do exist. Is it better to ignore such things or to deny they really exist, even when we are clearly confronted with them? Is it better to "put on a happy face" and treat others who have a catastrophic, debilitating, or deadly disease as though they were exactly the same as a healthy person? These are the sorts of questions critics would raise on this issue.

Moreover, a secondary rebuttal is to be found in clause 7. If the misfortune is undeserved, then by acknowledging it, or by responding to its badness, one is not implying that the person who suffers from it is at fault, or is any less of a person for being in this situation.

Potential violations of clause 7 are found in cases where persons who appeal to pity for their bad situation were themselves instrumental in bringing about that situation. One kind of case is the person whose house is destroyed by a natural disaster, and who appeals to pity to get aid to rebuild it. Then we find out that he or she was well aware of the hazard of building a house in this particular location. An editorial (*Register-Dispatch* 1993) asks whether insurance companies should be "in the business of subsidizing stupidity":

> *Case* 3.1: From hurricanes on the East Coast to flooding in the Midwest to fires on the West Coast, the nation is having to reconsider the basis for disaster insurance.
>
> To put it bluntly, how much support does the rest of the country owe to people who build in unsafe areas?
>
> Certainly it's difficult to watch people's lives being damaged without wanting to help. In many cases, however, people have built homes and other buildings in areas unsuited for development or they have built buildings that don't take into account natural occurrences such as hurricanes, floods and fires.
>
> Should we be in the business of subsidizing stupidity? If people build their homes in unsafe areas, are we obligated to bail them out when the inevitable disaster strikes? . . .
>
> There probably is not a state in the country that hasn't benefited from emergency relief and natural insurance programs. We need these kinds of programs.
>
> But we also need to push our senators and representatives to make sure those programs reward only the people who take reasonable precautions against disasters. Rewarding people for stupidity is a quick way to go broke.

We should be sympathetic to and help those who suffer from disasters. But perhaps our response of pity for the suffering, in such cases, should be somewhat qualified or reserved, in those cases where the "victim" had a hand in his or her own undoing.

Another case (*Vicksburg Evening Post* 1993) concerned a lawsuit where a jury felt pity for a paraplegic:

> *Case* 3.2: A 23-year-old mugger robbed a 71-year-old man by holding him and choking him. While fleeing the police after the assault, he was shot, after being

ordered to halt. Suffering a spinal injury, he lost the use of both legs. After pleading guilty and being sent to prison, he sued the Transit Authority for "excessive force" and won 4.3 million (U.S.) in damages.

Here too the question of the appropriateness of feeling pity for this individual is tempered by our awareness of his own role in causing his injury.

Clause 4 can also be questionable in some cases. By empathy, the pitier is supposed to put herself or himself into the mind of the pitied person. But this can be difficult to do, in some cases, and errors or deceptions can occur. Recently, psychologists have studied cases of psychopaths who may be described as "social predators who charm, manipulate and ruthlessly plow their way through life, leaving a broad trail of broken hearts, shattered expectations and empty wallets" (attributed to Robert Hare in Hess 1994, A4). Psychopaths show a lack of empathy. However, it is quite possible to be deceived into feeling pity for them, because they are very glib and manipulative, for example (p. A4):

> *Case* 3.3: While Joseph Fredericks shed tears over his vicious attacks on boys, he peeked between his fingers to see the effect his show of remorse was having on the psychiatrist interviewing him.
>
> A sadistic pedophile, who was killed while serving a life sentence for the savage rape and murder of an Ontario boy, Mr. Fredericks was a classic psychopath. The only suffering he cared about was his own.
>
> Although they do not feel normal emotions, psychopaths learn to mimic such feelings brilliantly as a means of getting their own way.

According to Robert Hare, a psychologist at the University of British Columbia, psychopaths frequently fool prison staff, and even psychologists, and it is difficult to spot them (Hess, A4).

Hence there can be a problem with appeals to pity, because they are based on empathy. The structure of the appeal to pity, because of the concept of pity itself (as defined above), presumes that the ways of thinking of the one party are similar enough to, or have enough in common with, those of the other party. The presumption is that they can relate to one another so that one is feeling (roughly) what the other is feeling, in response to similar circumstances. But this requirement can fail to be met in some cases. The following translation of a Greek fable of Babrius is given in Perry (1925, p. 187):

> *Case* 3.4: Fable 143: To Pity the Pitiless is Folly
> A farmer picked up a viper that was almost dead from the cold, and warmed it. But the viper, after stretching himself out, clung to the man's hand and bit him incurably, thus killing (the very one who wanted to save him). Dying, the man uttered these words, worthy to be remembered: "I suffer what I deserve, for showing pity to the wicked."

The problem generally is that a response of pity may seem to be appropriate in a particular case when, in fact, one of the clauses (requirements) of pity is not met.

In considering cases like 3.2, the banishment of pity argument known in the ancient world (Stevens 1944) should be kept in mind. Does a 23-year-old, like the man in case 3.2, who robbed a 71-year-old man by holding him and choking him, deserve our pity or sympathy for what happened to him as a result? Did the 23-year-old show any pity for the advanced age of the other man when he choked him and robbed him? If he didn't show any pity or compassion then, does he deserve our pity now? The banishment of pity argument could be used to point out that not only did the mugger show no pity in attacking an old man, he was also responsible for his own injury through his act of fleeing from the police.

In the definition of pity above, the first ten clauses are essential requirements for pity, but the eleventh clause, although it is important, could possibly be qualified as only being typical or normal, and subject to exceptions. Having now gained at least some provisional basis for clarity on the concept of pity, we can go on to analyze the related concepts of mercy, empathy, sympathy, and compassion.

4. MERCY AND PITY

Mercy (clemency) implies a situation where one individual has some power over the other, and is about to apply some sanction or penalty to the other (or at any rate, may do something that would hurt or cost the other party).

According to this definition of *mercy*, there is a clear contrast between pity and mercy, especially if we require condition 11 of the definition of *pity* in section 3, above. The pitying person can't change the bad situation of the other significantly, whereas the merciful person can.

Ben Ze'ev (1993, p. 14) cites the OED definition of *mercy* with approval, as "holding oneself back from punishing, or from causing suffering to, a person whom one has the right or power to punish." This is similar to pity, in that the subject is superior to the object, but is dissimilar to pity in that the subject has the power to change the inferior position of the object (p. 14).

However, the way that the subject is superior is different. With pity, the object is in a bad or distressful situation, but it is not one that is due to either party, or that either party can do much about, directly. With mercy, the object party is owing some penalty or debt to the subject party, and the subject party has the right to collect this debt, or perhaps to waive it. Thus the bad situation that the object party finds himself in is one that is (at least generally) in the power of the subject party.

In general, although pity and mercy have several elements in common, they are really quite distinct concepts. Mercy requires a structured situation where one party has power over the other. The bad situation that the other party finds himself in may be his own fault—it may be a situation he has caused himself, and deserves to be in—see the contrast with clause 6 in the definition of *pity* given in section 3, above.

Also, mercy requires a particular well-structured power relationship between the two parties that pity does not. Mercy is very well defined in a fragment from the writings of Seneca preserved in a letter by Hildebert of Tours (Basore, p. 449):

> It is the part of mercy to cause some abatement of a sentence that aims at revenge. He who does not remit the punishment of wrong-doing is a wrong-doer. It is a fault to punish a fault in full. He shows himself merciless whose might is his delight.
>
> It is a shining virtue for a prince to punish less than he might. It is a virtue to be forced by necessity to take vengeance, not to visit it voluntarily. The merciful man when injured savours of something great and godlike.

The kind of situation characteristic of mercy is where one party has the power to punish another person for a transgression, but punishes him "less than he might." This is mercy, and one can see that it is quite different from pity, and need not (in all cases) be based on pity.

Seneca (*On Mercy* I. IX.2–I. IX. 9; Basore, pp. 381–89) gives a very good illustration:

> *Case* 3.5: The emperor Augustus was informed that one Lucius Cinna, a dull-witted man, was concocting a plot to kill him. At first, he decided to have Cinna killed, but then he changed his mind, and had a long talk with him, which revealed Cinna's knowledge of the plot. Nevertheless, Augustus not only spared Cinna's life, but gave him a consulship, and he ultimately proved to be a loyal friend and supporter. For this act, Augustus was widely admired for his mercifulness.

In this case, we have all the elements of mercy. Augustus had the right, and perhaps even the obligation, to exact the normal penalty for plotting to kill the emperor. But, in this case, he showed mercy by making an exception to the rule, showing a kindness and intelligent flexibility that turned out to be wise.

A comparable case is given by Rainbolt (1990, p. 169):

> *Case* 3.6: In Shakespeare's *The Merchant of Venice*, Antonio borrows 3,000 ducats from Shylock. Antonio signs a contract stating that if he does not repay the loan within three months, Shylock may have one pound of flesh from any part of his body. Antonio, because of some business setbacks, is unable to repay the loan within the specified time. Antonio's friends beg Shylock to accept late payment of the debt rather than a pound of flesh. If Shylock had accepted late payment, this would have been an act of mercy. (In fact Shylock does not act mercifully. Antonio gets out of the contract on a technicality.)

The idea of mercy is that obligations or debts—as specified, for example, by a legal contract—should not always be exacted in a rigid or absolutistic way. There should be room for some flexibility, so that a humane person can show generosity or mercifulness by waiving a penalty or obligation that she or he is strictly entitled to. Mercy is a *supererogatory* quality, meaning that it is like a gift—it is something freely given, beyond the requirements of duty. It shows that the benefactor is a humane and kindly person who is willing to forgo some things that may be owed by strict legal requirements.

Mercy is related to pity and compassion, because the merciful person would normally, or at least very often, be a compassionate person who sympathizes with the plight of the other party.

However, there is a difference. Pity, as our definition above indicates, is essentially based on empathy, the ability to "step into" and appreciate the situation of the other. Mercy, although presumably often a result of empathy or sympathy for the plight of the other party, is not linked essentially to empathy. Mercy could be granted for any reason, even to enhance one's reputation, and it would still be a merciful act. Pity, on the other hand, is a mental attitude that is essentially dependent upon empathy.

5. A PRAGMATIC CONCEPT OF EMPATHY

The first four clauses of the definition of pity define a concept that can be called empathy. So defined, the concept of empathy is built into the concept of pity. It is correct to say that pity is a subspecies of empathy, a particular type or use of empathy.

But what is empathy? It seems to be a term that is derived from the social sciences.

The term *empathy (Einfühlung)* was invented (circa 1907) by Theodor Lipps (1965). It refers to a kind of "kinesthetic mimicry" whereby a person can attribute to an object feelings or attitudes aroused in the person by the depicted position or surroundings of the object. For example, viewing a Doric column holding up a heavy stone arch may evoke a kinesthetic mimicry in the observer, like a feeling of doggedly straining to hold up a heavy weight.[9] Lipps also wrote of empathy between persons, using the example (p. 409) of someone who sees a glimpse of a laughing face, and is stimulated to feel free and happy.

Although introduced as a social science term, *empathy* is now widely used as an everyday term in conversational English. To *empathize* is to make a kind of imaginative leap into the mental states of another person. Piper (1991, p. 737) offers a good definition:

> To *empathize* with another is to comprehend viscerally the inner state that motivates the other's overt behavior by experiencing concurrently with that behavior a correspondingly similar inner state oneself, as a direct and immediate quality of one's own condition. Empathy, in turn, requires an imaginative involvement with the other's inner state because we must modally imagine to ourselves what that state must be as we observe her overt behavior, in order to experience it in ourselves.

It seems then that empathy is a more minimal idea than sympathy. Sympathy requires empathy. And sympathy is empathy plus something else.

An excellent, very clear account of the difference is given by Chismar (1988, p. 257):

> To empathize is to respond to another's perceived emotional state by experiencing feelings of a similar sort. Sympathy, on the other hand, not only includes empathizing, but also entails having a positive regard or a non-fleeting concern for the other person. This would explain why to say, "I sympathize with you" seems to suggest more support and compassion than, "I empathize with you." I don't make my appearance at the funeral home to express my empathy, but to convey my sympathy, and while I may empathize with all the characters of a drama, I am likely in sympathy only with the hero. A "sympathizer" is one who goes along with a party or viewpoint, while an "empathizer" may understand, but not agree with the particular cause.

According to Chismar's account, sympathy is a more positive or supportive concept that includes empathy, which is a more neutral concept, not implying agreement or support.

Piper (1991, p. 740) agrees with this account of the difference between the two terms:

> By contrast with empathy, to *sympathize* with another is to be affected by one's visceral comprehension of the other's inner state with a similar or corresponding state of one's own, and to take a pro attitude toward both if the state is positive and a con attitude toward them if it is negative. In order to feel sympathy for another's condition, one must first viscerally comprehend what that condition is. Therefore, sympathy presupposes at least a partial capacity for empathy. But once one has achieved an empathic interpretation of the other's behavior, sympathy is, of course, not the only possible response.

What is especially important to note in this account is that sympathy is a species of empathy, because it is equivalent to empathy plus an attitude. This attitude can take two forms. If the state the second person is feeling is positive, it is a *pro* attitude. If negative, it is a *con* attitude. Thus sympathy can be either positive or negative in nature, whereas pity, as we have seen above, is inherently negative in nature.

It seems then that we can define pity as a species of sympathy, and sympathy as a species of empathy. But how can we define empathy? Is it only, or exclusively, a psychological term of the empirical social sciences, as its origin with Lipp suggests? Or can it have a normative meaning as a pragma-dialectical concept for argumentation that may be different from its broader, popularly accepted psychological meaning?

Empathy is very important as an interviewing skill in medicine. Bellet and Maloney (1991, p. 1831) define empathy as "the capacity to understand what another person is experiencing from within the other person's frame of reference, i.e. the capacity to place oneself in another's shoes." They give (p. 1831–32) the following example of the use of empathy in interviewing, where a mother refused to give consent for her son to have a diagnostic lumbar when meningitis was suspected:

> *Case* 3.7: PHYSICIAN: What concerns you about the spinal tap?
> MOTHER: I refuse to give consent.
> PHYSICIAN (remaining calm and showing genuine interest): Tell me more about why you are worried.
> MOTHER: I think my son will get better without that long needle.
> PHYSICIAN: You are concerned about the length of the needle. (The physician reflects to the mother her concern about the needle; this conveys to her his understanding of the problem. He purposefully avoids lecturing about the known safety of the needle.)
> MOTHER: Yes, I am concerned. It could make him bleed into his back.
> PHYSICIAN: What do you mean? (Again, the physician tries to understand the fear rather than repeat his explanation of the procedure.)
> MOTHER: My neighbor's father had a bad time with headaches after a spinal tap, and Johnny is sick enough already.
> PHYSICIAN: So you don't want your sick child to suffer more discomfort. It is difficult for you to put him in that painful situation. (The physician must not only understand the fear but also verbalize that understanding to the parent so that the parent knows the physician understands.)

MOTHER: Yes, I'm confused. Maybe it wouldn't hurt
him like it did my neighbor's father. How long is the
needle? (Now the mother relaxes and is able to listen
to the physician and follow his advice.)

Bellet and Maloney (p. 1832) add that although many physicians
may feel that they do not have time for this kind of questioning,
empathy, in the end, may save much time and expense.

From a point of view of informal logic, however, one sees that
empathy is necessary to make informed consent really work in practice. In order to persuade the mother that this procedure is more
likely to help, and not harm her son, the physician needs to use
arguments based on premises that express the real concerns and
commitments of the mother, and that relate to how she sees the
situation. This focus on the mother's viewpoint is absolutely necessary for the physician's arguments to inform and rationally persuade
the mother to be successful.

Thus from a pragma-dialectical and normative point of view of
the success of the dialogue between the physician and the other,
empathy—that is, the physician directing his arguments to the
expressed commitments and concerns of the mother—is necessary
for the argumentation to be successful.

6. A DEFINITION OF SYMPATHY

Although *empathy* is a relatively new word, *sympathy* comes
from the Greek word *sympatheia*, which was fundamental to Greek
philosophy almost from its beginning. The theory of cosmic sympathy, associated with the philosopher Poseidonius saw the *kosmos*
as a living creature, having things within it that are "naturally akin"
(Peters 1967, p. 186). Accordingly, both organic and inorganic things
have a "mutual interaction" or *sympatheia*, illustrated by the effects
of the sun and moon on the earth. Peters cites references to *sympatheia* (p. 187) in Sextus Empiricus, Cicero, Marcus Aurelius, and
Plotinus. The idea of *sympatheia* naturally raised questions of con-
tact, and the existence of a medium between the affected parties.
Peters (p. 188) even mentions Aristotle's case of being "touched by
grief" as a "possible escape" from having to postulate the existence
of a medium as necessary for *sympatheia*.

One can certainly see all kinds of philosophical problems relating to defining the concept of sympathy generally, like the problem
of "other minds." For sympathy presupposes some connection

between two parties, so that one can understand or relate to the viewpoint of the other.

The concept of empathy is a natural way to fill this gap, by defining sympathy as based on, and requiring, empathy. Scheler (1954) discussed different types of sympathy, but based them all on an underlying emotional identification between two parties that he called fellow feeling, that could also be called empathy.

Mercer (1972) defines *sympathy* as a relation between two individuals x and y such that x sympathizes with y *about* some circumstances of y or *in* some of y's feelings (p. 4). Mercer sees this relation as *interpersonal* in the sense that it holds between persons, and *intentional* in the sense that we sympathize *about* something, another person's circumstances, or *in* something, another person's state of mind (p. 5). Mercer (p. 19) expands this initial definition by adding four other required conditions:

(a) x is aware of the existence of y as a sentient object;
(b) x knows or believes he knows y's state of mind;
(c) there is fellow-feeling between x and y so that through his imagination x is able to realize y's state of mind; and
(d) x is altruistically concerned for y's welfare.

We see in clause (c) that "fellow-feeling" or empathy is a basic component of the definition.

Following the basic structure of Scheler's analysis, Rescher (1975, p. 5) defines *sympathy* as a kind of positive empathy by which we can "enter into the fortunes of others" and "share vicariously" in the experiences they feel:

> *Sympathy* (communion = *Mitgefühl*): deriving satisfaction (pleasure, enjoyment) from other people's satisfaction and dissatisfaction (displeasure, chagrin) from their dissatisfaction

What is especially notable about this definition is that sympathy does not always have to be a negative feeling of displeasure relating to another person's misery or dissatisfaction. According to Rescher, it can also be a positive feeling of satisfaction (pleasure or enjoyment) relating to another person's satisfaction.

The difference been sympathy and empathy, on these accounts, is that empathy is neutral. It is the ability to enter into another person's point of view, or personal situation, but without necessarily responding to it positively or negatively, by supporting it, or by being sorrowful about it. Sympathy, on the other hand, would go beyond empathy by involving a positive or negative reaction of "pleasure" or "displeasure" at the other person's situation.

According to this approach, sympathy could be defined by conditions 1 to 4 in our definition of pity, and then C in clause 5 could be good or bad. Pity, in contrast, is bound to the negative evaluation of the bad situation or distress suffered by the other party. Thus the difference is that sympathy requires a reaction or evaluation to, or of the situation of the other, but it can be positive or negative. Pity essentially, by its nature, requires a negative reaction of "feeling sorry" for the other.

Snow (1991, p. 197) thinks that sympathy is different from pity and compassion because it is an appropriate response to relatively minor misfortunes. When we feel grief, pity, or compassion, she thinks, it is because we are more deeply affected by the other's condition (p. 197):

> Sympathy differs from grief, pity, and compassion by being an appropriate response to a wider range of misfortunes, including those less serious. For example, we sympathize with someone whose car has been scratched or who suffers from indigestion, but we would not ordinarily feel grief, pity, or compassion for that person. Because the conditions that evoke it can be relatively minor, sympathy is often a less intense emotional reaction than these other emotions. When we sympathize with someone, we're inclined to believe that what he or she is undergoing is bad, but not a terrible or tragic event.

But is this really the basis of the difference? We do send cards expressing "sympathy" to someone who has just lost a loved one. We don't send them a "pity" card.

In our definition then it is not the magnitude or the seriousness of the misfortune that is the crucial factor in distinguishing between pity and sympathy. It is that pity is inherently negative, whereas sympathy can be either positive or negative.

Is pity a species of sympathy? It could be arguably, if we redefine condition 5 of pity more broadly for sympathy, as follows:

5 (*alternative*): C is a situation that is good for y or bad for y (an event that would generally be judged as particularly fortunate or unfortunate).

So defined, sympathy would have conditions 1 to 4 along with condition 5 (*alternative*) as its defining clauses. Since 5 (*alternative*) is a more general criterion than 5, and includes 5 as a special case, then pity would be a species of sympathy. This assumes, however, that pity is only defined by clauses 1 through 10, and that clause 11 is not included. Pity, by these lights, can be defined as sympathy for someone who is in a bad situation.

There is another problem, however. Some would argue that sympathy implies a willingness or ability to help. Mercer's clause (d) of his definition of sympathy requires that *x* has an altruistic concern for *y*'s welfare. But those who advocate clause 11 as essential to pity, might tend to see a conflict here. So a lot depends on clause 11, and on whether some comparable clause, indicating a willingness or ability to help, should be attached to the definition of sympathy.

It remains debatable just to what extent condition 11 is required of pity, and exactly what form such a clause should take. But the point is that there is no comparable worry that clause 11 in some form is an essential requirement of the concept of sympathy. This does suggest a difference.

Defined in this way, sympathy has none of the negative aspects found objectionable by those who have criticized pity, or seen it as a condescending and dehumanizing attitude.

According to Mercer (1972, p. 19) *sympathy* is different from *pity* and *feeling sorry* in two important respects: (1) *pity* and *feeling sorry* do "not necessarily imply a concern for the welfare of the other person," and (2) both "nearly always carry with them overtones of condescension" that are not typical of *sympathy*.

For our part, we see clause 11 as something that has taken on more prominence, or been emphasized more in recent times, by those who are more negative about pity. And we do not see it as essential to sympathy that there be an ability or willingness to help or intervene (perhaps more the former than the latter is a defining condition). But we recognize that there are differences of opinion on these matters. Moreover, even if we define pity as a species of sympathy, conditions 6 through 10, which apply to pity but not to sympathy, bring out several important differences between the two concepts.

One key difference between pity and sympathy is that pity separates the two individuals, making the one appear more like an object of fear or apprehension—the concern is not for the other person, as a person, to help him or her—but is an apprehension or fear that this awful situation could happen to me. The other aspect of this separation or distancing is the feeling of difference, that the object of pity is worse off than I am, and that it puts me on a higher footing. This perception of the difference of our situations implies an us-them relationship—the object of pity is looked down on as unfortunate.

A relationship of sympathy, on the contrary, draws two people closer together—it is based on a bond of closeness. But it does not have a negative aspect that leads to a rejection or distancing of the other, in the way that pity does.

Both pity and sympathy are based on an initial relationship of fellow feeling, or identification with the circumstances and feelings of another (empathy). But with pity, this leads to a curious driving apart or us-them separation. Sympathy is neither this complex nor this divisive.

7. COMPASSION AND PITY

Compassion, like sympathy, also is free of some of the negative connotations that are typically attributed to pity—for example, by the protesters in the Jerry Lewis case. Ben-Ze'ev (1993, p. 7) distinguishes between pity and compassion on the basis of what he calls "the inferior-superior difference." Pity involves the belief that the object of pity is inferior to the subject. Compassion, in contrast, does not require this belief: "Accordingly, one can feel compassion, but not pity, for someone in circumstances no worse than one's own, because compassion does not require one to consider the other inferior." Thus somebody in an equally bad situation can feel compassion for the other.

One key to this essential difference between pity and compassion resides in clause 8 of our definitional framework of section 3. Compassion can, so to speak, be a relation between equals, or persons in the same or a comparable situation that is bad or unfortunate for both.

Compassion then is less negative than pity, but compassion can still have negative implications, because the person one feels compassion for must be in a bad, evil, or unfortunate situation. So defined, compassion would require conditions 1 through 7 of the definition of pity, but it would not have conditions 8 through 11 as essential requirements.

Compassion, then, does have some of the negative implications that were found objectionable by the protesters, but fewer than pity. We could say that pity is more negative than compassion, from this perspective. So defined then, compassion would be halfway between pity and sympathy.

Ben Ze'ev (p. 13) thinks that pity and compassion are both negative emotions, based on a negative evaluation of others having bad fortune. However (p. 13), the crucial difference between pity and compassion is that compassion assumes "a certain equality in common humanity," whereas pity "assumes that the object is in some important aspect inferior to the subject." Thus according to Ben Ze'ev (p. 17), "Compassion has far higher moral value than pity." It implies a greater "commitment to actual help" (p. 17). Pity is inferior, or less "morally recommended," because it involves a "feeling of superiority and satisfaction with the subject's own position" (p. 17). It seems that pity involves a distancing between the two parties, whereas compassion involves a drawing closer.

Snow (1991, p. 197) thinks that the difference between pity and compassion is that pity is more "spectatorlike:"

> Compassion contrasts with pity. There is an immediacy or urgency about compassion that pity lacks. Perhaps this is best described by noting that pity is more spectator-like than compassion. We can pity someone while maintaining a safe emotional distance from what he or she is undergoing. When we feel compassion this emotional distance is crossed. We desire to relieve the other's plight, and in so doing, relieve ourselves of the burden of sharing the trauma caused by his or her condition.

This takes us back to a consideration of condition 11 again, suggesting that x cannot do much to mitigate or relieve y's plight. It suggests an even stronger extension of condition 11 for pity.

Condition 12: x does not desire to relieve y's plight—to make the bad situation C disappear.

This would certainly drive a wedge between pity and sympathy. But is condition 12 essential to the definition of pity? Probably not. It seems more like an implication added in by those who see pity in a dubious moral light.

But when Snow cites this spectatorlike quality that seems to be characteristic of pity, but not of compassion, it could be attributable to conditions 8 through 10. These conditions imply that x is not in the same type of bad situation y is, and this implies a certain distancing between x and y. This could be the basis of the "emotional distance" between the two parties cited by Snow.

But probably that is not all there is to the view expressed by Snow. The crux of the difference here really seems to reside in something like condition 12.

The consensus of opinion generally, in any event, is that there is a big difference between pity and compassion, and that (for a variety of reasons) compassion is not a term that has the same negative implications that pity has. But not everyone agrees on this question.

Contrary to the point of view advocated above, Spinoza (*Ethics*, book 3, p. 178) seemed to think that there is little or no difference between pity (commiseration) and compassion:

> XVIII. *Commiseration* is sorrow with the accompanying idea of evil which has happened to some one whom we imagine like ourselves.
>
> *Explanation.* Between commiseration and compassion there seems to be no difference, except perhaps that commiseration refers rather to an individual emotion and compassion to it as a habit.

So not everybody agrees that there is a difference, and indeed, as we saw in the definitions of *misericordia* given in chapter 2, section 10, there has often been a tendency to think of pity and compassion as being not much different from each other.

But once we do make a clear distinction between pity and compassion, as above, many of the objections to pity expressed in section 2 fail to apply to compassion. And once we distinguish clearly among the triad, pity, compassion, and sympathy, it appears that all of the negative aspects found objectionable so far in connection with pity or compassion are removed in the case of sympathy.

The logic textbooks generally define *argumentum ad misericordiam* as appeal to pity. This makes it easy to dismiss the argument as fallacious, precisely because of the negative implications articulated in our analysis of pity above. But could there also exist, in everyday conversational argumentation, uses of appeal to sympathy or appeal to compassion? If so, these kinds of argument would be not so easy to dismiss as fallacies. And could some of the cases currently treated under the label *appeal to pity* be better reclassified under one of these other labels?

8. THE SPEECH ON HEALTH SECURITY

In a televised speech before a joint session of Congress on September 22, 1993, U.S. President Bill Clinton made a plea on behalf of his forthcoming health reform proposal. His speech was entitled "Health Security for All Americans" (Clinton 1993). The speech outlined a number of problems in the current system of funding health care in the United States, and pleaded with the Congress to look past their partisan interests, and come together to support these much needed reforms.

To support his contention that the current system created serious problems for people, and needed reform, Mr. Clinton, during the speech, in three places, cited several individual cases of people in situations that would elicit strong feelings of empathy and compassion from the viewers in the television audience.

All three of these brief cases are instances of a type of argumentation that could definitely be called appeals to sympathy or compassion. They are the very kinds of cases that would fall under the traditional textbook treatments of the *argumentum ad misericordiam* outlined in chapter 1.

Were these arguments fallacious (as suggested by the usual treatment of the *argumentum ad misericordiam* as a fallacy)? Before attempting to answer this question, there is a prior question of identifying the *ad misericordiam* as a type of argumentation—Would these three arguments be best classified as appeals to pity, compassion, or sympathy? Let us look at the cases.

The first case, we are told in the speech, came from a letter written to the Task Force by an "ordinary citizen." It relates the case of someone who had "worked hard" but was "hurt by this system that just doesn't work":

> *Case* 3.8: Kerry Kennedy owns a small furniture franchise that employs seven people in Titusville, Florida. Like most small business owners, Kerry has poured his sweat and blood into that company. But over the last few years, the cost of insuring his seven workers has skyrocketed, as did the cost of the coverage for himself, his wife, and his daughter. Last year, however, Kerry could no longer afford to provide coverage for all his workers because the insurance companies had labelled two of them high risk simply because of their age. But, you know what? Those two people are Kerry's Mother and Father who built the family business and now work in the store.

Clinton draws the conclusion that there are certain things wrong with the current system of coverage, and he goes on to cite a number of faults in the system calling it costly and wasteful.

The argument in this case could be called an appeal to sympathy or compassion for the plight of the Kennedy family. But it probably should not be classified as an appeal to pity because (1) it is not looking down on the Kennedys, or condescending to them, and (2) according to Clinton, Congress can help their situation, and others in the same situation, by passing the bill he is arguing for.

The second appeal occurs later in the speech, where Clinton argues that under the present system, "the medical care industry is drowning in paperwork":

> *Case 3.9*: A few days ago, the Vice President and I visited Children's Hospital in Washington, where they do wonderful, often miraculous things for very sick children.
>
> Nurse Debbie Freiberg in the cancer and bone marrow unit told us that, the other day, a little boy asked her to stay at his side during his chemotherapy. But she had to tell him no. She had to go to yet another meeting to learn how to fill out yet another form. That's wrong.

Clinton concludes from this case that if doctors could be relieved of the burden imposed by the paperwork required under the present system, doctors could spend much more time with children.

This argument seems more like an appeal to sympathy or compassion, as opposed to an appeal to pity, because the argument is that Congress can help by supporting this new bill, which will introduce a universal claim form, reducing the unnecessary paper work greatly. From this point of view, it seems like a reasonable kind of argument, based on practical reasoning. The case is used to illustrate the problem.

The third case occurs near the end of the speech:

> *Case 3.10*: As Representatives in Congress, you have a special duty to look beyond such arguments. I ask you to look into the eyes of a sick child who needs care. Look at the face of a woman who has been told not only that it is malignant, but also that it's not covered by her insurance. Look at the bottom lines of the businesses driven to bankruptcy by health care costs. And at the forest of FOR SALE signs in front of homes of families who have lost their health insurance. Then look in your heart and tell me that the greatest nation in the history of the world is powerless to confront this crisis. Our history and our heritage tell us we can meet this challenge and we shall meet this challenge.

This case is even more emotional than the other two, and is clearly meant to have a rhetorical impact of leaving an impression, as the speech draws to a close.

In this case, a survey of several types of bad situations is given, including types representing the previous two cases. But although this may seem initially to evoke pity, the appeal is not put in such a way as to separate "us" from "them" in a separating or condescending way. The Congress is being asked to confront the crisis by supporting this new bill, which would change the situation for the better. Their support, presumably, would prevent the occurrence of the bad situations described in the case.

Over all, these three appeals to compassion do take the form of the argument from need to help the individuals cited, or at any rate to take political action to help people in this kind of situation generally (including ourselves). The Congress is being asked to take action to alleviate the bad situation of people under the present system of health care funding. All three cases fit in with the sequence of practical reasoning throughout the speech, designed to convince the Congress, and the wider audience, to take a particular course of action.

If the foregoing interpretation of these cases is reasonable, it follows that there do actually exist cases of arguments that can (and should) be classified as appeals to compassion or sympathy, but not appeals to pity. This is a very significant result. It means that there are arguments that are appeals to compassion that are not appeals to pity. It means that there are (probably plenty of) arguments that appeal to sympathy or compassion that are not, in a narrower sense, true *ad misericordiam* arguments.

9. CLASSIFICATION OF THE TYPES OF APPEALS

Now that we have defined the concepts of pity, compassion, sympathy, and empathy (as well as mercy) more carefully and exactly, or at least proposed a framework for such definitions, and articulated a basis for discussing the ethically negative implications often felt as flowing from them, we need to turn to the logical question of how appeals to these concepts are used in argumentation. The problem is to define, or more clearly articulate, the types of argumentation commonly used to appeal to emotions like pity and compassion that are so much the subject of attention in the informal logic textbooks. Clearly defining these distinctive types of argumentation is a necessary first step in the task of providing a set of normative standards for evaluating arguments of these types as correct or fallacious in a given instance of their use.

To help resolve the ambiguities inherent in the *argumentum ad misericordiam*, we first of all have to make some attempt to classify the ethical concepts that are appealed to. We do this, as shown in Figure 3.1, defining the traditional category of the *argumentum ad misericordiam* characterized by the textbook treatment as the umbrella category to stand for the whole group of concepts below it (sympathy, mercy, compassion, and pity).

Mercy is seen as a separate concept from the other three, in principle, even though in many cases it is typically based on one of the other three. These other three, however, are defined as more closely connected to each other.

There are three distinct types of arguments categorized as appeal to sympathy, appeal to compassion, and appeal to pity. Going by the literal meaning of the word *misericordia* (with an emphasis on *miser*), presumably only the appeals to compassion and pity should properly be classified as *ad misericordiam* arguments.

However, we need an umbrella term to cover all these various types of appeals that come under *ad misericordiam* as traditionally cited by the textbooks. I will use *appeals to feeling* as the generic category for this whole class of appeals.

Thus I use Yanal's term *appeal to feeling* as the umbrella term to include appeals to pity, compassion, and sympathy, making this term correspond to the inclusive use of *argumentum ad misericor-*

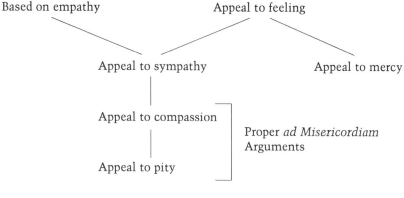

Figure 3.1
Classification of Ethical Concepts

diam favored by so many of the textbooks. Fearnside and Holther's term *appeal to pathetic circumstances* would apply primarily to appeals to compassion and pity, but perhaps to mercy as well, making it close or equivalent to my preferred narrower meaning of the phrase *argumentum ad misericordiam.*

In my new framework, according to the definitions advocated in this chapter, pity is defined as a special type of compassion. Compassion, in turn, is defined as a special type of sympathy. And sympathy, in turn, is defined as a special type of empathy. Many arguments are based on empathy, especially in persuasion dialogue, where it is crucial to base your argumentation on premises that are commitments of the other party. But appeal to empathy is not a specially distinct of appeal used in such a way that it marks off a special type of argument of the appeal to feeling type.

Appeal to pity is especially problematic as a type of argument, for, as Hume was aware, it contains a contradiction—or at least two opposed forces. On the one hand, pity draws the two parties, the pitier and the pitied, closer together, because it is based on empathy, and on sympathy and compassion. But it also has the effect of putting an emotional distance between the two parties, making one to appear to be on a superior footing to the other. This leads to the condescending attitude cited by the protesters in the Jerry Lewis Telethon case, as a perceived implication of pity.

This is why it is so vitally important to distinguish between appeals to pity, on the one hand, and the other types of appeals, to sympathy and compassion especially, on the other. We need to be clearly aware that the appeal to pity presents some special ethical problems, has some negative implications, and even has some inherent contradictory elements within its meaning. Our system of classification enables us to identify this problem when appeals to feeling are used in argumentation.

When these appeals are used in argumentation, however, it can be not so easy to determine whether the given argument should rightly be classified as an appeal to sympathy, compassion, or pity. The Jerry Lewis Telethon is a good case in point. Lewis claimed that it should be seen as an appeal to compassion, not pity. But the protesters seem to have plenty of evidence on their side, to the effect that Lewis has portrayed the disabled as "half a person," and so forth, in his *Parade* article. Countering this allegation, the defenders of the telethon claimed that it had evolved, due to the criticisms of the protesters, and was no longer a "pity approach" in the later years.

Gill (1993, p. 30), for example, cited the case of Duncan who was a Muscular Dystrophy Association "poster kid," but who saw through the Lewis appeal to pity and turned his "outrage" into becoming an antitelethon activist:

> But as long as Duncan remained the poster boy/man in the center, he remained distanced from all the supporters cheering him on from the circumference of the circle. There was no equality. Suddenly, Duncan realized the telethon promoted and played on inequality. It reinforced the view that disabled people had inferior lives. In Jerry Lewis' words, people with disabilities are "less," and "half a person." The telethon amplifies people's worst fears and prejudices about disabilities. Then it shows them a way out: Give a donation; then put it all out of your mind. [p. 30]

Like the other protesters and critics of Lewis cited in section 1 above, this one too focuses on Lewis's use of the phrase "less" and "half a person" to charge him with portraying disabled people as "inferior" and pitiable.

Reading over the original *Parade* article by Lewis (1990), it is interesting to see that the whole article is an attempt at empathy. Lewis hypothetically puts himself in the position of having muscular dystrophy, and going through the experiences of daily life in a wheelchair. Most of the article does not express a pitying or condescending attitude of the emotional distancing kind that separates "us" and "them." On the contrary, the whole article is directly aimed at overcoming this distance or separation by performing an empathetic thought experiment of imagining daily life from the point of view of a person with muscular dystrophy.

Unfortunately however, Lewis (p. 5), right at the end of the article, does use the phrase "half a person" and this became the focus of the protesters' criticism. The part quoted below (p. 5) is at the center of the controversy:

> I'd like to play basketball like normal, healthy, vital and energetic people. I really don't want the substitute. I just can't half-do anything—either it's all the way, or forget it. That's a rough way to think in my position. When I sit back and think a little more rationally, I realize my life *is* half, so I must learn to do things halfway. I just have to learn to try to be good at being half a person . . . and get on with my life.

I may be a full human being in my heart and soul, yet I am still half a person, and I know I'll do well if I keep my priorities in order. You really cannot expect the outside world to assist you in more ways than they already do, and I'm most grateful for the help I receive. But I always have the feeling in the pit of my stomach that I want to scream out: "Help!" or: "See what has happened to me!" or: "Is anyone watching?" But those screams are usually muffled by the inner voice that tells me what to do and when, and tells me softly and strongly: "Be still . . . Hush . . . Drive quietly . . . Try to make as few waves as possible."

I have never really found out why, when someone is dealt a bad hand, they immediately feel inferior and out of touch with the mainstream of life—when in fact, we're more productive, more creative, more educated and more apt to excel than most of the fortunate people who are either indifferent or just don't care.

If you examine this passage in the context of what Lewis is trying to say in the article, you can see that it is empathy, not pity, that is the theme of the argument. However, unfortunately, certain phrases like "cripple," "half a person," and "inferior" are used that, quoted out of context, make the argument look much worse than it really is.

In short, a sympathetic reading of the notorious *Parade* article indicates that the unfortunate wording used by Lewis in the passage has been wrenched out of context and used by the protesters as a straw man argument. A look even at the last part of the passage quoted above shows that Lewis was supporting the same view as that advocated by the protesters themselves.

In short, the evidence (generally, but subject to the controversial cited exceptions), supports the rebuttal made by Lewis that his argument was an appeal to compassion, and not an appeal to pity.

10. WHAT'S IN A NAME?

What you call a particular fallacy, or type of argument associated with a common fallacy, turns out to be very important. This can be shown to be true not only for the *argumentum ad misericordiam*, but for other fallacies as well.

Recent researches on individual fallacies have found that the types of argumentation traditionally classified as fallacious are, in many instances of their use in everyday conversation, nonfallacious, and even quite reasonable. One could cite, for example, recent work on *ad hominem*,[10] slippery slope,[11] arguing in a circle,[12] many questions,[13] and *ad ignorantiam*.[14]

On the other hand, some fallacies have a name that suggests they are inherently wrong or fallacious as types of arguments. For example, *argumentum ad verecundiam* is usually translated as the argument from respect, modesty, or reverence, suggesting too much of a deference to authority, of a kind that is generally exploited, or subject to exploitation.[15] If we were to label it "appeal to expert opinion," the connotations would be more favorable, suggesting a kind of argument that can be nonfallacious in many cases, and even reasonable as a basis for drawing a conclusion for prudent action, even if it is fallacious in some cases.

The *argumentum ad misericordiam* also fits into this category of being generally or always fallacious (at least easily), especially if you translate it as standardly done in the textbooks—appeal to pity. For pity has all negative connotations brought out in the telethon case, suggesting an attitude of condescension toward the person who is pitied. Thus it is easy for the textbooks to dismiss the *argumentum ad misericordiam* as being fallacious without having to justify that claim, or to provide criteria to distinguish between the fallacious and nonfallacious uses of this type of argumentation.

But what if we translated *misericordiam*, and conceived the argument as referring to compassion, or perhaps to sympathy or empathy. These terms are much more positive. Arguments appealing to one of these feelings are, as shown above, more morally positive, in the sense that the objections to the negative implications of the "term" pity are removed. So it would be much harder to dismiss them as fallacious without adding qualifications or further criteria to determine when the argument has been misused, or employed fallaciously, in a given instance.

The first step, then, in analyzing an argument that uses appeal to feeling, of the kind typically cited as *argumentum ad misericordiam* in the textbook treatment, should be to identify specifically what type of argument it is. Is it an appeal to pity, an appeal to compassion, an appeal to sympathy, or an appeal to mercy? If it (on the evidence) falls into one category but not the other, this will greatly affect how we should deal with it when it comes to evaluating it as fallacious or not. This is the task of identification of the type of appeal.

Of course, in some cases, it is hard to classify it, and the classification may be uncertain, or itself subject to argument. For example, in the Jerry Lewis Telethon case, the protesters classified the argument as an appeal to pity, while Lewis categorized it as an appeal to compassion. In other cases, the argument may fall into two categories. For example, in the case of the Clinton speech on health care, the argument could be classified as an appeal either to sympathy or to compassion. It seems to be both, and of course generally, an appeal to compassion is also ipso facto, an appeal to sympathy, by our definitions above. But the point in this case is that by classifying it as an appeal to compassion (or sympathy), as opposed to an appeal to pity, we prepare the way for an evaluation of it. We forestall the standard problem of generically identifying any such argument as an appeal to pity (the dominant traditional *ad misericordiam* category), and then routinely dismissing it as fallacious, without having to look at any further evidence.

The bottom line then is that each case of the so-called *argumentum ad misericordiam* or appeal to feeling, to use the better generic term, needs to be judged on its merits. It is no longer enough to classify such an argument as fallacious exclusively on the grounds that it is an emotional appeal to feeling, or *ad misericordiam* argument in the traditional sense.

On the other hand, we have seen that ethically there is a gradation of connotations from positive to negative as we go from sympathy to compassion to pity. This gradation also seems to hold true of arguments based on these appeals. In general, appeals to pity have certain characteristics that make them more dramatic and powerful, yet more problematic than appeals to sympathy. This may be because sympathy brings two parties closer together in empathy, whereas pity is also based on an exclusionary us-them relationship.

In general, it seems that appeal to pity is more of a red flag, indicating a possible fallacy, than appeal to sympathy. Appeal to compassion lies somewhere between the other two.

The textbook cases of the *argumentum ad misericordiam* in the standard treatment were devised to fit as illustrations of fallacious appeals to pity. It is therefore not too likely that many of them will fit the category of the nonfallacious argument from sympathy, or that of argument from compassion. To further study this question then, we are pointed towards reexamining the examples used in the textbook treatment, and expanding our corpus of examples beyond this base.

But now we have opened up this identification question, another question is posed. Do the argument from sympathy and the argument from compassion really exist, as common types of argumentation used in everyday conversation? Now we have defined *sympathy* and *compassion* as terms expressing feelings that have an important moral status. This suggests the hypothesis that such appeals would commonly be used in human discourse with great power to convince rational persons of conscience and feeling, and to move them to actions through the use of practical reasoning in persuasion and deliberation. But is this hypothesis confirmed by experience? The answer is now probably yes, if our analysis and classification of the argumentation in the Clinton speech is an acceptable interpretation. It would appear to be very likely that appeals to compassion of this kind are very common in everyday argumentation, and bear investigation as an important type of nonfallacious argument.

Even if it should turn out, however, that appeals to sympathy and compassion are not as common or as powerful as I have anticipated, in everyday conversational argumentation, still it is worth investigating such appeals. For as we saw in the Jerry Lewis Telethon case, one of the most important defenses against the criticism of having used appeal to pity is the rebuttal that your argument is really an appeal to compassion. Hence the first step in any useful analysis of the *ad misericordiam* as a fallacy, or as a type of argument, is the conceptual clarification of this distinction.

4

The Structure of the Argument

In this chapter an analysis of the underlying structure of the argumentation used in *ad misericordiam* arguments is given. It is shown to be a species of practical reasoning used by one party to try to get another party to take some kind of action. Three particular forms of argument used for this purpose are identified and analyzed.

Of course, appeals to pity can be used for many different purposes in different conversational frameworks.[1] But I will focus on one particular use—the use of appeal to pity to raise money by charitable relief agencies. I will argue that this use is basically nonfallacious. I will explore why, and give a structure to back up the normative judgment of this kind of case.

In this chapter, it will also be shown how the appeal to feeling is added onto the underlying structure of argument used to appeal for relief from distress.

1. ARGUMENTS FROM NEGATIVE CONSEQUENCES

It has already been noted in chapter 1 how many of the *ad misericordiam* arguments cited by the logic textbooks are species of argumentation from consequences. Yet another vivid example of the student's plea type of case will illustrate this aspect very clearly.[2]

Case 4.1: A student who is on a visa from his home country *x*, appeals to the university admissions committee: "If I

am not admitted to the university, I will lose my
visa, and be deported. When I go back to *x* I will be
shot!"

Here the student's argument has the form of a negative argument
from consequences. The argument is that bad consequences will
occur if the admissions committee takes a certain line of action or
decision. Therefore, the conclusion of the argument runs, the committee should not take the action of denying admission.

The committee may not be in a position to verify whether the
student's claim that he will be shot is true.[3] Still, the argument puts
a lot of pressure on the committee, because if the claim is true then
the result of their decision not to admit could be loss of life—quite a
serious negative consequence for the student!

When we unpack the argument in this case further, it becomes
apparent that it involves a sequence of practical reasoning.[4] The student's plea presumes that the goals of the committee include preser-
vation of human life, so that there would be a strong presumption
against any line of action that might likely result in loss of human
life.

In this case, then, the argument takes place in the context of a
dialogue exchange where the first party is asking the second party, or
trying to direct or counsel the second party, away from a certain
action, on the grounds that this action will probably have negative
consequences for the first party. In other cases, the second party is
already in a situation where the negative consequences are having an
impact, and the perception of these consequences is the basis of the
argument.

The following case concerned the practice of stubble burning by
farmers in the countryside around the city of Winnipeg. Because of
concerns that the drifting smoke had been causing respiratory difficulties for asthma suffers in the city, the provincial government
declared a partial ban on burning of stubble. However, in the autumn
of 1992, there was a late harvest, which did not leave enough time to
work the straw into the ground, and some farmers "felt impelled" to
burn stubble, saying it was the "only alternative" (Billinkoff 1992,
p. A7):

> *Case* 4.2: Unfortunately that alternative caused problems for
> those with asthmatic conditions. Everyone knows
> someone with such a condition. For instance, I know
> a severe asthmatic who regularly uses sprays and
> medication to breathe. When the burning began, her

breathing worsened. After a week of burning, she woke up in the early hours of a morning with acute respiratory distress. It was caused by smoke from stubble burning which had permeated the house even though all doors and windows were closed. She was compelled to use special breathing equipment.

Others, particularly children, were rushed to hospitals and, as the burning continued, the numbers rose. Within four days, about 60 children, some in life-threatening condition, had been taken to the emergency ward of Children's Hospital.

The case cited here, of the severe asthmatic, plus the citing of the cases of the children taken to hospital, is a use of argumentation from negative consequences. The conclusion advocated is that in the deliberations on whether or not to ban stubble burning—a continuing debate with advocates on both sides—these negative consequences constitute an argument against stubble burning. That is, they are being cited as an argument for banning the practice, or for finding some other way (if there is one) of preventing these bad consequences.

In response to this argument, officials of the provincial government argued that it is difficult to enforce any ban on stubble burning, and that "wet soil conditions had made burning the only viable way to remove stubble in some areas" (Billinkoff, p. A7). In this argumentation, the government officials are using practical reasoning to oppose the argumentation from negative consequences used in case 4.2.

So what is the difference between the argumentation being used in case 4.1 versus that in case 4.2? Both are instances of argumentation from negative consequences that cite life-threatening outcomes, and use this to argue for a particular line of action or decision. But there does seem to be a difference. In the stubble burning case, the article is citing consequences in an attempt to influence public deliberation on a controversial issue. Distress to persons is involved, but the argument does not seem to be so much of a direct or explicit plea for help in this case as it does in the student's plea case.

2. ARGUMENTS FROM NEED FOR HELP

It will help us to see that arguments of the kind we have been considering frequently take the form where one party is asking the other party for some kind of help. The asking party is generally in a situation where the other party sees that she or he can give some kind of help. The argumentation that is a plea for help in this kind of situation has a distinctive form, as a species of practical reasoning.

> *Case* 4.3: Alice is walking home from work, and is confronted by a shabbily dressed and unkempt man who tells her he is homeless and out of work. He asks, "Could you give me a dollar so I can buy something to eat?"

In this case, an explicit argument from need for help is used as the basis for a charitable plea for money to someone who appears to be in a position to give it. This general kind of argumentation is quite common and familiar. It may be said to have the following form:

Argument from Need for Help

For all x and y, y ought to help x, if x is in a situation where x needs help, and y can help, and y's giving help would not be too costly for y.

x is in a situation where some action A by y would help x.

y can carry out A.

y's carrying out A would not be too costly for y—that is, the negative side effects would not be too great, as y sees it.

Therefore, y ought to carry out A.

The previous case is an explicit use of argument from need for help. But in other cases, the argumentation can be nonexplicitly expressed or implied, without a plea being voiced. A typical kind of case of this type is the following:

> *Case* 4.4: Boyscout Bob sees a frail, elderly lady trying to cross the street, but she is clearly being in need of help getting across the busy intersection. Bob takes her arm and helps her to cross the street.

Here there is no explicit argument expressed. Let's say that the elderly lady makes no request for help. Bob, being a Scout, simply volunteers his help. Even so, in acting the way he did, Bob's basis of reasoning can be reconstructed as a sequence of practical reasoning, taking the form of an argument from need for help. We can presume, from the situation, and Bob's response, that he responded to the need for help.

When a visually graphic situation is the basis of the argument from need for help, the pull on the viewer is visceral. It produces a powerful primitive instinct (recounted from a televised program, June 1994, on the fiftieth anniversary of D-day):

> *Case* 4.5: A D-day invasion survivor, fifty years later, who had been one of the infantry carried to shore in a landing barge, described, with tears in his eyes, how they had seen tanks sinking in the water, unable to get to shore. He said the worst thing about the invasion had been that, because of military necessity, they could not stop to help the men in the tanks, many of whom drowned because they could not get out, or get help.

Years later, this man's feeling on this subject was still very strong. He had felt a strong pull to help these men, and was very disturbed by not being able to help them, while seeing them drowning in the water.

The pull of the argument from help in such a case is a powerful instinctive feeling, which, as we will see, in section 9 below, is based on a bias for group survival.

3. ARGUMENT FROM DISTRESS

An argument subtype of the argument from need for help is the *argument from distress*:

Argument from Distress

Individual x is in distress (is suffering).
If y brings about A, it will relieve or help relieve this distress.
Therefore, y ought to bring about A.

Here, A is some action that would help x. Hence the argument from distress is a special subtype of the argument from need for help. The first premise presents a particular case or example, usually in graphic detail. The second premise postulates a means of relieving or helping the distress cited in the first premise. The argument is a sequence of practical reasoning that directs the respondent to the course of action indicated by the second premise. This course of action becomes the conclusion of the argument.

The argument from distress is more sharply pointed than other arguments from need for help generally. Hence it calls up more of an urgency, and is more difficult to brush aside, or argue against by practical reasoning. It seems to demand immediate, urgent attention.

The following case was a letter sent to the author by Amnesty International (1994), enclosing a personal story about torture, requesting a tax deductible donation to help save people "detained in prison, tortured, or executed, because of their political or religious beliefs."

> *Case* 4.6: "I was taken downstairs blindfolded, while being beaten and kicked."
>
> Those are the words of Saadet Akkaya, who was 16 years old when Turkish officials arrested her 2 years ago.
>
> During her interrogation and torture, Saadet's ordeal included being stripped and tied to a cross with ropes. "When they took away the chair, I was hanging by my arms. Then they gave me electric shocks to sensitive parts of my body. At the same time, a policeman threw water over me." Saadet was also subjected to other forms of torture, abuse and ill-treatment.
>
> After undergoing 15 days of torture, she confessed to activities about which she knew nothing.
>
> Saadet is still imprisoned in Saqmalcilar.
>
> Under this story, it said "This barbarism can be stopped. Please help." In the accompanying letter, it said, "Our need for your support is so terribly urgent because, even as I write this letter to you, some place in the world—in Communist countries, in Western societies, in the Third World—innocent victims of government abuse are imprisoned, suffering unspeakable physical and mental agonies." In the letter it also gave details like, "the guards taunted the prisoner as they applied electrical shocks to her body," and "her cries were echoed by the screams of other victims."

This case is a use of argument from distress to solicit funds to help the kind of situation described in the case cited.

A comparable letter sent to the author by Amnesty International (1996) cited the arrest of a 23-year-old Kurdish journalist arrested by Turkish police in October 1994. After describing her interrogation and torture in terms comparable to the description given in case 4.6, the "true story" concludes: "After undergoing twelve days of torture she confessed to activities in which she was not involved." Added at the bottom in handwriting is the following plea: "Please help put an end to such atrocities. Your help is needed today!" The letter includes a form on which you can tick off the amount of your donation. In larger red letters on the form, the heading is: "STOP THE CRIES OF TORTURE." Payment can be made by check or credit card.

Having personally collected many such charitable appeals for funds that were sent in the mail in the past four years, I have noticed that the letters seem to follow a formula. They cite a particular case, in considerable graphic detail, of an individual person in some kind of distress. The theme of the letter is that the way to relieve this distress is to send money to the organization who wrote the letter.

4. CHARITABLE APPEALS TO PITY

The most common type of charitable appeal, however, is the type that features pictures of children in distress.

Examples of the use of this particular variant argument from need for help used in a charitable appeal are very common. A typical case is given by Walton (1992, p. 113)—a full-page ad in *Newsweek* (March 4, 1985, p. 75) showing an emaciated child with a distended belly, crying, below the headline, ETHIOPIA: THE MOST DEVASTATING HUMAN CRISIS OF OUR TIME.

> *Case* 4.7: THERE IS SOMETHING YOU CAN DO ABOUT THIS TRAGEDY . . .
>
> You've seen the news reports . . .
>
> • Thousands of people a day are starving to death!
> • More than 6 million people are threatened by starvation.
> • More than 100,000 could die from hunger and its related diseases in the next 60 days.
>
> THE TIME FOR ACTION IS NOW!
> HERE'S WHAT YOU CAN DO TO HELP!
>
> Your gift of $15 is all it takes to feed a hungry child for a month! Just $30 can feed two children for a month. And $75 will provide emergency food for an entire family of five for a month!

Especially the picture makes it clear that this ad does use a highly graphic appeal to pity, but underlying this appeal is a sequence of practical reasoning, using argumentation from need for help. And factual evidence bears on whether this practical reasoning can be justified in the given case, or not. Practical considerations relevant here are whether agency personnel sponsoring the ad can deliver the food if they get the funds. Also relevant is the consideration of whether they will do so effectively, and what proportion of their income goes to administration costs. These are straightforwardly factual questions, and the practical reasonableness of the argument—quite apart from its appeal to emotions like compassion or pity—stands or falls on what is known, or what can be found out, about these practical aspects of the situation.

Brinton (1993, p. 16) calls this kind of appeal the "supplicatory" *argumentum ad misericordiam*, identifying as a typical type of case the television plea from a relief agency:

> *Case* 4.8: The viewer is presented with visual scenes of starving Somalian children with distended bellies, in the arms of their malnourished parents. Facts about the situation are presented (verifiable claims are made, that is) by a spokesperson for the relief agency (usually some well-known person, an actress, for example). Information may also be presented about the proposed relief efforts by the agency to which we are implored to send contributions. [p. 16]

We are all familiar with the type of case of *ad misericordiam* argument. How should it be evaluated?

Seeing that the argument in this type of case is an instance of argument from distress, the first two factors to be evaluated correspond to premises of this type of argument. Two critical questions are posed. First, is individual (or group) x really in distress (as claimed)? And second, if the respondent brings about the cited action (giving money, in this case), will that actually help to relieve the distress? If the answer to either of these questions is no, or even maybe not, then doubts are raised about the worth of the argument. However, even if the argument is dubious or questionable, on the given evidence, it need not follow that the argument is fallacious, or commits the *ad misericordiam* fallacy. We need to evaluate the argument by the standards appropriate for practical reasoning.

One common problem with arguments of this type is that the second (means) premise may turn out to be highly dubious. This kind of questioning, for example, has been raised about the U.N. peacekeeping effort in Bosnia (Koring 1993, p. A1):

Case 4.9: Few aid workers and fewer UN peacekeepers will say so officially, but amid the frustration over being continually thwarted and harassed by the warring parties in the former Yugoslavia, there also is despair: Is the massive international aid effort, coupled with a Herculean road-building program aimed at getting food to more than two million people, actually saving lives or simply prolonging the war?

No one knows how much of the food aid is winding up in the bellies of fighters or how much is being diverted to the black market, where the hard currency it earns buys weapons and ammunition and lines the pockets of corrupt officials who often double as military commanders. Estimates of the amount of food being diverted range from 20 to 80 per cent.

The argument from distress in this case was based on a humanitarian effort to help the starving. But the suspicion is that the aid is being diverted to feed soldiers, and build roads used for military offensives, so that in fact the outcome is the prolongation of the conflict.

These same questions can be asked in case 4.8. In this case, the plea for funds is to get money for food to relieve the starvation. But is that a direct form of help that will solve the problem? It may be too late to do much for the children with distended bellies in the photograph used in the appeal. And, of course, there are always many practical questions of whether the food stands good chances of getting to the starving people, and even if it does, whether that is really helping them by solving the underlying problem.

5. PRACTICAL REASONING

Arguments from negative consequences, arguments from need for help, and arguments from distress, as used in charitable appeals of the kind we have been considering in the last section, do not seem to be inherently fallacious. This general observation suggests that these three types of arguments are, or can be, under the right conditions, reasonable arguments of some sort. But what sort? This is a pointed question. For they do not appear to be deductive or inductive arguments, of the kind usually dealt with in logic textbooks. What kind of structure of reasoning do they fit into then, so they can be evaluated as good (reasonable) arguments when used in a certain way, and bad (fallacious, weak, erroneous) arguments when used in another way?

The purpose of a charitable appeal is to get the respondent to send money. This is done by convincing him that sending the money will provide help to some persons in distress—that is, that the act of sending money will relieve that distress. This argument could be a good one if in fact the people cited are really in distress, as claimed, and the money will be used by the relief agency to relieve that distress. At least, it can be a good argument in the sense that it is instrumentally reasonable in linking certain goals of helping people to actions that will carry out or contribute to these goals.

The key to understanding the logic of such arguments lies in realizing that they are not purely "academic" or abstract arguments designed to prove that a particular proposition is true or false. They are practical arguments that pose a problem and then propose a means of solving the problem, or at least dealing with it somehow, by taking a course of action. They involve deliberating on what to do to confront or change an allegedly bad situation that requires some sort of action to make it better. This kind of argument primarily uses a kind of reasoning that seeks out means to carry out ends or goals. As Aristotle puts it in the *Nicomachean Ethics* (1112 b 12–1112 b 17):

> We deliberate not about ends but about means. For a doctor does not deliberate whether he shall heal, nor an orator whether he shall persuade, nor a statesman whether he shall produce law and order, nor does any one else deliberate about his end. They assume the end and consider how and by what means it is to be attained; and if it seems to be produced by several means they consider by which it is most easily and best produced, while if it is achieved by one only they consider how it will be achieved by this and by what means *this* will be achieved.

This kind of reasoning is described, in general terms, as follows. A goal is assumed to be given, and the reasoning process looks around for a means, or some means (an action or several actions) that would result in the goal, if carried out. However, there may be several possible actions that would have this effect. Hence the line of reasoning is to select out one of them as the best or the easiest to produce.

But there is another complication also indicated by Aristotle. Once a means or action is designated as the chosen one, it may be necessary to carry out other actions first, in order to produce this action. Thus there will generally be a chain or sequence of actions that may need to be carried out, to get to the desired goal.

What Aristotle describes here is a distinctive type of reasoning that he identified with *phronesis* (practical wisdom), the art of judging a prudent (practical) course of action to achieve a stated or assumed goal. In recent times the study of the characteristics of this distinctive type of reasoning has been revived (Clarke 1985; Audi 1989; Walton 1990b), and it is called *practical reasoning*. It is described in Walton as a distinctive species of goal-driven, knowledge-based, action-guiding argumentation. This structure of reasoning involves an agent a who is assumed to have a goal G, and is considering a set of possible actions $A_1, A_2, \ldots, A_n$, as means of carrying out this goal.

As Aristotle puts it (*Nicomachean Ethics* 1112 b 34), "deliberation is about things to be done by the agent," and these things are seen by the agent as means to some goal of the agent's. It is this selection of means that is the subject of deliberation, and the sequence of reasoning used to arrive at such a selection is the primary type of argumentation contained in deliberation. This is practical reasoning.

The simplest general form of practical reasoning as a type of inference is given in Walton (1990b, p. 41):

(PR) G is a goal for a.
  A is the means to bring about G.
  Therefore a should (practically speaking) bring about A.

This is the simplest type of practical reasoning, but there are many complicating factors in particular cases that require more complex forms of practical reasoning. There may be several alternative means to carry out G, for example, or a might have more than one goal. Such goals could even conflict, or need to be priorized. Or a sequence of actions may be necessary. And some means may be necessary conditions for G, or for other actions, while other means may be sufficient conditions. More complex forms are analyzed in Walton (1990b, chapter 3).

6. EVALUATING PRACTICAL REASONING

Practical reasoning is practical because it is used in argumentation where chaining together of a sequence of practical inferences occurs in a context of dialogue. One very common context is action-directed deliberation where two or more parties are discussing what to do in a problematic situation and there is a conflict of opinions on how to proceed. In such a context of discussion, one participant puts forward a proposal for action based on practical inferences, while the other participant raises critical questions. There are four kinds of critical questions appropriate for countering practical inferences:

Q1. Are there alternative means of realizing G, other than A?
Q2. Is it possible for a to carry out A?
Q3. Are there other goals for a, aside from G, which might conflict with a's realizing G?
Q4. Are there negative side effects of a's bringing about G that ought to be considered?
Q5. Are other actions by a needed in order to carry out G?

Practical reasoning is typically based on defeasible presumptions concerning the agent's knowledge or estimation of his given circumstances. Such circumstances are often subject to change, however. Therefore a given practical inference is generally subject to rebuttals by the raising of critical questions. A practical inference is typically used to shift a burden of proof in deliberation by bringing forward presumptions. Critical questioning in the dialogue by a respondent can, however, shift the burden of proof against the conclusion of a practical inference.

Practical reasoning can be faulty or incorrect in one particularly simple way that is important to note. It can be a simple argument from negative consequences of the form, "Don't do action A because bad consequences $C_1, C_2, \ldots, C_n$ will occur if you do A!" where it is not adequately proved that $C_1, C_2, \ldots, C_n$ will in fact follow from doing A. In itself, this may be not so much a fallacy as simply an argument from consequences that is unproven. It is an incorrect argument only in the lesser sense of being a weak argument that has not been proved. Requirements of burden of proof have simply not been met by the proponent. Even if the premise is false, it may not be appropriate to say that such an argument from consequences is fallacious. The observation will have important ramifications later.

So we should note that if an argument from consequences can be a reasonable kind of argument in some instances, as legitimate practical reasoning, it can also be incorrect or unreasonable in other instances.

But it is also instructive to see that practical reasoning can be faulty or incorrect for various reasons. It has a premise-conclusion distinctive structure with distinctive critical questions imposing requirements of correctness on its use in argument.

Practical reasoning, in the simplest kind of case, concerns a solitary agent who is deciding how to proceed in a situation, based on his or her own goals and assessment of the situation. But it is also very commonly used in argumentation where one party is trying to advise another on how to act, or where one party is trying to convince the other party what a certain course of action is the best way for that other party to proceed with a course of action. Here, one party says to the other: "Your goals are such-and-such—so this is what you ought to do" (or something to that effect).

Practical reasoning is a knowledge-based type of reasoning where the agent is in a given situation (set of circumstances) and knows or is aware of these circumstances. The sequence of reasoning is for the agent to find a line of action from the given situation (as the agent sees it) to the end point represented by the goal. This tends to be a defeasible type of reasoning because the agent's knowledge of the situation tends to be imperfect and incomplete, and the reasoning may have to be altered if new information comes in, or if the circumstances are changed.

This knowledge can flow in from an external source, in a case where deliberation is joined to another type of dialogue, like advice-seeking dialogue. For example, consider the following hypothetical case:

> *Case* 4.10: Suppose I am deliberating with my spouse on what to do with our pension investment fund—whether to buy stocks, bonds, or some other type of investments. We consult with a financial adviser, an expert source of information who can tell us what is happening in the stock market, and so forth, at the present time.

In such a case, my spouse and I are engaged in a deliberation dialogue. But then joined to that dialogue, we are also engaged in an expert consultation (advice-seeking) dialogue with a third party. Presumably, the advice-seeking dialogue is bringing in external knowledge to the deliberation dialogue by way of appeal to expert opinion (a distinctive type of argumentation in its own right),[5] and hereby improving the quality of the deliberation dialogue.

Thus practical reasoning is not the only type of argumentation that can be used in a deliberation. Deliberation is very much based on opinions or knowledge of what is true, or taken to be true as information. And determining what is true or false does not rely on practical reasoning alone. But practical reasoning is the primary type of reasoning used in deliberation. It is highly characteristic of deliberation, and may be described as the type of reasoning that is the main thread of reasoning woven through the fabric of a deliberation.

Practical reasoning can be used in argumentation in five main kinds of conversational exchanges recognized in Walton (1989, p. 10) other than deliberation—the quarrel, the critical discussion, the negotiation type of dialogue, the inquiry, and the information-seeking dialogue. So the context of dialogue in which *ad misericordiam* arguments of the kind typified in chapter 1 does not have to be that of a deliberation.

But the kind of case studied in chapter 4, especially the kind of appeal to pity used in charitable appeals typified by case 4.6, does seem to have elements of deliberation that are an important part of the context of use of the argument. The relief agency is asking the respondent, to whom the appeal is directed, to take action to relieve a kind of distress that has been cited. The argument says, in effect, "Join with us as a trusted partner in taking action to relieve this pitiable distress, because you share our goals (our common feelings of humanity and caring for the suffering)."

An interesting problem in evaluating some charitable appeals, however, is that some groups purporting to be charities really seem to be engaged in a kind of persuasion or advocacy dialogue, rather than a deliberation type of dialogue. Such groups are really political action groups that are supporting a cause, or advocating one side on a controversial issue. For example, Human Life International and Childbirth by Choice Trust are two groups on opposite sides of the abortion debate that are registered as charities in Canada, meaning that donors can claim a tax credit in Canada when they give to either of these organizations. However, Revenue Canada, according to Matas (1994, p. A11) wants to take away the registration of these two groups, on the grounds that they have crossed over the line separating charitable work from political action.

Human Life International has used aggressive tactics like showing the severed head of a fetus held in a pair of forceps during an abortion, indicating how strongly they are advocating one side of the abortion issue. Childbirth by Choice publishes booklets on topics like abortion information for teens. Both groups appear to be one-sided advocates on the abortion issue, and this approach conflicts with the requirement of Revenue Canada that an educational activity—which both groups claim to be involved in, as charities—must give "information about various points of view on an issue and cannot be restricted to one side" (Matas, p. A11). Other groups like Physicians for Life and Save the Baby Seals are suspect on comparable grounds, because they advocate one particular point of view or cause, instead of taking a balanced approach to solving a problem, or responding to a need for help.

The problem posed by these kinds of appeals to pity is that the shift from a balanced, collaborative deliberation to a one-sided advocacy of a cause may not be apparent to the donor who is solicited for funds. It may appear to donors that they are simply responding to an appeal based on argument from distress or argument from need to help, but something else may be going on under the surface of the appeal, that may reveal that the plea is not what it purports to be. The funding may go to support a political action group that spends it to support a narrowly defined cause.

7. WHAT DELIBERATION IS ABOUT

The purpose of a critical discussion is to resolve a conflict of opinions by rational argumentation.[6] And deliberation often seems very similar. In deliberation, typically, there is a decision to be made between incompatible courses of action. And so it seems to come down to a resolution of a conflict of opinions as to whether this or that is the best (or most prudent) course of action. Both types of dialogue require balanced and open-minded argumentation.

However, there does seem to be a difference. In a critical discussion, the aim is to present evidence that will prove, or at least support the claim, that a particular proposition is true (or false). In deliberation, it is a decision between two courses of action (or policies for action), and the aim is to decide which one is the best (or preferable) one to take, in the circumstances.

But perhaps this distinction is not so significant. For to say that a course of action is prudent, or is the best thing to do, is a kind of proposition. Hence it is a kind of opinion that can be supported by evidence in argumentation, or not.

On the other hand, deliberation does seem to have essential characteristics that sharply define it as a distinctive type of dialogue. The clearest account of these characteristics comes from Aristotle.

When Aristotle sets out to analyze deliberation in the *Nicomachean Ethics*, he begins by asking what its subject is. What do we deliberate about? To narrow down the answer to this question, he sets out several positive and negative conditions (1112 a 20–1113 a 13):

1. No one deliberates about eternal things, for example, about the incommensurability of the diagonal and the side of a square (1112 a 22).
2. We do not deliberate about "things that involve movement but always happen in the same way"—for example, the solstices or the rising of the stars (1112 a 25).
3. We do not deliberate about "things that happen now in one way, now in another"—for example, droughts and rains (1112 a 26).
4. We do not deliberate about chance events, like the finding of a treasure (1112 a 27).
5. We do not deliberate about all human affairs. For example (1112 a 28), "no Spartan deliberates about the best constitution for the Scythians."
6. "We deliberate about things that are in our power and can be done" (1112 a 30).

The first five conditions are negative. Aristotle writes that when you have eliminated all of these (1112 a 31), what is left is condition 6.

Aristotle even divides up the arts and sciences, to indicate which contain deliberation. The best examples of arts that contain deliberation are medical treatment and money-making (1112 b 4). We deliberate less in the sciences than in the arts, because we have more doubt about the arts (1112 b 7). Note that, for Aristotle, medicine is an art (*techne*). Aristotle also notes that we do more deliberation in the art of navigation than in the art of gymnastics.

Having narrowed down the subject matter of deliberation by these six conditions, so that we now have an account of what it is we deliberate about, Aristotle goes on to pinpoint this more exactly:

> Deliberation is concerned with things that happen in a certain way for the most part, but in which the event is obscure, and with things in which it is indeterminate. We call in others to aid us in deliberation on important questions, distrusting ourselves as not being equal to deciding.

This is a very important passage, which may seem obscure initially. But it points to two essential characteristics of deliberation: (1) deliberation is appropriate where an event is "obscure"—that is, where we don't know everything about it—there is a lack of (exact knowledge). But (2) with this type of event, things generally happen (for the most part) in a certain way. In a situation where deliberation is appropriate, we can normally expect the events to follow an expected pattern, but this is only a defeasible presumption. We have no exact knowledge of such things, and it may very well turn out to be the case that something unexpected happens. The characteristic situation then is one of ignorance (lack of knowledge) and uncertainty. Plausible guesswork based on assumptions about what normally happens in a situation of this type is our guide.[7]

Finally, it is very important to see that deliberation is seen by Aristotle as a type of dialogue or conversational exchange, in those cases where the question is an important one, and we do not trust ourselves to decide on a solitary basis. Although deliberation can, in many cases, as mentioned above, be a solitary process, it can be viewed as a normative structure of dialogue between two parties, or two points of view entertained by one. One immediately thinks here of political deliberation, where a group of citizens have a meeting to deliberate on some policy, problem, or course of action.[8]

Even in the solitary case, deliberation could be seen as a kind of devil's advocate debate with oneself, where two sides of a decision are examined critically. But it is clear that in the cases of multiple person deliberation, there will be public records of such speech exchanges—for example, in the form of transcripts of political or parliamentary debates, and the like. Such cases contain argumentation, and it is appropriate to judge such argumentation in the framework of deliberation as a goal-directed type of dialogue.

8. THE CASE OF WALTER
THE HARD-NOSED LOGICIAN

Now that we have a better understanding of the structure of the argument from need for help as used in a case of an appeal to pity, we are in a much better position to begin to try to explore why such arguments are so generally condemned as fallacious by the logic texts. And eventually, we will be in a better position to judge whether and why such evaluations are justified. For the present, we can already see how these arguments can fall short in certain ways. An appeal to pity can rightly be criticized as a bad argument if in fact the distress it portrays is not real, or if the means cited for relieving it are in fact ineffective. These are criticisms of the practical reasoning used in the argument.

But what about an argument like the one in case 4.2, where the factual information given in the appeal is correct, or at least can be reasonably justified by the evidence? Could there still be grounds for criticizing it as a fallacious *ad misericordiam* argument? The problem can be stated even more explicitly by posing another case.

Brinton (pp. 35–36) asks us to imagine the reaction of a particular type of person to the televised appeal in case 4.8:

> *Case* 4.11: Let us suppose (a quite reasonable supposition in the case of certain well-known relief agencies) that we have good reason to believe that the agency in question will do, efficiently, what the spokesperson says it will do with our contributions. Walter, a hard-nosed logician who sometimes watches television, at first a little irritated at the interruption of his favorite episode of *Star Trek*, takes in the relevant information. He is offended by the actress's plaintive tone of voice, and also by the blatant attempt to arouse his sympathies by means of the photographic techniques typically used in such advertisements. On the other hand, he takes some pride in his ability to make his judgments on the basis of the facts and his moral principles, which in this case lead him to go get his checkbook and write out the recommended donation.

Walter is offended by such a blatant appeal to feelings, and at first he may well be tempted to dismiss this argument as a fallacious *ad misericordiam*. But, as noted in our discussion of case 4.7 above, there could be good reasons for not judging this kind of case as a fallacious appeal to pity. For as a sequence of practical reasoning, the argument from request for aid in it could perhaps be reconstructed as quite a reasonable sequence of goal-directed argumentation. Let's say that the relevant information in case 4.11 is given along with the "plaintive" appeal to pity, so from a practical reasoning viewpoint, there is good evidence given to support the conclusion.

The way Walter assesses the situation, according to Brinton (p. 36) is to be influenced only by "the facts and his moral principles." Walter understands that the agency probably has to take an emotional approach to get money, "human nature being what it is." But he resents this, and wishes they would simply present people with the facts.

According to Brinton (p. 36), Walter is mistaken and the relief agency's appeal is "perfectly appropriate," not just a compromise required by the "deficiencies" of a mass audience. This conclusion seems like it could be justified. But before we can go ahead and do this, it is necessary to clearly separate the two parts of the argument.

What is presumed is that there is a distinctive "factual" type of argument typically contained within charitable advertisements of this sort. On our analysis, the core argument within the advertisement has the structure of the argument from need for help. This part of the argument is a species of practical reasoning and, as such, the kinds of critical questions it properly elicits are more "factual" (or more practical—questions of ends, means, and efficient action) in nature than emotional appeals to feelings like compassion or pity (which have to do more with feelings).

How do the appeals to pity, compassion, sympathy, and mercy come into such arguments then? For they are commonly there, as illustrated by the cases cited above. How does the appeal to one of these emotions get grafted onto the practical reasoning in a given case to generate an *argumentum ad misericordiam*? How can we separate between the core argument and the appeal to feeling grafted onto it?

The argument from distress species of the argument from need for help is close to an appeal to compassion already, because the sight of a person in distress is normally enough to provoke sympathy. However, in some cases, the appeal to feeling is more distinctly presented.

In some cases, the argument is explicitly an argument from negative consequences and the appeal to pity is indirect and unstated as an appeal to feeling. For example, in case 4.1, the student said he would lose his visa, and as a result be shot, if the committee did not decide to admit him. Because of this distressful consequence, we know that this argument does make an appeal to pity, but the appeal is not made in an explicit or direct way.

We could contrast this case with one described by Alan Brinton (in conversation).[9]

> *Case* 4.12: A student had failed his logic course, and pleaded, on his knees, with tears flowing down his face, before the instructor, saying, "If I pass this course, I will be headman in my village when I go home. If I fail I will be nobody!"

Here too, the argument is one from negative consequences, but the emotional appeal to feeling is much more explicit and evident. The appeal is accompanied by, or conveyed in, an emotional plea that could be described as "theatrical," even though it may have been quite sincere.

Now we can rephrase Walter's question more sharply. When the argument from need for help is accompanied by an appeal to feeling, over and above the practical reasoning and argumentation from negative consequence, what is the function or value of this emotional appeal to pity or compassion, from a logical point of view? What is its worth as evidence in prudent deliberations on choosing a course of action? Walter doubts that it has any such value. He thinks it is just a primitive instinct that is being appealed to, appropriate for a mass audience, but of no value as evidence to a critical thinker.

9. EVOLUTIONARY LOGIC OF
APPEAL TO FEELING

The answer to Walter's question is that the intense feelings of sympathy and compassion we have are useful in human deliberation because they influence us to support, to help, and to relieve others we empathize with. We feel pity for persons who are in distress, and from a purely calculative point of view, it may cost us something to help them or do something to try to alleviate their distress. But still, this kind of feeling can be important to group survival, which in turn contributes to the prospects for individual survival. That same individual may never help me when I am in distress, but somebody else might, influenced by the same feeling of compassion. Thus while the feeling of sympathy that influences our deliberations in such a case may be a kind of primitive bias that needs to be moderated by the calculations of practical reasoning, in order to be of value, it does have a function that can contribute to successful deliberation, from a broad evolutionary perspective. By adding an element of urgency, the appeal to pity or compassion contributes an emphasis to an argument used in deliberation that makes one respond to it with heightened attention and energy. So the appeal to pity does have a useful function, when grafted onto an argument from appeal for help.

This explanation of the logical function of appeal to pity is an evolutionary or Darwinian approach to the feeling of compassion as a built-in human bias in the general sense of Marks (1994). By *bias* however, I do not mean something inherently negative—it is possible to have good (functional) bias as well as bad (critically harmful) or negative bias, of the kind that distorts or devalues an argument.[10]

The assumption is that the bias toward pity is not fixed or absolute, and needs to be moderated by practical reasoning in the known circumstances of a particular case. This approach then is Aristotelian, in the sense that feelings or emotions are being portrayed as valuable when they are moderated, or more accurately, when they are given weight appropriate for the circumstances of a case, and acted on in light of the broader picture of evidence known in a case.

This justification of the evidential value of appeals to feeling is also Aristotelian in another way. Walter's view of the shortcomings of such appeals in argumentation is that they have a dramatic, but short-term impact. A critical thinker needs to take long-term consequences into account, in judging such arguments, and look to the wider picture of the network of practical reasoning in such a case. Walter takes a dim view of these short-term emotional responses.

However, in the real world of deliberation on personal questions of practical reasoning in the conduct of one's life, very often there just is not enough time to look into all the relevant consequences and long-term effects before making a prudent decision. In an emergency, it may be better to respond with heightened arousal of emotions and go with one's "gut instincts" or feelings.

Damasio (1994) examined a number of case histories of patients who had suffered brain damage. Although these patients had unimpaired use of language, motor skills, and skills of rational thinking, they kept making bad personal and social decisions that resulted in loss of jobs, property, and spouses. But the only thing that appeared to be missing in these patients was the capacity to experience normal emotions. This lack of capacity, however, could be described as bringing with it an inability to engage in reasoning of a sort—the kind of practical reasoning that is used in everyday deliberations. Damasio concludes that Descartes was in error to neglect the emotions as important to thought and reasoning. He concludes that feelings or emotions function as somatic markers that raise alarm signals about the possible future negative consequences of choosing a particular course of action.

In section 5 above, Aristotle noted that an essential characteristic of deliberation is that it is appropriate where an event is "obscure," in the sense that there is a lack of knowledge about its long-term consequences. In such cases, we must reason by *ad ignorantiam* argumentation on a basis of presumption—if we don't know that a particular proposition is true (false), we operate on the provisional assumption that it is false (true), until more information comes in to enable us to make a correction (if needed).[11]

What Walter was objecting to is that the appeal to pity is a kind of short cut way of arriving at a conclusion. Walter thinks that logical reasoners should do their homework, and collect the evidence, then decide on the basis of this larger and more reliable body of data. This attitude is partly right. But what it overlooks is that in the practical realities of everyday personal deliberation on what to do in an uncertain and changeable world, it may sometimes be best to go with the short cut argument, as long as you are open to changing your conclusion if new knowledge comes in that supplies a broader picture of evidence. Walter committed Descartes' error of overlooking the role of emotions in practical reasoning in deliberation.

10. CONCLUSIONS SUMMARIZED

In this chapter, the underlying structure of argumentation, common to kinds of cases cited as *ad misericordiam* arguments in chapter 1, has been analyzed as taking particular, identifiable forms of reasoning. The argument from negative consequences, argument from appeal to help, and argument from distress have been shown to be species of practical reasoning used in deliberation to try to get a respondent to take some particular form of action.

Then we showed how the various appeals to feeling studied in chapter 3 are grafted onto these arguments to produce the composite type of argumentation known as *argumentum ad misericordiam*. I have justified this type of argument, contrary to the general presumptions of the textbook treatments of it, as being reasonable (non-fallacious) in some cases.

There are important questions that need to be answered, however, before we can go on to the task of giving general criteria for evaluating the *argumentum ad misericordiam* as fallacious or not, in a given case. For Brinton is right, I think, to judge that an argument of this kind in the sort of case of charitable appeal we have been considering, should not be evaluated as fallacious simply on the grounds that it is an appeal to feeling or emotion of the kind that successfully moves an audience. True, such an argument has a "factual," or better, practical core. But when the argument goes beyond this practical reasoning part to appeal to feelings like compassion, that, in itself, should not make it a bad argument. Only where the emotional appeal has been somehow blown out of proportion as a

powerful feeling that is exploited, or used in place of the proper factual backing needed to support the practical reasoning—or even
worse, when it has been misused to distract attention away from
such deficiencies—should we call such an argument fallacious.
Brinton's investigation supports Hamblin's general line (1970), and
our own (1992a) that appeals to compassionate emotions should not
be condemned, purely on grounds that such feelings are appealed
to, in instances where practical reasoning is being used in argument
as a basis for action.

Practical reasoning in deliberation should not exclude appeals
to gut feelings or emotional attitudes as a basis for its calculations
used in arriving at a conclusion on how to act, in an imperfectly
known situation. In case 4.7, for example, there was a blatant appeal
to pity or compassion in the picture showing starving children in
Ethiopia. But can we say, just in virtue of the use of this appeal in the
case, that the argument for funding is an instance of the *ad misericordiam* fallacy? I do not think so, in virtue of our analysis so far, but
more work needs to be done on the reasons why the *argumentum ad
misericordiam* should be judged fallacious in a given case before
this question can be adequately answered, one way or the other.

Implied by so many of the textbook accounts is the objection
that the argument in case 4.7 is an appeal to pity, and therefore (for
that reason alone) it can be judged to be an instance of the *ad misericordiam* fallacy. The objection here could cite the use of the photograph of the children with distended bellies as a tactic that makes
the problem seem remote, and fixable just by sending money, instead
of having any real empathy or sympathy for their real situation. So
construed, this case could be equated with many of the aspects of the
Jerry Lewis Telethon found objectionable by the protesters—that is,
that the plea for funds using "pathetic" visions of children in distress
does not really address the real problem of how to make the lives of
the affected parties better, by creating conditions making it possible
for them to help themselves.

A television documentary cited by Cuff (1996) presented a
film that elicited sympathy for children by featuring two families
living in cramped, shabby accommodations provided by government social services:

Case 4.12: *Family Rooms* is described in the accompanying
bumpf as "an intimate look at children living in
hard times." There are two families featured, and by
the end of the film I wasn't quite sure who belonged

to what family and frankly didn't much care. All had been evicted from whatever places they were renting and were living hand to mouth in cramped, shabby accommodation provided by Social Services.

The mothers were mostly mute, and viewers were given little information about their histories other than the very visible evidence that they had (and were still) giving birth to numerous children they obviously could not feed nor care for adequately.

At the top of the program, viewers are told that one million children are living in families who are on welfare and that the number represents an estimated increase of 300,000 since Parliament vowed (in 1989) to end child poverty by the year 2000.

In commenting on this case, Cuff (1996, p. A12) asks some hard questions: Why do the people portrayed, who have so many problems (one father is in jail, and one mother was in drug rehabilitation) have so many children? And why do documentaries like this one always seem to absolve the parents of any responsibility for their situation? And why do so many of these children go on to perpetuate the cycle of self-abuse, criminal behavior, and irresponsible reproduction? Instead of posing these hard questions, the documentary film just presents "victims" and appeals for more government funding of social services.

This kind of documentary film definitely presents an argument—an argument from distress, pleading for more government funding to end child poverty—but it bases the argument exclusively on a one-sided appeal to pity, failing to even ask the kinds of critical questions that might lead to any real relief of the distress. Instead of looking at the whole picture of the practical reasoning in the case, the documentary presents a very narrow focus on one angle. Such a view looks at the situation through the rose-colored glasses of appeal to pity. It is a feel-good culture of feelings viewpoint that ignores any realistic assessment of the consequences of the practical courses of action.

Here then is an important clue to what should be logically objectionable about appeals to pity of the kind that have become so familiar in recent times. It is not the appeal to sympathy, or the argument from distress, that is (in itself) objectionable. It is what the appeal leaves out, by omitting to take into account all the considerations of practical reasoning needed to get a practical solution to the problem that would realistically enable the affected parties to get out of the bad situation they are in. The problem with so many familiar appeals to pity of this kind is that they avoid the hard questions, and propose some easy solution like sending a check to a charity, or spending more tax money on welfare programs that are dubiously effective in solving the problem cited, and may even be worsening the problem.

However, it would be a mistake to leap from the criticism identified in case 4.12 to the conclusion that all appeals to pity, like the one in case 4.7 showing starving children in Ethiopia, are fallacious. While the argument in case 4.7 can certainly be criticized on several grounds, it would be too hasty a conclusion to reject it as fallacious, simply on the grounds that it uses an appeal to pity. For the problem here is that the inference from criticizing pity on ethical grounds of its negative moral implications, to condemning an argument using an appeal to pity as a premise, on logical grounds, by judging it to be an instance of the *ad misericordiam* fallacy, is too much of a logical leap to be sustained generally, without filling in many further conditions and qualifications that need to be met.

One can go on to ask hard questions about whether the aid agency advertising the appeal really can deliver the food needed to relieve the distress of the starving children. The evaluation of the case then turns on the practical issue of whether the distress can really be relieved by this means. One important question would be whether this form of aid is effective in the long term, by enabling these starving people to get over the immediate emergency situation so that there is some reasonable chance they can eventually get to a normal life where they can provide for themselves.

It seems then that appeals to pity can be reasonable arguments in some cases, but they need to be evaluated in a context of practical reasoning that takes into account the consequences of going ahead with a particular action that is being advocated. It is one thing to bask in a rosy glow of sympathy and self-congratulation for having charitable intentions. It is quite another thing to do your homework, and ask critical questions about how to really achieve one's goal of giving help or relieving distress. Such a practical assessment of an appeal to pity involves taking a look at the broader realities of the situation—including an assessment of the likely consequences of the course of action recommended.

It seems then that evaluating *ad misericordiam* arguments intelligently on a basis of practical reasoning requires a balanced assessment. Some of these arguments are reasonable, even though defeasible and tentative, while others can be misleading, one-sided, and highly questionable. Just because an argument from need for help is based on an appeal to sympathy, it does not automatically mean that this argument should be judged (without further questioning) to commit an *ad misericordiam* fallacy.

In case 4.11 then, I would reject the conclusion of Walter the hard-nosed logician, who pays attention only to the practical reasoning in the plea for aid, and rejects the emotional aspect of the appeal to pity as being merely rhetoric for the uncritical and uninformed mass audience. Instead, we see the *argumentum ad misericordiam* as a legitimate appeal to deep human feelings, based on empathy, that can have a proper function in arriving at a decision on how to act. The argument from request for aid is a use of practical reasoning that is properly based on an appeal to sympathy or compassion—and yes, in some cases, even appeal to pity. When such an argument is partly based on a premise that appeals to sympathy, compassion, or pity, it can function as a reasonable kind of default argumentation, subject to criticism and correction once further information on the situation comes in, but provisionally reasonable as a practical guide to action where the situation is imperfectly known. But if appropriate critical questions of the practical kind are suppressed or ignored, and the respondent is invited to leap directly to the conclusion (or course of action) advocated, without taking a realistic and balanced view of the larger evidential picture, then caution should be in order.

5

The Nayirah Case

When we go beyond the examples cited in the textbook treatment, and examine real cases of *ad misericordiam* arguments in more detail, we find that it may not be so easy to definitely prove, one way or the other, whether a fallacy has been committed or not. Despite the difficulties posed by trying to deal with real cases, however, the effort can be instructive.

In this chapter I present one particularly interesting case study as a case of the use of the *argumentum ad misericordiam* that raises interesting questions on whether it should be evaluated as fallacious. This case illustrates how powerful the *argumentum ad misericordiam* can be, as an effective tactic of argumentation. It also involves the concepts of bias and deception. It also raises interesting general questions about how the concept of fallacy should be defined.

I begin by stating the known facts of the case in chronological order, as reported by the news sources I have collected. Then I proceed to an analysis and evaluation of the case, based on this given information. Finally, I raise some general issues for the study of the *ad misericordiam* fallacy posed by the case.

1. FACTS OF THE CASE

The invasion of Kuwait by Iraq took place on August 2, 1990. Not long afterwards, there were rumors of a shocking incident. In a letter circulated at the United Nations on September 6, 1990, Kuwait charged that Iraqi soldiers had removed hospital equipment that resulted in the deaths of many patients, including premature infants, in intensive care (Reuters 1990, p. A14):

127

In a letter to Secretary-General Javier Perez de Cuellar, Kuwait's UN representative, Mohammad Abulhasan, did not say how many deaths have resulted.

"The delicate medical equipment used in the intensive-care units of many Kuwaiti hospitals has been seized and taken to Baghdad," he wrote. "This has led to the death of many patients who were receiving intensive care."

Mr. Abulhasan said incubators in maternity hospitals used for premature children were removed, "causing the death of all the children who were under treatment."

On September 28, 1990, the emir of Kuwait visited George Bush at the White House to discuss ending the Iraqi occupancy and restoration of Kuwait's government. Brent Scowcroft, then National Security Adviser, said (MacKenzie 1990, p. A10) that Iraqi behavior in Kuwait was "accelerating the timetable" for considering the "options" on how to proceed.

> He said the emir outlined Iraq's stripping of Kuwait's assets in graphic detail during his meeting with Mr. Bush. The Iraqis, he said, were removing babies from incubators and patients from life support and shipping the equipment to Iraq. At the same time, Iraqis were being moved into Kuwait, presumably to act as colonists.
>
> "What I'm saying is that the atrocities, the devastation inside Kuwait merit world attention," Mr. Scowcroft said.

At this meeting, Mr. Bush pledged to restore the emir to power, but there was no talk of any immediate U.S. military action being planned.

On October 10, 1990, in a hearing before the Congressional Human Rights Caucus, a fifteen-year-old Kuwaiti girl identified only as "Nayirah" testified, while crying, that Iraqi soldiers had pulled babies from incubators in Kuwait. The quotation below is from *60 Minutes*, but the words in the second paragraph were initially reported in Shepard (1990, p. 4):

> Mr. Chairman and members of the committee, my name is Nayirah, and I just came out of Kuwait.
>
> While I was there, I saw the Iraqi soldiers come into the hospital with guns. They took the babies out of the incubators, took the incubators, and left the children to die on the cold floor. *[crying]* It was horrifying. [*60 Minutes*, 1992, p. 8]

After this testimony, it was reported that George Bush repeated the story at least ten times in the following weeks, using the words "Babies pulled from incubators and scattered like firewood across the floor" (*60 Minutes*, p. 8). This story was widely publicized. Portions of a video release featuring Nayirah's testimony eventually reached a total estimated audience of thirty-five million (Rowse, 1992, p. 28).

On November 27, 1990, two days before the United Nations vote on whether to respond with military force if Iraq did not pull out of Kuwait by January 15, there was a presentation at the U.N. that included a videotape showing Iraqi soldiers firing on unarmed demonstrators, and the walls of the U.N. council chamber were "covered with oversize color photographs of Kuwaitis of all ages who reportedly had been killed or tortured by Iraqis" (Rowse, 1991, p. 20). In a report in *The Toronto Star* (Ward, 1990, A2), a surgeon named Mohammed was quoted as saying that under his supervision one hundred twenty newborns were buried. He himself buried forty "newborn babies that had been taken from their incubators by the soldiers." The mounting evidence of Iraqi atrocities in Kuwait culminated on December 19, 1990, in the publication of an Amnesty International report that had a dramatic impact on developments (*60 Minutes*, 1992, p. 8):

> *SAFER: [voice-over]* There was plenty of evidence of Iraqi brutality, but the incubator story became almost a rallying cry. It has Presidential confirmation and the confirmation of Amnesty International, which published a report after Nayirah testified, quoting her and claiming 312 babies were killed when Iraqi troops pulled them from their incubators.

According to the Amnesty report (Reuters, 1990a, A1), widespread abuses of human rights by Iraqi occupying forces in Kuwait included executions, torture, beatings, castration, and rape. According to the report, Iraqi troops "left 300 premature babies to die after stealing incubators" (A1). It said that an Amnesty investigation team talked with several doctors and nurses who "gave details of the deaths of 300 babies removed from incubators in hospitals by Iraqi troops and left to die on cold floors" (Reuters, 1990a, A2).

On January 10, 1991, the U.S. Senate voted to authorize going to war against Iraq. The measure passed by five votes. Seven senators cited Nayirah's testimony in speeches backing the use of force.

Then in March, 1991, after the invasion of Kuwait, a number of revelations came out that threw doubt on Nayirah's story, summarized by Rowse (1992, p. 16) below. These developments were precipitated by the investigations of John Martin of *ABC*, who interviewed Kuwaiti hospital officials who said that the incubator story was a falsehood. It also came out that the story had been promoted by America's preeminent public relations firm, Hill and Knowlton:

> In March 1991, *ABC News* interviewed Kuwaiti hospital officials who denied that any babies had been dumped out of incubators by Iraqi troops. A month later, Amnesty International, which earlier had reported the figure of 312 dead, said it had "found no reliable evidence that Iraqi forces had caused the deaths" of any incubator babies. The big bombshell, however, was a story by *Harper's* magazine publisher John R. MacArthur, which appeared in January 1992 on *The New York Times* op-ed page, revealing that Nayirah was the daughter of the Kuwaiti ambassador to the United States. MacArthur also revealed that Reps. Tom Lantos and John Edward Porter, who sponsored the congressional hearings, had started a group called the Congressional Human Rights Foundation that had received $50,000 from Citizens for a Free Kuwait, as well as free office space in Hill and Knowlton's Washington headquarters.

The *Times* article by MacArthur revealed in January 1992 that Nayirah was the daughter of Saud Nasir al-Sabah, and a member of Kuwait's royal family. MacArthur had gotten suspicious, while working on a book on propaganda in the Gulf war, and had found out Nayirah's identity by asking questions at the Kuwait embassy (*60 Minutes*, 1992, p. 9). According to MacArthur, her identity was known to caucus co-chairmen Lantos and Porter at the time of the senate hearings, but they did not disclose it. Both had close political ties to Hill and Knowlton, the firm that had promoted a public relations campaign, including the presentations for the U.N. and the U.S. congress.

It turned out that Hill and Knowlton had many close connections to Kuwait, and that the campaign was financed mainly by a group of wealthy Kuwaitis, using a front organization "Citizens for a Free Kuwait." According to an estimate of *The Washington Post* (Rowse, 1991, p. 20), the total amount paid to Hill and Knowlton by Citizens for a Free Kuwait was more than eleven million dollars.

According to the *60 Minutes* report (1992, p. 11), Hill and Knowlton is "by far, the biggest, most influential PR firm in Washington." John MacArthur in the *60 Minutes* interview (p. 11) indicated how Nayirah's story made an enormous difference in their campaign:

Mr. MacARTHUR: When the Kuwaitis hire Hill and Knowlton to represent their interest, to get them to argue the case for military intervention, Hill and Knowlton desperately needs a defining moment, a defining atrocity, something that is so emotional that the American people will not be able to ignore the plight of Kuwait. And Nayirah and the baby incubator story provide that defining moment.

Had Americans known that Nayirah was the daughter of the Kuwaiti ambassador, a man desperately trying to find friends to help liberate his occupied country, their reaction to the story would have been quite different.

Subsequent investigations, by John Martin of *ABC*, broadcast in a *20/20* program (1992), confirmed by interviews with Kuwaiti medical officials that there was no evidence of the incubator story (*20/20*, 1992, p. 4).

We found the incubators that the Iraqis supposedly had taken away here at Maternity Hospital. Doctor Soad Ben-Essa is a pediatrician who stayed behind in the hospital during the war. She said Iraqi soldiers lived in Ward Nine.

[interviewing] Did you ever see them take the babies out to take the incubators away?

Dr. SOAD BEN-ESSA, Pediatrician: No.

MARTIN: [voice-over] Dr. Fawyiza al Qattan was an obstetrician at the Maternity Hospital. When we found her living outside London, she told us there had been atrocities there, a staff doctor had been murdered, but none involving incubators.

[interviewing] So between August and November, no Iraqi soldiers came to take incubators from the Maternity Hospital.

Dr. FAWYIZA al QATTAN, Obstetrician: Not from Maternity Hospital.

MARTIN: [voice-over] Nayirah, the ambassador's daughter, said atrocities took place at the al-Addan Hospital. The obstetrician Dr. Fahima Khafaji worked there during that period of the occupation.

[interviewing] Did the soldiers come into the hospital and take the incubators away when babies were in the incubators?

Dr. FAHIMA KHAFAJI, Obstetrician: No, I didn't see.

MARTIN: [voice-over] Some babies did die. Why?

Dr. FAYEZA YOUSSEF Obstetrician: There was no service, no nurses to take care of these babies, and that's why they died.

MARTIN: [voice-over] Dr. Muhammad Matar directed Kuwait's primary health care system. His wife, Dr. Fayeza Youssef, ran the obstetrics unit at Maternity Hospital. We talked in Cairo, where they fled after the atrocities supposedly took place.

[interviewing] This is very specific. "Iraqi soldiers took them out of the incubators and put them on the floor to die."

Dr. MUHAMMAD MATAR: I think this is something just for propaganda.

MARTIN: [voice-over] We asked human rights investigators.

ANDREW WHITLEY, Executive Director, Middle East Watch: We haven't found any evidence that any incubators were taken. I do believe that there were some exaggerations, politically inspired exaggerations, of the atrocities that were taking place.

The body of evidence collected on the alleged incident indicated the absence of any verification of the incubator story, and strongly suggested that it was not true.

2. ANALYSIS OF THE CASE

The sequence of argumentation in this case breaks down into two phases—see Table 5.1.

The first phase goes from the initial circulation of rumors about the incubator story, continuing through the events that culminated in Nayirah's testimony, and ending after the Senate's vote to approve the invasion of Kuwait. The second phase begins with John Martin's broadcast in March 1991 interviewing the Kuwaiti medical officials, and John MacArthur's article revealing Nayirah's identity. The appeal to pity was a successful argument during the first phase of its deployment, and played a key part in influencing American public opinion and getting action to support the invasion. But then, during the second phase, critical doubts were raised, and it gradually became apparent that the argument had been a deception. The critical point in this turnaround was the revelation of the identity of Nayirah.

The context of argument for the first phase is that of the Senate deliberation on whether to back the use of force in Kuwait, and the testimony of Nayirah as a key part of the argumentation in these deliberations. During this first phase, the appeal to pity seemed to be appropriate in context, and played a legitimate (and very important) role in influencing the outcome of the deliberations.

Table 5.1
Chronology of Events

Phase One

Aug. 2, 1990:   Iraq's invasion of Kuwait
Sept. 6, 1990:   letter to U.N. from Kuwaiti ambassador
Sept. 28, 1990: emir of Kuwait visits White House
Oct. 10, 1990:   hearing before Congressional Human rights Caucus: testimony of Nayirah
Nov. 27, 1990:   U.N. presentation on atrocities
Nov. 29, 1990:   U.N. vote on Jan. 15 deadline for Saddam
Dec. 19, 1990:   Amnesty International Report
Jan. 10, 1991:   U.S. Senate authorizes use of force against Iraq

Phase Two

March, 1991:   John Martin broadcasts interviews of Kuwaiti medical personnel denying incubator story
April 18, 1991: Amnesty International retraction
May, 1991:   financing of Hill and Knowlton public relations campaign by Kuwaiti backers revealed
January, 1992: identity of Nayirah becomes known

The precise moment that the identity of Nayirah became general knowledge is a little difficult to pin down to an exact date. But January 1992 is probably a good rough approximation to go by. Knoll (1992) has outlined the details of what happened. Arthur Rowse's article, "Flacking for the Emir," appeared in May 1991 in *The Progressive*. Rowse said he expected the story to set off a lot of alarm bells, "but did not hear from anyone in the U.S. media, and only received inquiries from Italian television, the BBC, and the CBC" (Knoll, 1992, p. 4). According to Rowse, as reported in (Knoll, p. 4), it was not until January 1992 that the story became widely known:

However, it wasn't until this past January that the corrected account became widely known. That was when John R. MacArthur, the publisher of *Harper's*, and Leslie Fruman of the Canadian Broadcasting Corporation, working separately, learned that Nayirah was actually a daughter of the Kuwaiti ambassador to the United States. MacArthur, who was writing a book on Gulf War propaganda (to be published soon), found her identity by simply calling the Kuwaiti embassy on a hunch.

Fruman had heard rumors, and then confronted the ambassador in a camera interview.

"MacArthur told the world in a *New York Times* op-ed piece on January 6," Rowse continued, "The CBC broadcast the news that night, then presented a lengthy segment the next night on its *Fifty Estate* program. This was soon followed by news clips on CNN and extensive footage on the BBC's *Late Show*, ABC's *20/20*, CBS's *60 Minutes*, and Thames Television, as well as articles in the print media. And the story is still reverberating.

Apparently, the most newsworthy part of the story was the fact that it was the ambassador's daughter who made the plea.

During even earlier points of the second phase of the case, however, more came to be known about how the argument making the appeal to pity was being used. According to MacArthur (1992, p. 68), Alexander Cockburn openly challenged "the incubator myth" on January 17, 1991, in the *Los Angeles Times*, but his article came too late to make a difference. It became widely apparent only later that the appeal to pity was a key part of a public relations campaign designed for purposes of advocacy, to influence public opinion and the Senate toward supporting a particular course of action. Such advocacy argumentation for a "cause" is not, in itself, fallacious. But viewed in context, in light of the supposed purpose of Nayirah's testimony, a definite contrast between what originally appeared to be the use of the argument and its real underlying use became apparent. One needs to appreciate the sequence of how the argument was used, in context.

In this case the *argumentum ad misericordiam* was used effectively to shift an important outcome of a deliberative debate in a balance-of-considerations decision to one side, by a narrow margin. Here the situation was in a delicate balance, at one point in the debate, and the emotional appeal to pity function as a tie-breaker. It seems that there is a great inertia in public opinion against an action like going to war or undertaking an invasion, and some emotional picture or "icon" is needed to give a kind of morally compelling reason for taking such an action (what MacArthur, above, called a "defining moment").

According to MacArthur (1992, p. 52) a London *Times* dispatch of August 1941 reported a story of a man who saw "with his own eyes German soldiery chop off the arms of a baby which clung to its mother's skirts." The French propaganda bureau then produced a photograph of the handless baby, and even carried a drawing of the German soldier eating the hands. Subsequent investigations failed to substantiate the truth of such an incident. But manufactured reports of atrocities of this sort have long been used by all sides, both to justify declaring war, and to keep alive the "war fever" needed to sustain public support for continuing the war.

In the invasion of Kuwait, the picture of babies being pulled from incubators and scattered like pieces of firewood on a cold floor was the icon. It is an icon that everyone immediately reacts to as outraging basic human instincts to protect vulnerable children. Here then there was a powerful appeal to human emotion that was relevant to the context of dialogue, yet it became apparent during the second phase of the case that the intended recipients of the argument had taken it to be something it did not turn out to be.

3. BIAS AND EVIDENCE

One important factor in judging evidence based on the testimony of a witness is the perceived bias of the witness. If the witness is perceived as having something to gain by advocating a particular viewpoint, or if the witness has some connection or involvement with advocating, or with those who advocate one side of the issue, then doubts tend to be raised about the testimony as evidence. Testimony, as evidence, depends on the honesty and sincerity of a witness. In a court setting, the witness takes an oath, and in cross-examination the opposing attorney is allowed to raise questions about the potential bias of a witness (Degnan 1973; Waller 1988). This is the bias of a person.

But our concern is narrower than bias per se (see Adler 1993). I want to focus on biased argumentation. Here Nayirah's plea was part of an argument.

Biased argumentation is hard to measure, or even to define (Walton 1991). But generally, it is a presumption that a speaker advocating only one side of an issue in a context of dialogue where it is appropriate that both sides should be considered in a balanced way, has argued in a biased way.[4] If an arguer has a lot to gain by advocating one side of an issue in which he is supposed to consider both sides, for example, then there can be a suspicion that his argument is biased.

One key aspect in evaluating the argumentation in this case is the concealment of the identity of Nayirah. The finding that she was the daughter of Kuwait's ambassador to the United States threw a new light on the evaluation of her plea as a supposedly neutral witness, by indicating a source of bias. Initially, she was identified only as a fifteen-year-old Kuwaiti girl. But the subsequent revelations that she was a member of the Kuwaiti royal family, the daughter of the ambassador, and also the link with Hill and Knowlton's campaign, financed by the government of Kuwait, raised a presumption of bias that plays a large part in judging her testimony as evidence. These facts suggested a presumption of manipulation and a deliberate public relations campaign to influence U.S. support for an invasion of Kuwait. Hence the element of perceived bias in the case made before the Senate and television viewers is very significant in evaluating the *argumentum ad misericordiam* in this case. Whether the witness, or her backers, had something to gain is a key question in judging the appeal to pity.

One defense against the presumption of bias used by the participants was the claim that Nayirah's identity had been concealed to protect her family against Iraqi reprisals. The two senators who may have known Nayirah's identity, according to John R. MacArthur, the publisher of *Harper's* magazine (Facts on File, 1992, p. 31), responded to the charge that they concealed Nayirah's identity because of their ties to Hill and Knowlton, in different ways:

> MacArthur suggested that caucus co-chairmen Reps. Tom Lantos (D. Calif.) and John E. Porter (R. Ill.) might have concealed the girl's identity at the hearings because of their close political ties to Hill & Knowlton, a U.S. public relations firm. One of the firm's clients was Citizens for a Free Kuwait, a Kuwaiti-financed group that had lobbied for U.S. military intervention during the Persian Gulf crisis. The group had helped to organize the atrocity hearings and had also donated $50,000 to a human-rights foundation founded by the two congressmen.
>
> Lantos Jan. 6 admitted that he had known Nayirah's identity at the time of the hearings, but he insisted that her family connections "did not diminish her credibility." Lantos said he had withheld her full name in order to protect her family against Iraqi reprisals.
>
> Porter Jan. 6 told reporters that he had not learned of Nayirah's identity until recently, and he said the Human Rights Caucus would investigate her allegations in an effort to restore the group's credibility. Both men denied that their ties to Hill & Knowlton had influenced their handling of Nayirah's testimony.

Lantos admits he knew Nayirah's identity, but uses a dual defense, including the claim that her full name was concealed in order to protect against reprisals.

Another defense used was the argument that Hill and Knowlton were paid by an organization of private citizens, and not by the government of Kuwait (*20/20*, 1992, p. 5):

> *[interviewing]* Who hired Hill and Knowlton to handle this account? Was it the Citizens for a Free Kuwait, or the Kuwaiti government, or the Sabah family?
>
> *LAURI FITZ-PEGADO, Senior Vice President, Hill and Knowlton:* Our client was Citizens for a Free Kuwait, an organization of private citizens. It was a group that consisted of former government people, opposition members, students, academicians, a broad cross-section of people. And they were our client.
>
> *MARTIN: [voice-over]* Hill and Knowlton kept emphasizing to *20/20* that Citizens for a Free Kuwait was a private organization.
>
> *[on camera]* But Citizens for a Free Kuwait collected about $12 million in its campaign, and these documents, filed by law with the United States government, show that $11.8 million of the $12 million came from the Kuwaiti government.

As the *20/20* report showed, once the facts about the amounts of funding were revealed, the defense that Hill and Knowlton were paid by a citizens coalition, and not by the Kuwaiti government, was shown to be a deception. This was a ploy that was easily refuted, with investigation of the amounts given by the sources of funding.

Another curious defense against the presumption of bias came from Nayirah's father, as reported in an interview with Morley Safer on *Sixty Minutes* (1992, p. 10):

> *SAUD NASIR al-SABAH:* I think the girl came *[unintelligible]* and spoke, and told them what she actually saw with her own eyes.
>
> *SAFER: [voice-over]* That's Nayirah's father, Kuwait's ambassador to the United States. He didn't respond to our request for an interview with him or his daughter, but he did talk to the Canadian broadcast, *Fifth Estate*.
>
> *Amb. al-SABAH:* Whether she was my daughter, my friend, or she was somebody else, I could have much more easily—if I

wanted to lie, or if we wanted to lie or we wanted to exaggerate, I wouldn't choose my daughter to do so—I could easily buy other people to do it.

Here the defense is used by the ambassador that if he wanted to lie, he would not have chosen his daughter, for he could easily buy other people to do it.

Needless to say, none of these defenses was a convincing rebuttal against the presumption that the concealment of Nayirah's identity was an indication that the argument she put forward by testifying in the way she did was biased, and that the use of appeal to pity was open to critical questioning on grounds of personal involvement of the witness. This aspect is an important element in evaluating her appeal, in context, as a fallacious use of the *argumentum ad misericordiam*.

4. EVALUATION OF THE CASE

In the first phase of this case, the appeal to pity seemed like good evidence being furnished in the form of eyewitness testimony. And this testimony was relevant to the deliberations that were taking place on the question of American support for an invasion of Kuwait. But then during the second phase, several developments altered this assessment. First, Nayirah's identity was revealed, throwing into doubt her impartiality as a witness. Second, investigations found the lack of any evidence supporting the incubator story, indicating that it was (likely) false. Third, the revelations about the public relations campaign by Hill and Knowlton threw new light on the purpose and context of how the argument was used to promote the interest of its advocates.

In the summer of 1992, an investigation of the allegations of infant deaths was made by the internationally respected firm of Kroll Associates, hired by the Kuwaiti government. The results of this investigation are described by Rowse (1992, p. 17):

This summer, the voluminous Kroll Associates study was released to virtually no attention. The only mention in the national press was by *The Washington Post*. For that, Hill and Knowlton is probably grateful. Based on more than 250 interviews over a nine-week period, the Kroll report concluded that at least seven babies died because of the looting of incubators.

However, Kroll also reported that there was no written record and no consensus among nurses on how many such deaths may have occurred. It said Nayirah had told Kroll of seeing only one baby outside its incubator in an incident lasting "no more than a moment." Also, she told Kroll that, contrary to her testimony, which she said had been prepared with the help of Hill and Knowlton, she had not been a volunteer at the hospital, but had only stopped by for a few minutes.

Knoll also tracked down the physicians who had been widely publicized as witnesses to the incubator claim, and found no real basis to substantiate them (Rowse, 1992, p. 18). It seems that, in the end, no real evidence could be found to substantiate the story. The original "witnesses" all retracted their stories, claiming they had never made the statements cited in Nayirah's testimony to the Congressional Human Rights Caucus.

The appeal to pity, it turned out, was not only based on a premise that was not substantiated by the evidence, and showed strong indications of being false, but it was engineered as part of an elaborate public relations campaign to promote one side of the issue.

There is nothing inherently wrong or fallacious about public relations campaigns, or with trying your best to support the interests of your country by appealing for help and support in a desperate situation. The appeal to pity or sympathy is not, in itself, fallacious. This is our basic point of departure in evaluating this case.

But the fallacy charge comes in when you perceive the shift between what the argument was supposed to be, and how it was (understandably) taken, and what it really was underneath the surface appearance, relative to the information given in phase one of its use. The appeal to pity seemed appropriate and reasonable at first, but then, once more information came in, the evaluation of it changed radically. It was not what it seemed, and in fact was revealed as a deceptive tactic that was successful in achieving its goal of influencing action.

This dynamic aspect is typical of the *argumentum ad misericordiam*. It is a nonmonotonic type of argumentation that is properly used to shift a burden of proof in a balance-of-considerations dispute, but can sometimes be revealed as an incorrect, or even fallacious, argument, once further information comes into a case. It is a tentative and defeasible type of argument (chapter 4, section 9) that is subject to qualification and potential retraction or rebuttal, as an argument unfolds sequentially in a dialogue.

The Nayirah case provides good evidence, however, that the appeal to pity should be evaluated as fallacious in some cases. In this case, the argument not only undergoes a dialectical shift, so that it needs to be reevaluated in the second phase of its use, but the shift was unilateral in that it involved concealment of relevant information on one side of the dialogue.

5. GENERAL ISSUES

Currently there are questions being raised on how the concept of a fallacy should be understood (Hamblin 1970; Walton, 1992c; van Eemeren and Grootendorst 1992). According to longstanding tradition, a fallacy is a deceptive argument that has an appearance of being correct or reasonable, but in reality is not a correct or reasonable argument. To sum up this aspect of the involvement of appearances, one could use the traditional slogan to the effect that a fallacy is not only a bad argument, but one that seems good (Hamblin 1970).[6]

In the Nayirah case, timing was vitally important in making the argument seem good. Opinion was divided at the time, in the Senate debate, and Nayirah's testimony was the kind of tie-breaker needed to swing the weight of presumption in favor of taking action. In context, because of its timing, and its powerful emotional appeal to a particularly devastating form of child abuse, this appeal to pity was just the icon (defining moment) needed to mobilize public opinion in favor of the invasion.

Here the appeal to pity was effective in persuasion because, in phase one, it seemed to be relevant evidence based on eyewitness testimony which, at the time, there appeared to be no reason to doubt. As phase two unfolded, however, it became apparent that a deliberate campaign of advocacy by interested parties was behind the testimony, that the witness was a member of this group of interested parties, and that her testimony did not square with that of the leading participants on the scene available for questioning afterwards.

In phase one, the appeal to pity seemed like a reasonable argument, as part of a sequence of argumentation in a context of dialogue. In fact, it was very powerful and moving as an emotional appeal. But then, as phase two unfolded, there was evidence of a dialectical shift. The testimony was revealed as not only being open to questioning on grounds of bias, but it was not corroborated by the body of other evidence. It even showed strong signs of being manufactured by an advocacy group as part of a deliberate campaign of influencing public opinion, and the Senate decision in particular.

One might reply: yes, the premise of the witness's appeal to pity turned out to be false, but that does not make the appeal to pity a fallacy. The suggestion is that more is needed than a false premise to license the conclusion that an argument is fallacious. A fallacy (Hamblin 1970) has generally been taken to be a structural failure in an argument (of some sort—that is, an unlicensed inference) as opposed to merely an argument with a premise that happens to be false.

The question about the nature of the fallaciousness of the *ad misericordiam* in this case can be sharpened by posing a prior hypothetical question—What if Nayirah's story about the incubator babies had been true?[7] As a thought experiment, let us suppose her claim true, keeping all the other known facts in the case, as described above, constant. Suppose, that is, her story about the incubator babies turned out to be supported by the subsequent investigations. Would her *ad misericordiam* appeal still be a fallacy or not? This question could be studied empirically by taking two groups of student respondents who have been told the two versions of the case (one the existing case, and the other where Nayirah's claim is found to be supported by the subsequent investigations), and querying each group to see whether they judge the *ad misericordiam* in their case as fallacious or not.

Without having conducted such a poll, on the basis of experiences of using similar cases in classroom discussions, one would be inclined to predict that it would be easier to convince students that there is definitely a fallacy in the existing case, as opposed to the hypothetical case where Nayirah's claim is verified.

Polls aside, would it be justified and reasonable to describe the *ad misericordiam* appeal as a fallacious argument in this latter (hypothetical) case? There are two sides to this question.

On the one side, the baby incubator story is a relevant consideration, a small but relevant item of evidence among the masses of information collected by the Senate investigation. If the story were true, and is conceded to be relevant evidence on the issue, what grounds are there for classifying it as an *ad misericordiam* fallacy?

6. THE KAIROS FACTOR

What this case reveals is that the strongest justification of the appeal to pity (or sympathy) as a legitimate kind of appeal in argument can also be its most significant weakness. The evolutionary justification of the appeal to pity was that the appeal to feeling can be a valuable basis for deciding on a course of action or inaction in deliberation when there is insufficient knowledge available, at the time, to come to a conclusion on the basis of practical reasoning utilizing the facts of the situation. The appeal to pity then comes in when a decision is urgent, and it is used as a tie-breaker, on balance of considerations. This justification of the appeal to pity as reasonable basis of argument rests on the idea of *kairos*, "the timely" consideration in an argument.[8]

But in the Nayirah case, the aspect of *kairos* was precisely the weakness that was exploited, making the appeal to pity so deadly as a rhetorical tactic of deception. The incubator story, with its appeal to pity, was the tie-breaker, the defining moment that swung the deliberations toward the decision to go ahead, in a situation of uncertainty. Here the problem was the lack of information available from Kuwait in time to verify or refute this story, or to give enough information generally for the Congress to have a full picture of the situation.

Once the deadline for the date of the decision had been set by President Bush, an important practical constraint on the decision was fixed in place. Given the conditions in Kuwait at that time, it was not possible for the U.S. Senate investigation to confirm or refute Nayirah's story by getting direct access to evidence, by the deadline. Hence the deliberation had to be made on the basis of (partial) ignorance of the facts. And presumably, Hill and Knowlton would have been well aware of this factor in their deliberations, when promoting the Nayirah story as part of their campaign. Thus the factor of whether or not the story turned out to be verified by the facts or not, played no role in its usefulness as an *ad misericordiam* argument to influence the U.S. Senate and U.S. public opinion to support the decision to go ahead with the invasion. So it appears that there are good grounds for evaluating the *argumentum ad misericordiam* in this case as fallacious, even if the premise were true.

7. STAGED APPEALS TO PITY

In the Nayirah case, the fact that the appeal to pity was apparently based on a lie, or false premise, tends to occupy our attention as the main fault of the argument. But there is another aspect to it, as well, that could be called *staging* or *contriving*. In the Nayirah case, the tearful appeal was part of a contrived or elaborately staged strategy of public relations. When an appeal to pity is deliberately staged in this way, it is deceptive. But once this staged aspect is revealed, we tend to evaluate the appeal to pity quite differently as an argument. We find it not nearly so persuasive.

In malpractice cases in law, the plaintiff's attorney will often use a tactic of "arousing so much pity for the tragic victim that the facts of the case became virtually meaningless" (Azvedo, 1990, p. 102). The jurors, overwhelmed by the appeal, will award millions of dollars in damages.

As part of the evidence routinely admitted in these cases, the plaintiff's side shows videotapes to the jury that depict the everyday life of the injured party. Skillful editing and filming of the tapes often results in a "hearts and flowers" appeal that has a terrific impact on the jury. Azvedo (p. 105) cites cases where a child was depicted as screaming and crying in frustration over daily routines, or where a mother was holding a brain-damaged baby and crooning to her. A defense lawyer, James Penrod, cites one kind of case of this type he has experienced:

> *Case* 5.1 We've also had scenes where the plaintiff falls or has some other accident. In one case, a child was using complicated crutches and fell down. When the parents testified as to how the scene was set up, one of them admitted it was staged. That cut the heart out of the film's credibility, and we ended up with a favorable settlement.

These kinds of cases show how the videotape uses the visual impact to convey a powerful appeal to sympathy that jurors find very persuasive. In fact, it can be so persuasive that it is overwhelming, causing the jurors to cast other relevant information aside and focus on the appeal to pity.

However, once the jurors are shown that the scene was staged, that "cuts the heart out of its credibility." Its impact on their assessment of the total evidence is considerably reduced. This kind of evidence of staging is one of the things the defense attorney looks for in order to fight back against the appeal to pity in videotaped evidence.

This staging element is a very important indicator of the *ad misericordiam* fallacy. The evidence of systematic use of tactics of deceptive persuasion tends to cut the credibility of any argumentation of a testimonial kind, because there is always a Gricean presumption that the presenter of evidence is sincere or honest. Once this is cast into doubt by some evidence of staging, then there is immediately a basis for the suspicion of bias and advocacy entering the picture. This is deadly to an appeal based on sympathy, because once we see the testifying party as an interest-based participant in the dialogue exchange, we no longer see them as vulnerable or helpless, and the impact of the plea for help is diminished. Instead, we see ourselves, as respondents of the argument, as being deliberately manipulated, and for financial gain at that. It seems now that the "victims" are more like "perpetrators."

In the Nayirah case, you have to consider the massive Hill and Knowlton campaign to make Nayirah's testimony on the baby incubator story a big issue, a defining moment, of the public deliberations. Even if the story were true, the use of it as the key part of a public relations tactic to mobilize public opinion and the U.S. Senate at just the right moment to tilt the burden of persuasion, is a strong indicator of a fallacy (in the sense of a sophistical tactic of persuasion cleverly exploiting appeal to feeling).

8. TWISTING OF THE ARGUMENT

One subtle aspect of the Nayirah case is that the appeal to pity is part of argumentation that is an argument from need for help. And it can also be classified as an argument from distress. However, in the specific cases of the babies being pulled from incubators cited by Nayirah in her appeal, it is too late to do anything to help them. The argument then is not directed to the audience to help these particular babies, or to relieve their distress. Instead this argument from distress is being used for a different purpose. It is being used as a "defining moment" a kind of picture or story as part of a rhetorical argument to break a deadlock, or shift a balance of considerations, in deliberations of the U.S. Congress on whether or not to go to war.

The key observation here is that the argument from need to help is not being used for its usual or normal purpose of seeking help for someone in distress. Instead, this argument is being twisted around, so that it is used for quite a different purpose. Ostensibly, American military intervention in Kuwait will prevent possible future occurrences of this type of alleged child abuse. But that is not really the main use of the argument from need for help in this case. Really, what the argument is being used to project is the following message to the American people: "The Iraqi soldiers have committed this terrible abuse, which is outrageous and intolerable.

The pitiable victims are small, dependent children, abused by the Iraqis. Therefore, the Iraqis deserve being punished, and we are fully justified in going to war against them." The argument from need for help is being used here to tilt the balance of considerations, in the deliberations on whether to invade or not, to the one side. It is being used to give a kind of permission or justification for taking a decision for military intervention.

This turning of the argument from need for help, from the use it would normally be put to, is an important feature to notice. It reveals how the appeal to pity, in the incubator story and its tearful telling, is being grafted onto the argument from need for help, and then projected into the deliberation in a clever, even artful way.

But would the twisting or using of the argument in this way be regarded as fallacious if the incubator story were true? There seems to be room for divided opinions on this question.

The usual way that embarking on, and continuing to wage a war, is justified to the public is by means of atrocity stories that demonize the enemy. And cynically speaking, it probably doesn't matter much to the success of the argument, at the time, whether the story is really true or not.

This is where Walter the hard-nosed logician would say that the use of appeal to pity, for example in the baby incubators case, is really just a gimmick, expressly made to cater to the "deficiencies" of a mass audience. They need a "story," an emotional appeal to feeling, that justifies being righteously offended as a basis for action. This story is only a kind of frill or added bit of theater, Walter would say. And we really need to judge the decision on the basis of practical reasoning—that is, deciding on the known facts whether intervention would be a prudent action for the United States to take.

9. FALLACIOUSNESS OF THE *AD MISERICORDIAM*

What, then, does the fallaciousness of the *ad misericordiam* lie in? It is not just the false premise, as argued above. And the *ad misericordiam* argument was relevant. The answer seems to lie in the exploitation of the story, the targeting of the Senate, and the wider audience of viewers, by using such a calculated and exquisitely effective appeal to pity as part of a planned campaign to win public support for the invasion, and to get action by influencing the Senate vote. This was more than just a picturesque, emotional story blown out of proportion by media coverage, as so often happens. It was a key part of a deliberate public relations initiative, carried out by professional public relations experts, and paid for by participants with a clearly defined vested interest.

Moreover, Nayirah herself, as daughter of the Kuwaiti ambassador, had a vested interest that was not made known during the period of the Senate deliberations. It was finally brought to light only by an investigative reporter.

What, then, is the proper basis for evaluating the appeal to pity in this case as such a strong candidate for being fallacious? One factor was, of course, the false premise—that is, the failure of the report to be verified. However, the decisive factors, I propose, are the following. First, in context of its use as part of testimony before a deliberating body, the appeal to pity should meet certain normative requirements, in order to be reasonable as an argument to play its role in shifting the burden of proof in the larger sequence of argumentation of which it was a key part. One of these requirements is that if the person testifying before the deliberating body has a vested interest, or personal connection with the case, then this indicator of potential bias should be identified and made known.

As noted above, the appeal to pity failed to meet this normative requirement, as revealed in phase two. But that, in itself, does not make the appeal to pity in this case a fallacy, as opposed to simply being an inadequate, questionable, or faulty argument. In this case, the bias that was eventually revealed turned out to be part of a deeper concealment. It was a twisting of the argument from distress, and also the revealing of the argument's having been used as a powerful and concealed tactic of deceptive manipulation, that marks it characteristically as a fallacy in this case.

Clearly there is much more to be discussed here on the meaning of the concept of fallacy, whether a fallacy is always a deliberate tactic of deception in a dialogue to get the best of a speech partner, and so forth. Suffice it to say that this case is an interesting one in studying these issues in relation to our understanding of the *argumentum ad misericordiam* as a fallacy. This case suggests that the *argumentum ad misericordiam* is well worth studying as a powerful type of argument, even if the problem of evaluating this type of argumentation as fallacious or not is a good deal more subtle and problematic than the traditional textbook treatments indicated.

Most of all, this case illustrates the power of the appeal to pity as a tactic of argumentation, used here successfully as a key part of a public relations campaign to influence public opinion and government decision-making at the national (and international) level to conclude to a specific course of action. This impressive display of the power of the *argumentum ad misericordiam* as a tool of persuasion suggests that this traditional type of argument, once it is more clearly defined and systematically analyzed, is well worth including in the informal logic curriculum.

As part of the context of dialogue of this case, it should be observed that the U.S. Senate inquiry lacked direct access to the facts on what happened in Kuwait, and had to depend on the evaluation of testimony of witnesses. Lantos, as co-chairman of the committee on human rights, was supposed to help that inquiry. Yet knowingly and misleadingly, he portrayed Nayirah as a volunteer health worker in the hospital in Kuwait—or at any rate, someone who was believable as a neutral observer. But MacArthur posed the right critical question: If you knew her (real) identity, was her story likely to be true? Amnesty International was also supposed to be a neutral fact-finder. The concealed bias is the key to understanding the use of the *argumentum ad misericordiam* as such a strong candidate for being a fallacy in this case.

Another part of the context of dialogue of the case was the broadcasting of the lachrymose appeal to such a wide television audience, and the increase in majority support for the invasion after the performance. The audience was presented with a misleading appeal to pity that became the defining moment in the argument that swayed public opinion to one side of the debate. This staged aspect of the manipulation of public opinion by a public relations firm is another strong factor in judging the *ad misericordiam* argument fallacious in this case.

But do all these factors add up, or blend in together appropriately, to enable us to justifiably conclude that the *ad misericordiam* argument was fallacious in this case? There remain grounds for doubt.

10. *ENSTASIS* AND FALLACY

There are two ways of criticizing an argument recognized by Aristotle. The first is to show a premise of the argument to be false or unsubstantiated. The second is to show that the conclusion does not follow from the premises—that is, that the argument is structurally weak or insufficiently supported. In the second type of failure, the reasoning from the premises to the conclusion fails to meet some standard for the argument to be sufficiently conclusive. *Enstasis* (objection), according to Post (1866, p. 198), is "either the solution of a fallacy by pointing out why the reasoning is inconclusive (*diairesis*), or the disproof of a false premise (*anairesis*)."

According to longstanding tradition, to show that an argument commits a logical fallacy, or what Aristotle called a sophistical refutation, the failure has to be of the second type. This traditional idea, that a fallacy is an incorrect argument, or failure of reasoning of some type (Hamblin 1970) is one that is worth preserving.

But on this assumption, we still have a problem with the Nayirah case. Our grounds for judging the argument to be a fallacious *ad misericordiam* should not, it seems, include, or have to rest on, the finding that the premise is false. If so, we come back to the same old hypothetical question—Would the argument correctly be judged fallacious if the premise—that is, the incubator story—were true?

The problem is that now we have justified the appeal to compassion as a kind of argument that does have a legitimate, useful function, and can be reasonable in many cases, some would argue that the appeal to pity in the Nayirah case—if the premise were true—could be seen as falling into this nonfallacious class of cases.

While it's true that hard-nosed logicians like Walter pooh-pooh this type of appeal to feeling, and see it as a gimmick for mass consumption, that does not make it fallacious—at least, necessarily. For some would argue that advertisers, politicians, and public relations firms have every right to use such mass media appeals to advocate their conclusions, or to influence public opinion for their clients, in the marketplace of democratic free debate. Nobody can guarantee that they have all the answers on controversial issues of public debate and national deliberations on policy. In the absence of hard, definitive knowledge to resolve or settle a controversial issue, appeals to feeling are legitimate and appropriate—at least so some will argue.

It seems, then, that even though there are grounds for saying that the argument in the Nayirah case would be fallacious even if the premise were true, but these grounds are not demonstrably sufficient. We can argue that the argument was a public relations tactic that exploited *kairos* in a clever and theatrical way. But if Nayirah's story were true, would this be provably sufficient to justify evaluating her argument as an instance of the *ad misericordiam* fallacy? Some would still say not, or have grounds for doubt.

Yet if we try to argue that the argument is fallacious because the premise used in the appeal was false (or is unjustified by the evidence), we run afoul of the tradition that this is an empirical matter, and should not be part of the reason for judging the argument to be fallacious.

Before the *ad misericordiam* argument in the Nayirah case can be definitively evaluated as fallacious or nonfallacious, then, a further investigation into the criteria for judging an argument to be fallacious must be carried out. We must resolve the issue of whether a finding of false premise in an argument can be part of the reason for judging the argument to be fallacious.

6

When Is It a Fallacy?

Now we have a firm basis for judging *ad misericordiam* arguments as meeting the proper requirements for arguments from distress used to appeal to pity. But the big question remains. How can we distinguish between the cases where the argument is merely defective in some way, and the (presumably) more serious cases where an *ad misericordiam* fallacy has been committed?

This is a hard question to answer definitively, given the current state of the art of argumentation theory, because the concept of fallacy has not yet been precisely defined in a theory that all agree to.

Even so, I have, in other works, put forward a pragmatic theory of the concept of fallacy.[1] It has already been applied, to some extent, to the problems posed by the *ad misericordiam* fallacy.[2] What can be done is to briefly sketch out the essentials of this pragmatic view of fallacy, and to conditionally apply it to the *argumentum ad misericordiam*, to give a provisional answer to this big question.

The theory advocated in this chapter is that the argument scheme has a set of matching critical questions that define a proper profile, or sequence of moves, for the kinds of arguments where appeals to feelings are used. The fallacious use of such an appeal is one that interferes with the proper ordering of such a sequence.

1. INFORMAL LOGIC AND FORMS OF ARGUMENT

One of the problems with the treatment of fallacies in the past has been that the argument corresponding to the alleged fallacy did not seem to have any identifiable form. Hence, it seemed impossible to evaluate these arguments in the way we are usually accustomed to doing so in logic—by checking to see whether the argument has a particular form in a given case.

Of course, traditionally in logic, the formal, deductive aspect has been stressed, and treated as the paradigm of logical reasoning. Hence, when it came to the informal part, and the study of fallacies, the tendency has often been to try to view it in the same kind of formalistic way. Hence the assumption was that fallacies should be reduced to errors of reasoning of some kind—that is, as some kind of semantic failure of inference.

An example of a textbook that reduces all fallacies to errors of reasoning is Lambert and Ulrich (1980). They take what could be called a *deductivist* approach. A formal fallacy, as defined by them, is "the logical form of an invalid argument" (p. 24), where *invalid* means deductively invalid. If two arguments have the same invalid form, according to their account, then they are both "instances of the same fallacy." The problem with informal fallacies, they contend, is that the logical form is "not discernible" or that the mistake in reasoning is not "due to the logical form of the argument in question" (p. 24). Therefore, they conclude, the study of the "alleged informal fallacies" has no basis in logical theory that would make it useful as a part of logic.

Lambert and Ulrich see the present state of fallacy theory as presenting a kind of dilemma. We can deal with formal fallacies in logic because they can be modeled as mistakes in reasoning due to the logical (semantic) form of the argument in question. But we can't deal with informal fallacies, except by ad hoc methods of memorizing examples, or by clever and subtle skills of recognizing the "myriad fallacies" that are impossible to duplicate or verify. Until we have a general way of telling when two arguments commit the same fallacy, Lambert and Ulrich conclude (p. 28), we must reject informal fallacies as "not useful" for "determining whether a given argument is acceptable."

The answer to Lambert and Ulrich's skepticism about informal fallacies is to be found in the pragmatic notion developed here that each type of argumentation—of the kind associated with an informal fallacy—is based on an argumentation scheme. The argumentation scheme is a structure or form that shows how this type of argument should be used correctly in a context of dialogue to shift a burden of proof or presumption in building or refuting a case. To be used correctly, or nonfallaciously, the argumentation scheme must be used in a dialogue, in a given case, in such a way as to allow for questioning, and to respond appropriately to the kinds of critical questions that match that scheme.

The concept of the *ad misericordiam* fallacy advanced here is deeply pragmatic in nature. A fallacy is not just a failure to meet a semantic standard of validity, or an incorrect argument from a designated set of premises to a conclusion. It is a failure to use an argumentation scheme correctly, as revealed by an extended sequence of question-reply argumentation in a two-party dialogue. The person who has committed a fallacy in this sense has performed badly in the dialogue, over a whole sequence of moves, which may, in some cases, be quite lengthy. It is a question of how he has performed in the dialogue, his attitude and willingness to engage collaboratively in the spirit of the dialogue. This is indicated both by the given text of discourse and by the goals and rules of the dialogue that this participant is supposed to be participating in.

I have now identified several argumentation schemes that are characteristic of the use of the *argumentum ad misericordiam*, in chapter 4. And I have defined the meanings of the terms *empathy*, *sympathy*, *compassion*, *pity* and *mercy* in a precise way. We can now tell, in a given case, whether the use of one of these argumentation schemes in that case makes an appeal to one of these feelings.

However, a special kind of problem presents itself in the case of the *argumentum ad misericordiam*. As used in the case studies so far, the *ad misericordiam* type of argument does not appear to have a single distinctive form of its own. Instead, what we find is an appeal to pity (or feeling) grafted onto several different argument structures. That is, putting the point negatively, the form of argument used in our cases (as one might have expected) does not simply have the following kind of structure:

> *pity appeal:* I advocate conclusion *C*.
>
> You should have pity for me, because I am in a bad situation.
>
> Therefore, you should accept *C*.

The *argumentum ad misericordiam* doesn't appear to be this simple, as a distinctive type of argument. There are other elements added to *pity appeal* in order to get an *ad misericordiam* argument, as shown in section 2, below.

Before going on to look at these various versions of the *ad misericordiam* argument, that are gotten by adding other elements to *pity appeal*, it should be noted that all of these arguments based on the *pity appeal* format can be attacked directly by posing a counter-argument that can take one of two forms. A respondent can counter-argue (i) that pleaders do not deserve our pity because they themselves showed no pity in a comparable situation (banishment of pity argument), or (ii) that their actions caused harm to someone else who is involved, and we should show pity for this person, instead of for the pleaders.

The second counter-argument usually takes the form, in modern trials, of allowing the family of the victim to present *victim testimony*. The problem with many appeals to pity, in murder cases particularly, is that the perpetrator appeals to pity as a basis for parole or a shortened sentence. But nobody remembers the victim, who is dead, and cannot present an equally emotional appeal to feeling for the other side. In such a case, a counter-argument to the appeal to pity on one side is to allow the family of the victim to testify emotionally to their loss.

2. USE WITH DIFFERENT TYPES OF ARGUMENT

The *argumentum ad misericordiam* is an unusual and distinctive type of fallacy in that it is more complex than other fallacies typically are, in the following respect. Usually a fallacy is the misuse of an argument scheme that represents a particular type of argument form or structure. However, the *argumentum ad misericordiam* is an appeal to feeling (*pity appeal*) that is used in conjunction with several different types of argument. Typically, it is used in conjunction with the argument from need for help or the argument from distress. Both of these types of argument have distinctive argument schemes, presented in chapter 4, above.

But appeals to feeling (pity, compassion, and sympathy) have also been used in instances of the *argumentum ad misericordiam* we have examined, in conjunction with excuses—for example, in the legal cases studied, and in the student's plea case. In such cases, as we saw in chapter 1, section 6, the kind of argument that puts forward a plea for exemption from a penalty is a distinctive type of argument in its own right. It needs to be evaluated in a distinctive kind of pragmatic framework.

Of course, in these kinds of cases, it could be argued that the appeal to pity is really functioning as a kind of argument from distress, or argument from need for help. And that could be partly how it is being used. But the primary function of the argument in such a case is to form the basis for an excuse. The pleader is arguing that his case should be exempted from the penalty normally attached to some general rule or law that he has broken, on the grounds of some excuse—for example, that he was under duress, did not act voluntarily, and the like. The subject of pleading excuses is a distinct pragmatic framework of argumentation in its own right—see Austin (1956–57), Hart (1968), and Smith (1992). In such a framework, the pleader admits a certain transgression, but claims special circumstances (usually of certain recognized types) that could justify an exemption, removal or reduction of penalty, or some other form of special handling of the case. In such cases, appeal to sympathy or pity may be used to support the argument. But the argument itself may be of a different type from argument from distress or argument from need for help.

The argument from plea for excuse has the following general form.

Argument from Plea for Excuse

Normally rule R requires or forbids a type of action or inaction T, which carries with it a sanction (penalty) S.
I (the pleader) have committed T.
But I can cite special circumstances that constitute an excuse, E.
Therefore, in this instance, I ought to be exempted from S.

As noted in chapter 1, section 6, standard types of excuses are often recognized for different types of cases and institutional settings. In the criminal law, standard excuses include items like coercion, mistake, ignorance, immaturity, and so forth.

It is important to note that argument from plea for excuse is *defeasible*, or subject to reversal in special circumstances, as indicated by the word *normally* in the first premise. Although such arguments are frequently reasonable, even when used in conjunction with appeal to pity, the use of such an appeal is often used to bolster up a weak case, or even make a fraudulent or ridiculous argument appear persuasive to a particular audience.

In legal cases, the use of the *ad misericordiam* argument is currently riding on a wave of fashionable victimology. It stretches the traditional categories of legal excuses to ridiculous lengths, especially where a particular type of excuse is highly fashionable at the moment. Thus juries award fantastic sums of money in damages to people who voluntarily caused their own harm. Social scientists invent all kinds of syndromes to excuse criminal behavior. And in cases like the Menendez case, individuals who have clearly committed a horrible crime voluntarily for financial gain, have their attorneys put forth fashionable but ludicrous excuses, like child abuse, backed by a chorus of social scientist expert witnesses.

In these cases, juries are asked—with amazing success—to surrender logic to the dramatic impact of the *argumentum ad misericordiam*.

3. SUPPRESSED CRITICAL QUESTIONS

Appeal to feelings is primarily used in conjunction with four types of arguments: (1) argument from need for help; (2) argument from distress; (3) plea for excuse; and (4) practical reasoning generally. Each of these types of argument is presumptive in nature, in that it is used to shift a burden of proof or disproof to the other side in a dialogue exchange of arguments. Each type of argument has a matching set of appropriate critical questions. When a proponent puts forward one of these arguments, it has a weight of presumption in its favor. But if the respondent poses any one of these appropriate critical questions, the presumption shifts against the original argument, at least temporarily, until the question is answered adequately.

The set of five critical questions matching the argument from practical reasoning has already been given in chapter 4, section 6.

The set of critical questions matching the argument from need from help are the following:

Q1. Would the proposed action *A* really help *x*?
Q2. Is it possible for *x* to carry out *A*?
Q3. Would there be negative side effects of carrying out *A* that would be too great?

The set of critical questions matching the argument from distress are the following:

Q1. Is *x* really in distress?
Q2. Will bringing about *A* by *y* really help or relieve this distress?
Q3. Is it possible for *y* to bring about *A*?
Q4. Would negative side effects of *y*'s bringing about *A* be too great?

As you can see, these critical questions are of a practical nature. They reflect the classification of both argument from need for help and argument from distress as being based on practical reasoning, as used in deliberation.

The critical questions for argument from plea for excuse are the following:

Q1. Does *E* fall under one of the recognized categories of excuses for this type of case, and if so, can this inclusion be justified in this case?

Q2. If *E* does not fall under a recognized category, then what about this case is special that justifies the claim to exemption?

Q3. If *E* does not fall under a recognized category, would it set a precedent, and if so, would this pose a problem in future cases?

The third question often relates to slippery slope considerations, where granting of a precedent might arguably lead to such a rush of new cases that it might overwhelm the rule, make it useless, or lead to some other dangerous ultimate outcome (Walton 1992b).

With any of these four types of argument, the use of the argument, in a particular case, can be weak or unjustified (insufficiently supported) if one or more of the appropriate critical questions has not been answered adequately. But the fallacious type of case is worse than mere failure to answer a critical question. Fallacies are associated with cases where the argument is put forward in such a way, in a context of dialogue, where the asking of critical questions is blocked by some tactic or other.

The *ad misericordiam* fallacy occurs in cases where an appeal to feeling (pity, compassion, sympathy, or mercy) is conjoined to the argument in such a way that critical questions are ignored or suppressed, so that asking them is ruled out or dismissed from the dialogue. There are four characteristic ways this is usually done, corresponding to the four subtypes of *ad misericordiam* fallacy: (1) the twisting of the argument, (2) the failure of relevance, (3) the exploitation of the timely aspect (*kairos*), and (4) the deployment of feeling as a staged effect. The effect of all four of these tactics in the *ad misericordiam* fallacy is to throw off or close off the respondent's attention or capability for asking the appropriate critical questions at the next move in the dialogue sequence of argumentation.

To evaluate individual cases of use of appeal to feeling as fallacious or not, it is necessary to examine the sequence of back-and-forth argumentation at the local level, in a profile of dialogue, and then relate this profile to the context of dialogue as a whole. Then you have to make an evaluation of how the appeal to feeling was used in that case—and in particular, whether it was used in such a way as to block off or suppress the asking of the appropriate critical questions for the type of argument that was used.

4. OUT OF CONTEXT AND PERSPECTIVE ARGUMENTS

The central fact about the *ad misericordiam* argument as an effective tactic in argumentation is that typically it is one small piece of evidence in a much larger body of evidence that is relevant to a given case. Hence its place in the longer sequence of argumentation is typically very important. If a balance of considerations argument has reached a stage where the burden of proof is relatively evenly met by the arguments on both sides, the *argumentum ad misericordiam* can very effectively be used as a tie-breaker.

This aspect of *kairos* was very evident in the use of appeal to pity in the Nayirah case. The appeal was put into the sequence of deliberations by the public relations campaigners exactly at the right moment to break the deadlock and shift public opinion, and the Senate deliberation toward the side of taking action.

Another factor that is important to notice with respect to the *ad misericordiam* argument is that it typically has a tremendous short-term impact, especially when presented visually, or with dramatic effect, but it tends not to have a lasting outcome on deciding an issue. The reason for this, as shown in chapter 4, is that typically, it is only one argument that is part of a larger, connected sequence of practical reasoning that contains many other subarguments relevant to a case. Hence to exploit this high but short-term impact effectively, placement within this larger sequence of argumentation can be very important.

Consider the use of *ad misericordiam* in a sales pitch like the kind of argument used in the case cited by Rescher (1964, p. 79) of a broom salesman who cites his sick wife and four kids. What may be most important in a case like this is that the salesman may begin with other types of arguments first, to sell his product. Gradually, through the conversational exchange, the salesman and prospective buyer begin to build up some elements of a personal relationship, instead of being complete strangers to each other. Once this bond has taken place, the basis has been put in place to make the use of an *ad misericordiam* argument, at the concluding stage of the sales pitch, much more effective. On the other hand, to start the appeal to pity too early might simply put the buyer off.

The *ad misericordiam*, conveyed through the visual appeal of images, especially on television, has an emotional appeal that tends to be misleading. The image presents a one-dimensional aspect of the argument, often in abstraction from any real context or perspective on the situation. Zuckerman (1993) describes the use of televised pictures of "emaciated elders" and "matchstick children covered with flies" to "evoke a wave of human sympathy" to justify U.S. intervention in Somalia. The problem with such a "feel good" approach to justifying foreign policy decisions is that it is one-sided. It may overlook other situations where intervention would do more good, or be more practical help. Television is misleading in that, by going with a visual, emotional impact, it overlooks perspective on a complex situation, making a simplistic argument (p. 84):

> How will we come to grips with the fact that the TV camera is one-dimensional? It sees what it sees and nothing else. It cannot apply a corrective lens to bring context, biography and history to the news. And as a practical matter, TV network news does not have the airtime to convey that kind of perspective. Often it cannot even convey the immediate provocation that produced the events. We are left in intellectual limbo, observing results with no apparent causes.

Television conveys action and excitement in its pictures of disasters, earthquakes, tears, suffering, and so forth, which have a terrific emotional impact. But the very visual power of this impact, along with a failure to put it in a proper context for judgment, is highly misleading. As Zuckerman puts it, "it may well add up to a lie" (p. 84), by leading viewers to make a judgment solely on one part of the story. It was precisely this failure to ask hard questions that was cited in case 4.12 as the problem with the misleading and exploitive use of the appeal to sympathy for children living in families on welfare. Supposedly a *documentary*, this film is really advocating a point of view.

The problem is that such appeals tend to lead the viewer or respondent to a simplistic conclusion. But why is this fallacious, when such appeals to sympathy are in fact fallacious? It is because the impact of the appeal to compassion can be exploited to seal off the asking of critical questions that would be appropriate for properly deliberating on the question at issue. It is not just the oversimplification of the issue, but the suggestion that asking further critical questions is unnecessary or inappropriate, before taking a particular course of action being advocated.

5. THE WHOLE EVIDENCE REQUIREMENT

Our analysis of the *ad misericordiam* fallacy is that it is sometimes a fallacy of relevance, but that even more typically and fundamentally, it is a fallacy of insufficient evidence. This can take the form of not only ignoring or excluding such evidence, but of using the dramatic effect of the appeal to feeling to block further questioning. The main fallacy is that the appeal to feeling, especially when presented in a visual or dramatic form, driven by images and emotions, has such an impact that it tempts the respondent to overlook and ignore hard evidence and factual circumstances that should be very important factors in weighing an argument in a given case.

Leo (1993, p. 24) cites cases where powerful pictures were used by the media to advocate conclusions, where other relevant evidence was ignored, or even covered up:

> *Case* 6.1: Dead fish from the Clearwater National Forest in Idaho were shown on *NBC Nightly News* on January 4, 1993, to show how logging by the timber industry fouls streams and kills fish. It was revealed later that the fish were stunned by forest officials, and weren't from Clearwater.

Such deceptive presentations used on a news program ignore the notions that the news report is supposed to present information. Where it does advocate a cause or conclusion, it should at least attempt to look at the evidence on both sides, or present a rounded, or fairly full account of the evidence. However, as noted by Leo (1993, p. 24), as a generation raised on television, people now are used to being influenced by images and feelings, and are not used to raising questions like "What evidence supports your view or contradicts it?" Emotional and image-based arguments tend to be accepted without questioning the larger evidential circumstances of a situation.

On this account, the *ad misericordiam* fallacy would seem to be a species of the *fallacy of suppressed evidence*, defined as the ignoring of an important piece of evidence, in a particular case, that

outweighs the presented evidence, and entails a different conclusion (Hurley 1991, p. 248). The requirement violated here is the one
that requires "telling the whole truth," or presenting all the important and relevant evidence in a case. But a problem is posed as well.
When exactly is such a requirement necessary, normatively, to make
an argument successful or adequate?

The problem is that this type of total-evidence requirement is
not always a necessary part of the context of dialogue in which an
argument has been put forth. In a persuasion dialogue, it is not
required, for an argument to be persuasive, successful, or appropriate
that it present all the evidence—or negatively, that it not omit
important evidence. In a critical discussion, for example, if an argument makes a good point, by presenting some convincing evidence
for its conclusion, then it could be a good and strong argument, even
if it omits other important evidence that could be relevant, either for
or against the conclusion. After all, in a persuasion dialogue, the
proponent's goal and obligation is to present arguments supporting
one point of view, and it is up to the respondent to ask critical questions, or to bring forward important arguments, against that point of
view, or for a different point of view. In this context, the whole evidence requirement does not seem to be necessary for the adequacy of
an argument, to make it nonfallacious.

For an argument put forward in deliberation dialogue, however,
the story is quite different. In deliberation, it is very important to
consider all the relevant, significant evidence. In making a prudent
decision on what to do in a situation, overlooking serious evidence, or
important probable consequences of one's proposed course of action,
can turn out to be disastrous. Many of the cases of the use of the *ad
misericordiam* argument we have examined have in fact taken place
in the context of deliberation. The Nayirah case is a good example.
Other examples are the cases of the use of visual appeals to pity to
support requests for charitable donations, relief appeals, and so forth.
As we have noted, it is crucial in such cases to ask critical questions
about the consequences of the intervention being advocated.

Our conclusion, then, is that the *ad misericordiam* is most
dangerous as a fallacy when the visual or dramatic appeal to feeling—in itself a legitimate type of argument—is blown out of proportion, due to its dramatic impact. Important evidence that should
also be taken into account is ignored. However, this analysis of the
fallacy is inherently pragmatic, because whether the whole evidence
requirement is reasonable, in a given case, depends on what type of
dialogue (conversational exchange) the participants are supposed to

be engaging in when they argue together. And it is especially in the deliberation, information-seeking, and inquiry types of dialogue that the whole evidence requirement tends to be important.

Many of the cases we have considered concerned arguments that are part of a deliberation. And it is not hard to see here why looking at all the available evidence and consequences is necessary for prudent practical reasoning.

6. SUBTYPES OF *AD MISERICORDIAM* FALLACY

Through examining the various cases where the *ad misericordiam* argument was judged to be fallacious, we have found four basic subtypes of the fallacy. These are (1) the twisting of the argument, as in the Thackeray and student's plea cases; (2) the failure of relevance; (3) the exploitation of the timely impact of the appeal to pity, where evidence in the context is ignored; and (4) the use of appeal to pity as a staged effect, as in the use of crocodile tears cited in case 1.26 and in the Nayirah case. Indeed, in the Nayirah case, all of elements 1, 3, and 4 were notably present.

These four aspects are explanations of what is wrong as an argument with the *ad misericordiam* when it is fallacious. So it is appropriate to designate them as various subtypes or special kinds of instances of the general *ad misericordiam* type of fallacy. However, there are cases that combine several of these subtypes of fallacy in the same case.

The other way of identifying several subtypes of *ad misericordiam* arguments is given in Figure 3.1. There we distinguished several kinds of appeals to feeling—appeal to sympathy, appeal to compassion, appeal to pity, and appeal to mercy. This classification applies to *ad misericordiam* arguments whether they are fallacious or not.

Thus the analysis and evaluation of an *ad misericordiam* argument that is alleged to be fallacious requires two stages. The first is the identification of what type of appeal to feeling it is, or is supposed to be. This stage is just the identification of the *argumentum ad misericordiam* as a specific type of argument. Then the second stage is the analysis of the basis on which the argument is alleged to be a fallacy. This stage involves the citing of one or more of the four subtypes listed above, along with the evidence from the text and context of discourse to back up this claim.

Van Eemeren and Grootendorst (1992, p. 139) see the *argumentum ad misericordiam* as having two subtypes: "An *argumentum ad misericordiam* can be used either to put pressure on the audience or to sway the audience in the protagonist's favor." In the former case, the appeal to pity is a violation of the rule that forbids participants in a critical discussion from preventing "each other from advancing or casting doubt on standpoints" (van Eemeren and Grootendorst 1987, p. 284). In the latter case, the fallacy is one of relevance (1992, p. 139). Thus van Eemeren and Grootendorst's analysis agrees with ours, that the *ad misericordiam* fallacy is sometimes a fallacy of relevance.

But it is less clear how their other type of *ad misericordiam* fallacy relates to our classification of subtypes. They describe this subtype as "putting pressure on the other party by playing on his feelings of compassion" (van Eemeren and Grootendorst, 1992, p. 213), and as typified by the argument "You can't do that to me" (van Eemeren and Grootendorst, 1987, p. 285). The idea seems to be that the playing on feelings of compassion by one party somehow prevents the other party from putting forward the argument he is supposed to be advancing, to support his point of view on the issue of the discussion.

The closest this kind of analysis seems to come to our classification of subtypes is to the twisting of the argument subtype. The fallacious aspect of the use of appeal to feelings of compassion in the student's plea case, for example, resided in the student's tactic of argument. This has the effect of preventing teachers from doing their job—that is, of arriving at a decision on giving a grade to the student's work on the basis of its merit.

The context is that of a deliberation in a kind of pedagogical and institutional decision that should be made by certain designated guidelines. Following these guidelines, teachers have a certain function or job to perform, and their weighing of deliberations should conform to these guidelines. However the appeal to pity twists the basis of the deliberations around, so that it, in effect, prevents, or has the effect of preventing, teachers from making the decision on the proper basis of evidence they are supposed to use.

Perhaps then, van Eemeren and Grootendorst's subtype of "putting pressure" on an arguer could fit in under our subtype of twisting of the argument.

7. THE PRAGMATIC VIEW OF FALLACY

It has been shown above how examples of *ad misericordiam* fallacies given in the textbooks often turn out to be reasonable, even if defeasible or weak arguments, based on presumptions that are subject to correction or rebuttal. But weak arguments, and blunders in argumentation of various sorts, need to be distinguished from fallacious arguments. To claim that an argument is fallacious is a particularly strong form of condemnation of the argument that needs to be backed up by certain kinds of evidence from the context of dialogue.

This general theoretical approach to the evaluation of argumentation makes it necessary to pay more attention to the subtleties and contextual factors, as known in a given case. In some cases, it can be quite difficult and tricky to judge whether an argument is just weak—a blunder, or an insufficiently supported argument that could be improved or corrected by further argument—or whether it is fallacious. A *fallacy* is a more serious error than a blunder. It is a systematic, underlying kind of error in an argument, or deceptive tactic used to try to persuade another party to accept the argument in a conversational exchange.

In a new approach to the concept of fallacy, expressed most fully in Walton (1995), a fallacy is defined as a species of failure of use of an argument in contributing to a conversation in which two parties are reasoning together.

The view put forward is one that looks at how an argument is used in a context of conversation. A fallacy is defined as a conversational move, or sequence of moves, that is supposed to be an argument of a kind that contributes to the purpose of the conversation, but in reality interferes with it. The view is a pragmatic one, based on the assumption that when people argue, they do so in a context of dialogue, a conventionalized normative framework that is goal-directed. Such a contextual framework is shown to be crucial in determining whether an argument has been used correctly or not.

This pragmatic and dialectical view of fallacy derives from the work of Grice (1975), and also fits in with the viewpoint of the Amsterdam school (van Eemeren and Grootendorst 1984, 1992), who define a fallacy as a violation of a rule of a critical discussion. However, this new conception goes beyond the Amsterdam account of fallacy by drawing an important distinction between a *fallacy* and a *blunder* in argumentation, the latter being a less serious type of error. The Amsterdam viewpoint also considers only one type of dialogue in defining the concept of fallacy—the critical discussion. This new view considers six basic types of dialogue—the critical discussion, the inquiry, negotiation, deliberation, the quarrel, and information-seeking dialogue. It allows for dialectical shifts in argumentation from one type of dialogue to another.

This new approach rejects the traditional, and widely current, notion of a fallacy as an argument that seems valid but is not. This is rejected as a concept that is too prejudicially biased toward a narrow psychologistic and deductivist point of view that is no longer useful for state-of-the-art methods in argumentation. Instead, a quite different conception is put forward—one that will initially appear to be radical and controversial. It holds that a fallacy is best conceived of as the use of a tactic of argumentation in a context of dialogue where two parties are reasoning together, and both of them can accept conclusions tentatively, on balance of considerations, even if these conclusions are not proved beyond all reasonable doubt. This makes cases of traditional fallacies somewhat harder to evaluate, however. It requires that arguments be evaluated by standards appropriate for the given context of conversation.

The first step in evaluating a sophistical tactic kind of fallacy is to identify the local conclusion of the particular argument advocated, and then the given premises. Having attained this grasp of what the local argument is, the next step is to place it in a context of dialogue.

According to the new theory of dialogue presented in Walton and Krabbe (1995), there are four types of procedural rules of reasoned dialogue: locution rules, commitment rules, dialogue rules, and win-loss rules:

1. *Locution rules* determine what types of locutions (speech acts) are permitted or required at any particular point in a sequence of dialogue. For example, an assertion by a participant may be required after a specified type of question has been asked by the other participant.
2. *Commitment rules* determine which propositions are inserted into or retracted from a participant's commitment-set, when that participant has made a particular move of a certain type at a given point in the dialogue.
3. *Dialogue rules* determine appropriate turn-taking moves in a sequence of play. In particular, the dialogue rules specify the range of permitted responses by one participant in relation to a previous move of the other participant.
4. *Win-loss rules* determine which sequences of dialogue-exchanges constitute a win or loss of the game for one participant or the other. To *win* is to correctly fulfill the goal of the dialogue.

Many examples of all four kinds of rules can be found in the various games of dialogue studied by Barth and Krabbe (1982), Walton (1989), Mackenzie (1981), and Walton and Krabbe (1995). There can be different goals of dialogue, and consequently there can be many different sets of rules appropriate to facilitate these goals. There are a plurality of different dialogues, but each distinctive type of dialogue has a normative model that articulates or stipulates its goal precisely.

In constructing formal systems of dialogue rules that represent normative models of question-reply argumentation in different contexts of dialogue, many technical problems arise in trying to design rules for moves of the game that represent fair turn-taking in the context. Formal systems of dialogue where care has been taken in attempting to deal with these technical problems are surveyed in Walton (1989). A *move* is defined as a sequence of locutions allowed at any particular point in a dialogue. A move can pose questions of various sorts (yes-no questions and why-questions are especially significant and central). And a move may also contain requirements that a question asked in a previous move must be given a certain type of reply. This does not mean that a question always has to be given a direct answer at the next move An answer is only one kind of reply.

It is important to distinguish between win-loss rules and strategic rules in games of dialogue. Win-loss rules specify the goal of a particular kind of dialogue. Strategic rules outline general methods or techniques a player can use to best achieve such a goal of dialogue.

It is also important to distinguish more carefully between strategic and tactical rules of dialogue. *Tactical* rules are practical "tips" or pieces of advice, applicable in a particular case, that help a player to attack and defend more effectively during a critical juncture in a game of dialogue. They can help you to play the game more effectively in tricky situations where you could easily lose to an opponent's move.[3] *Strategic* rules are more global. They give you general advice of what sort of overall patterns of play will contribute to your goal of winning a game. Tactical rules are more localized. They coach you on how to react to characteristic types of tricky situations that are likely to arise in the course of a game. Using defensive tactics, you may have to act quickly to respond to the sophistical tactics of your opponent (counter-tactics). Or using attacking tactics, you may be able to put your opponent on the defensive by exploiting a weakness in an argument.

Thus the new theory finds its roots in the Aristotelian conception of a fallacy as a sophistical refutation.[4] But the new theory, more radically, has the consequence that many of the argumentation

tactics traditionally labeled fallacious are in fact reasonable techniques of argumentation that can be used, in many cases, to support legitimate goals of dialogue.

With respect to the *argumentum ad misericordiam*, it has been
shown that the appeal to feeling grafted on to the argument from
need for help is not inherently fallacious, and that some instances of
its use involve a kind of presumptive, inconclusive type of reasoning
that can be used reasonably to shift a burden of proof in reasonable
dialogue. These species of argumentation involve a newly recognized (Walton 1992c) kind of reasoning—a presumptive and dynamic
kind of default reasoning that is inherently subject to correction and
rebuttal in a context of dialogue. Presumptive reasoning is inherently tentative, as used in a dialogue—it must be open to default as
new information comes in.

In our analysis of cases of *ad misericordiam* arguments, we
have seen that arguments from consequences and need for help are
presumptive arguments based on soft evidence, used as practical
guides to action or commitment when hard knowledge is not available.[5] Far from being inherently fallacious, such arguments are often
reasonable and important as guides to reasoned commitment in
deliberation. When they are fallacious, it is because they have been
misused as sophistical tactics in a dialogue as means for deceptively
getting the best of an opponent.

Presumptive reasoning is inherently subject to correction, and
as it is analyzed in Walton (1995), the concept of fallacy is redefined,
to bring it in line with the idea of argument being used to shift burden of proof appropriate to a context of dialogue. The arguments
traditionally classified as fallacious under the old deductivist conception of argument are now revealed, in many instances, as not
only nonfallacious, but as inherently reasonable, acceptable kinds of
arguments, even where they are weak, fallible, and less than totally
and overwhelmingly convincing.

8. SENSITIVITY TO CONTEXT

Because it is so well suited to the visual appeals to feeling that
television can portray so effectively, the *ad misericordiam* has become
a favorite vehicle of governments, advocacy groups, and advertisers
who hope to influence public opinion in favor of a certain course of
action. This can be seen in the Nayirah case and the baby seals case,
for example, where the visual impact of an appeal to feeling was used

with powerful effect on public opinion by a public relations firm, and by advocacy groups, respectively. In a democracy, public opinion is crucial to get action or support for a cause. The skilful manipulation of public opinion by exploiting the timely impact of visual appeals to feeling has now become a common practice of no small significance in political deliberation and in advocacy of causes.

However cynical we are about the exploitation of appeals to feeling in such arguments, we need to take care in recognizing that the normative judgment of them as fallacious *ad misericordiam* arguments is highly sensitive to the context of dialogue in which they have been put forth. Advocacy arguments, of the type used in the baby seals *ad misericordiam* argumentation, are basically interest-based arguments to promote the cause of a specific group, and as such they are free to use appeals to pity if they think that such appeals will win sympathy, and thereby support, for their cause. Such a use of appeals to feeling is not necessarily, in this context, fallacious. However, if the argument purports to be some other type of dialogue—like a critical discussion, a balanced deliberation, or a news report—a very different evaluation could be justified.

Frequently where such appeals to sympathy are used in advocacy arguments, there is a shift from one type of dialogue to another. To make its case appear more compelling, the advocacy of an interest may try to put itself forward as being some sort of objective news report, scientific inquiry, or prudent deliberation. Here the *ad misericordiam* argument can be fallacious, either because it is irrelevant, or because it ignores other important, relevant evidence.

In cases where advocacy of a product or cause is overt, and is clearly the purpose of the argument, however, the appeal to pity may not be entirely unreasonable. In the case of a salesman appealing to pity to sell brooms to a woman, by pointing out that he needs money to support his sick wife and four children (Rescher, 1964, p. 79), for example, what should we say? First, the appeal to pity is not really relevant to the main issue of whether the brooms are a good buy. Even so, if the salesman adds on this small appeal to sympathy as a final touch to his sales pitch, it is hard to condemn his sales tactic too heavily, as a fallacy or logical failure of argument. After all, the woman knows, presumably, that the salesman stands to profit from selling these brooms—indeed, that is at the basis of his appeal to pity—and she can judge his argument accordingly. She knows his argument is based on advocacy, and is not an objective report on the brooms.

Sales dialogue is a complex type of dialogue in which to judge arguments as fallacious or not. It would not be fair to hold up arguments in this type of dialogue to the standards appropriate for a critical discussion. They make an offer for acceptance (a "deal"), so they are primarily a form of interest-based bargaining. But they are often mixed—shifting to persuasion dialogue or to information-presenting dialogue or deliberation.

Political discourse is also a very mixed framework of dialogue. It would be naive to condemn many cases of the use of *ad misericordiam* arguments by advocates of a political viewpoint on the grounds that the argument has been put forward in the context of a critical discussion or deliberation type of dialogue. For political argumentation, quite legitimately, has an aspect of negotiation, because interests are at stake. It also has aspects of eristic dialogue, and is meant to be a bear pit arena where advocates of a cause can attack their adversaries and engage in contestive disputation.

9. DEFINING RELEVANCE

One of the most difficult problems inherent in the textbook treatments of the *argumentum ad misericordiam* as a fallacy is the failure to define relevance in a clear and useful way. The kind of definition of relevance needed to support a useful evaluation of the *ad misericordiam* as a fallacy of relevance is pragmatic and dialectical in nature, as opposed to being purely semantic. Relevance of an argument, of the dialectical kind needed to analyze the *ad misericordiam* fallacy, must be evaluated in relation to the type of dialogue that the argument was supposed to be part of. This concept of dialectical relevance is based on Grice's cooperative principle for the conduct of a conversation: "Make your conversational contribution such as is required, at the stage at which it occurs, by the accepted purpose or direction of the talk exchange in which you are engaged" (Grice, 1975, p. 66). As we have seen—for example, in case 1.6—whether an appeal to pity is best judged as a relevant argument, is determined not only by the type of conversation and its purpose, but also by the stage of that conversation the argument is in.

Six basic types of dialogue, or goal-directed contexts of conversation for argumentation, have been identified in Walton (*Informal Logic*, 1989, pp. 9–16), and relevance in these different types of dialogue has also been investigated in the same work (chap. 3). In a new research project (Walton, "Relevance: A Pragmatic Theory," unpublished) a pragmatic analysis of the concept of dialectical relevance has been given. This analysis shows how dialectical relevance of an argument should be defined by the use of the argument in one of these six types of dialogue—persuasion dialogue, inquiry, negotiation, deliberation, information-seeking dialogue, and eristic dialogue. The goals, stages, and main characteristics of each of these six types of dialogue are identified in Walton (1995). Whether an argument is dialectically relevant or not, in a given case, can be judged using these six conversational frameworks as normative models.

What is especially significant to note is that the *ad misericordiam* fallacy has been judged as a fallacy on the presumption that the context of dialogue is that of the critical discussion, a subtype of persuasion dialogue. In fact, van Eemeren and Grootendorst (1992, p. 139) based their analysis of the *ad misericordiam* fallacy precisely on this assumption. However, as we have seen repeatedly in our case studies, and as Hamblin (1970, p. 43) warned, often the context in which appeals to pity are used is that of the deliberation type of dialogue, as opposed to that of the persuasion dialogue. The problem is that while the appeal to pity might indeed be rightly judged to be irrelevant in a case if the participants were supposed to be engaging in a critical discussion, if the aim of the conversation was deliberation, the same *ad misericordiam* could be justified as relevant.

Hence what is significant about our analysis of *ad misericordiam* arguments is that we have taken deliberation into account as a distinctive type of dialogue in its own right. Especially important in this connection is the use of practical reasoning as a distinctive type of argumentation used in deliberation. It is in this special type of goal-directed type of reasoning that the concept of relevance appropriate for deliberation needs to be defined and evaluated.

Relevance of an argument is determined at the local level by the sequence of questions and replies (the profile of dialogue), in relation to how the sequence matches the proper normative profile determined by the argumentation scheme and the appropriate critical questions. But relevance is determined at the global level by the type of dialogue the argument is supposed to be part of, and by its contribution, at a given stage of this dialogue.

10. THE LOGICAL LEAP
FROM ETHICAL PREMISES

There is nothing logically wrong, or fallacious, in asking someone for help, or even arguing that they ought to help, if they are humane persons who can easily afford such help. But as soon as such an argument contains an appeal to pity, compassion, sympathy, or mercy, it can be classified as an *argumentum ad misericordiam*. As such, it is immediately open to suspicion—or on the standard treatment, even rejection—as being a fallacy. What are the reasons given for this rejection or suspicion by the standard textbook treatments? And how is this account different from the one advocated in this book? To answer these questions, we must go back to the distinctions, made in chapter 3, between argument from pity, argument from compassion, argument from sympathy, and argument from mercy.

Of this group, the argument from pity is the most likely to be condemned as fallacious. The feelings behind these reactions were very clearly brought out in the reactions of the protesters to the Jerry Lewis Telethon. And these reactions can be justified as reasons for rejecting appeals to pity, once we see how they involve various requirements for the definition of pity, as shown in our analysis of it, above. Pity is an us-them relationship that implies that the pitied person is "wretched" or "miserable," that the pitying person is "superior," and so forth. But are these only ethical reasons for rejecting the appeal to pity, as not paying sufficient respect to personhood, human dignity, or rights? Or are they also logical reasons for rejecting the argument from pity as fallacious?

The answer proposed here is that they are ethical rather than logical reasons, with one important exception. This concerns clause 11 of the definition of *pity* given above in chapter 3, section 3.

Clause 11, we recall, stipulated that the pitying party cannot do much directly to make the bad condition of the pitied party disappear. If this clause is required of pity, then it presents a problem in relation to the kinds of cases of charitable appeals studied in chapter 4, on practical reasoning and the argument from request for aid. The problem is that with clause 11 in place, it seems that the pitying party cannot help, or give aid to the pitied party. Thus the appeal to pity, as such, blocks the practical reasoning contained in the argument from request for aid. Since pity blocks or interferes with the basis of the argument, we can conclude that any argument from pity (in an appeal to charity case) is fallacious.

But is this conclusion really justified? It seems there are arguments on both sides. On the one side, it has to be admitted that clause 11 does, in general, imply a certain nonutility of pity. This was the objection of Seneca, who said that instead of indulging in pity, you ought to help the other person.[6] But on the other side, clause 11 does not imply total powerlessness to help. In the Jerry

Lewis Telethon, for example, the medical research and other activities in providing wheelchairs and so forth, were providing help of a sort, which was making the situation for those with muscular dystrophy better. This remained true, even if, as the protesters claimed, this form of help was not solving all the problems of those with muscular dystrophy, directly or completely, or in a way in which they felt was entirely appropriate for their needs.

Here there is no comparable problem for the argument from compassion or the argument from sympathy, however, because clause 11 is dropped as a requirement for defining these concepts. It seems that on this count, the argument from pity is most severely open to objection as being fallacious. And the argument from sympathy is the most positive, in the sense that such an appeal would not be likely to be dismissed per se as fallacious.

But clause 11 is an optional requirement of the definition that not all (notably including Aristotle) would agree ought to be included as a mandatory or essential condition. Also, even if clause 11 is included, there is room for argument on how much powerlessness to help it implies. Also, it should be asked whether it is the kind of powerlessness that conflicts with the practical reasoning in the argument from request for aid, to the degree that any argument from pity in a charitable appeal must be condemned as fallacious. It seems there is room for doubt here.

Moreover, a prior question also needs to be asked. If appeals to pity are morally bad, inherently because of reasons internal to the definition of pity itself, is this a sufficient reason for condemning all arguments from pity as fallacious? Although it is tempting to make such an inferential leap from ethical condemnation of pity to logical condemnation of arguments from pity, we need to reflect further on the nature of this kind of inference.

In judging appeals to pity versus appeals to sympathy as types of argumentation, there is a tendency to draw a defeasible inference from an ethical premise to a logical conclusion. The warrant for such an inference can take the form of one or the other of the two defeasible conditionals *(P)* and *(S)*, below:

> *(P): If pity is (morally) a bad quality, then appeals to pity in argumentation should generally be condemned (logically) as fallacious.*
>
> *(S): If sympathy is (morally) a good quality, then appeals to sympathy in argumentation should generally be acceptable (logically) as reasonable kinds of arguments.*

The kind of reasoning using *(P)* as a premise typically proceeds as follows, by way of illustration. *First premise:* pity is a negative attitude that reinforces an us-them relationship between the whole, superior pitier, and the wretched, less-than-whole individual who is the object of pity (the pitiable). *Inference from first premise:* therefore, pity is (morally) a bad quality. *Second premise: (P)* (above). Therefore (*conclusion*): appeals to pity should generally be condemned (logically) as fallacious.

The kind of reasoning using *(S)* as a premise typically proceeds as follows. *First premise:* sympathy (or it could be compassion) is a religious virtue that is the basis of giving help to the suffering, and is a fundamental feeling at the basis of ethics, according to Schopenhauer and Hume (in the case of sympathy). *Inference from first premise:* therefore sympathy (compassion) is (morally) a good quality. *Second premise: (S)*. Therefore (*conclusion*): appeals to sympathy should generally be acceptable (subject to exceptions, in cases where the appeal is irrelevant, based on a false premise, or otherwise improperly exploited) as reasonable kinds of arguments.

Here then we arrive at the basis of the problem with the textbook treatment of the *argumentum ad misericordiam* as a fallacy. Now we have defined the argument from pity and the argument from sympathy as distinctive types of argumentation, and brought out both the negative implications of pity and the positive implications of sympathy. Are these negative implications sufficient to support the ruling that all appeals to pity are fallacious, and that all appeals to sympathy are nonfallacious (leaving compassion somewhere in between)? Or is there more to the story than this? Are there other reasons why appeals to pity are fallacious, in addition to their being appeals to a concept (pity) that has negative ethical implications?

This way of putting the question appears to make the job of evaluating cases of the *argumentum ad misericordiam* more subtle and difficult than it was in the past. In the past, the general textbook presumption was that all instances of the *ad misericordiam* could be routinely classified as appeals to pity, the presumption being that, due to their negative implications, they can immediately (without further justification to students) be rejected as fallacious. We have now seen, in abundant detail, why this logical leap can no longer be accepted as the basis for evaluating *ad misericordiam* arguments as fallacious.

In place of the traditional textbook treatment of the *argumentum ad misericordiam*, I have presented a new method that requires examining each individual case on its merits, on the basis of the evidence provided by the case.

7

Evaluation of Case Studies

In the last chapter, we set out the criteria by which particular cases of the *ad misericordiam* should be judged as fallacious or not. But of course, not all the cases we have examined have been judged to be fallacious. There can be a range of outcomes. Sometimes the argument is weak or questionable, but not so bad that we are justified in calling it fallacious. In this chapter, I will evaluate the major cases studied in the previous chapters. A couple of new cases are considered as well.

A summary of the method is given in section 9. In section 4, a set of conditions for the effectiveness of the use of the *argumentum ad misericordiam* in gaining acceptance for a conclusion is given.

1. LEGAL USES OF APPEAL TO PITY

As noted in chapter 1, section 4, the modern textbooks generally classify the *argumentum ad misericordiam* as a fallacy in legal cases on the grounds that appeal to pity is not relevant as an argument in a court of law. As noted as well in chapter 1, this claim is often dubious, because appeals to compassion are generally regarded as appropriate during the sentencing stage of a trial. However, we can go even further than this, and say that appeals to pity are very often allowed as defense pleas, even during the earlier stage of criminal trial where guilt is being disputed.

This relevance comes in because a criminal trial may be not just about the factual issue of whether the defendant committed the act in question. Guilt can also be a factor of the defendant's state of mind at the time. For example, the defendant's attorney may argue that he did stab the victim, but that he was legally insane at the time, and therefore was not responsible for his action. Using the insanity defense, the attorney can argue that the defendant had an excuse, that because of the state of his mind at the time, he is not guilty of murder.[1]

Because the state of the defendant's mind is a relevant issue in this type of defense, appeals to sympathy or compassion cannot be excluded from a criminal trial as irrelevant, generally. If the defendant's insanity was caused by, or is related to his pathetic circumstances as a poor, deprived child who suffered child abuse, then introducing this line of evidence would generally have to be regarded as relevant by the judge.[2]

There are special rules of relevance governing the conduct of criminal trials in different jurisdictions. But judging from recent trials, where appeal to pity is used very effectively as an argument to persuade a jury, *argumentum ad misericordiam* should not be regarded as fallacious in this context, on grounds that it is an irrelevant type of argument for a lawyer to use.

But the North American legal system is very much an adversarial system, and we can also take the point of view of external critics of the system. Even if the *ad misericordiam* is allowed, and even if in fact it often does work very well to persuade juries not to convict, or to award huge settlements to accident victims, we could still question whether these lawyers, judges, and juries are using, and being persuaded by, fallacious arguments. But here we are judging the argument by a standard external to the legal standard itself, with its internal rules of evidence and conduct used to regulate trials.

For example, in a recent case, a lawyer admitted his client was "idiotic" for jumping off a roof into a pool, breaking his neck, and leaving him a quadriplegic But the jury found the pool owner partly responsible, awarding the defendant two million dollars (*Canadian Press*, 1994, p. A2). In cases like this, juries see the insurance company who has to pay as impersonal, whereas they are moved by sympathy to help the defendant. Thus the *ad misericordiam* argument works very well.

But one can question the logic of the argumentation used by juries, and by the lawyers who advocate the arguments, on several grounds. Have the courts expanded the concept of warning of a danger beyond what ought to be expected of a reasonable person? Should we feel pity for someone who had a leading hand in causing his own misfortune, and could have easily prevented it with a little prudent foresight that one would normally expect a reasonable person to have? What are the consequences for insurance costs to homeowners of paying out awards to guests on this kind of scale?

Recent cases indicate that people on juries are willing to extend their pity well beyond the boundaries of what would have been considered reasonable in the past. The popular wave of victimology as a currently effective way of influencing judges and juries to expand the boundaries of traditionally accepted excuses has already been noted in chapter 6, section 2.

This issue has been sharpened in the public consciousness by the recent case of two brothers who admitted that they killed their parents, but pleaded a history of sexual abuse in a tearful defense that was portrayed by their attorneys as a "cry for help." The judge ruled that their case did not meet California's standard for "perfect self-defense," which required that they show that they were in "imminent fear for their lives." Instead, they pleaded "imperfect self-defense," which "requires only that the defendants honestly believed that their lives were endangered" (Adler, 1993, p. 103). Crying on the witness stand and biting their lips, the brothers described a history of abuse by their parents that half the jury members found moving and persuasive. However, the remaining jurors did not find the appeal to pity so persuasive. The jury could not agree on a verdict. The end result in 1994 was a mistrial. The case was then scheduled to go to court again for another trial.

2. THE MENENDEZ CASE

The basic facts of this case are that two brothers, Erik and Lyle Menendez, burst into their parents' bedroom on the night of August 20, 1989, and killed them with fifteen shotgun blasts. After the killing, the brothers went on a spending spree. Lyle bought a Porsche sports car and businesses in Princeton, New Jersey, while Erik hired a coach and turned into a professional tennis player (Reinhold, 1990, A20). Once circumstantial clues started coming in and the brothers were arrested, and they confessed to the killing.

When the case came to trial, attorneys argued that the brothers were not guilty of murder on the grounds that they had been sexually abused as children by their parents. The parents were portrayed as monsters, who had sexually and physically abused and humiliated them over a period of years. The argument used by the attorneys is a form of self-defense plea called *imperfect self-defense*. If successful it would mean that the brothers would not be held legally responsible for having murdered their parents, on the grounds they acted out of fear for their lives.

The argument used is an extension of the battered-wife defense called the battered-child-syndrome defense. Even though the victims were placidly sitting and watching television at the time of the killing, the argument was that the brothers defended themselves proactively because of the threat they perceived due to their emotional abuse. A *Time* article (Church 1993, p. 68) summarizes the basis of this argument:

> The law sometimes recognizes self-defense pleas from people who are not under attack but who reasonably fear imminent death unless they get their potential assailants first. The battered-child-syndrome defense holds that a child can be so terrorized by years of sexual, physical and emotional abuse that he or she genuinely reads menace—accurately or not—into a look, a gesture, an ambiguous word that an outsider might not consider a threat.

The ages of the brothers was a complicating factor in this defense. Lyle was twenty-one and Erik eighteen at the time of the killing. In this respect, as noted by Professor Peter Arenella, of the UCLA law faculty, the defense was more like that of a battered wife case (special to the *New York Times*, Sept. 1, 1993, p. A17):

> Professor Arenella said the brothers' ages made the case more like a battered wife case, in which women assert they killed their husbands in self-defense because of repeated sexual or physical abuse. But such killings tend to occur during or immediately after violent physical confrontation, he said, and thus far no clear evidence has emerged that such was the case with the Menendez brothers.

Comparable to the battered wife syndrome, the argument was that the defendants had grounds to be afraid of being killed by their parents.

The defense argued that the brothers had killed out of fear, and not out of greed for the fourteen million dollars inheritance. The defense argument was backed up by a succession of expert witnesses (Mydans, Nov. 7, 1993, p. 34):

One expert, Ann Burgess, a professor of psychiatric nursing at the University of Pennsylvania, said the pattern of the 15 gunshots seemed to demonstrate fear.

"A large number more shots were fired than were necessary," said Dr. Burgess, who has studied homicide scenes for the Federal Bureau of Investigation. She said it was notable that the shots, 13 of which struck their targets, seemed random rather than focused on one part of the body. "That would speak to a more pervasive emotion than just one emotion such as anger or rage," she said. "It would speak to a wider aspect such as fear."

Another expert, Jon Conte, a professor of social work at the University of Washington, who interviewed Lyle Menendez for 60 hours, said the brothers seemed genuinely to have been in fear for their lives even if that fear was not reasonable.

He said many years of sexual and mental abuse by their father had made them irrationally susceptible to threatening signals. "They began to put all the clues together and say, 'They're going to get rid of us'," Dr. Conte testified.

Legal experts say a history of abuse and fear can diminish a person's ability to assess the extent of a threat and reduce his liability for turning to violence.

This expert testimony on the emotional state of the brothers made them appear as victims of a threat, raising a feeling of sympathy for them. This feeling of sympathy played a key role in the defense argument.

"I think that ultimately it's going to come down to how much do the jurors feel some sympathy for these defendants, and do they really perceive them as victims in some way," Erwin Chemerinsky, a law professor at the University of Southern California. [Mydans, Sept. 1, 1993, p. A30]

Judge Weisberg complained that the issue of the linkage between the killing and alleged molestation was being "blown out of proportion." But the defense case seemed to overwhelm him, according to Mydans' report of the trial (p. 26).

The defense attorney, Leslie Abramson, argued that the defendants "cannot be held to the cold standards of accountability of a legal system that lags behind social and psychological theories of behavior," as quoted in a *New York Times* report of Mydans (Dec. 20, 1993, p. D9):

"These boys were not responsible for who they turned out to be," she said. "They were just little children being molded. They were never free of the clutches of their parents. When you terrorize people and they react from terror, you pretty much get what you sowed."

"It's not an issue of individual responsibility, it's an issue of people getting caught in events, and they act precisely as you would expect them to."

It is noteworthy that Ms. Abramson continued to call the Menendez brothers "the boys" before the jury, putting her arm around them, suggesting how lovable they were. She portrayed herself as motivated by a "gentler impulse to protect people who have been rejected by society" (Mydans, Dec. 20, 1993, p. D9):

"I'm drawn to cases where very nice people and very good people are accused of crimes because the law lags behind psychology, like people who have been abused and battered," she said. "I don't like to see people suffer, and I don't like the hard-heartedness of other people towards them. Human beings are very sensitive creatures, and they suffer terribly when they are treated badly."

"I'm very drawn to these people because they are delightful clients and they are decent human beings and they need me."

Portraying "the boys" as warm and lovable was a key part of the appeal to sympathy projected to the jury.

Lyle Menendez's testimony of alleged child abuse by his father was described as "gripping" in a *New York Times* report (Mydans, Sept. 12, 1993, p. 30):

On the other hand, Lyle has not exactly shown the brothers to be lovable enough to deserve outright acquittal. Witness part of his testimony about killing Kitty: "I could see somebody moving where my mother should be. So I reloaded. I ran around and shot my mom. I shot her close."

The media coverage of this case captured public interest during the period of the trial. According to *Newsweek* (Adler, 1993, p. 104), a cable channel that has been carrying as much as eight hours a day of live Menendez coverage, reports viewers "split almost evenly between those who accept the defense story and those who think Erik and Lyle are lying."

Although Leslie Abramson became a "media star," very little was heard about the Menendez case in the media until March 1996, when the brothers were convicted of murder by a new jury (Kaplan and Foote, 1996). In this new trial, the judge found insufficient evidence of self-defense, and excluded most testimony about abuse.

In the first trial, when the "abuse excuse" was allowed as relevant by the judge, the prosecuting attorney should have used the banishment of pity argument to contend that the brothers did not deserve our pity. However, Abramson's defense countered this argument by contending that the brothers were abused by their parents, and were thus driven to this desperate act of killing in self-defense.

What one suspects, from the account of this case given above, is that the imperfect self-defense line was being used as an entry device by the defense lawyers so that they could introduce their really persuasive argument to the jury—namely, the appeal to pity—portraying the defendants as victims of child abuse. For once imperfect self-defense has been chosen as the defense that will be argued, then the introduction of the motives, character, circumstances, and family background of the defendants is relevant. For in the plea of self-defense, the motives and intentions of the defendant are both relevant and important.

Judge Weisberg was evidently frustrated by this tactic, and felt the jury was being overwhelmed by the appeal to pity. As we know it, the appeal to pity tends to have an overwhelming impact when presented in graphic detail. Before making a final comment on this case, let us examine another case that has already been introduced.

3. THE BABY SEALS CASE

The case of the photographs of cute little baby seals being killed, cited by Soccio and Barry (1992, p. 135), was noted in case 1.22. This type of picture, used by animal rights groups, has had an overwhelming impact in influencing public opinion, leading to bans on seal hunting. Should this kind of case be called an instance of the *ad misericordiam* fallacy?

The first thing to note is that if the animal rights group that uses such a photograph as part of their campaign is frankly advocating their cause, then if the appeal to pity works as a powerful argument tactic to influence public opinion, then they are free to use it for this purpose. There is no deceptive tactic of argument used in such an appeal to feeling, and it should not be called an *ad misericordiam* fallacy.

However, when such an appeal is used in political deliberations—say, in a government congressional or parliamentary hearing on whether to ban seal hunting, the broader circumstances of the case, including the consequences of such a ban—are relevant to the case.

Pictures of cuddly baby seals being slaughtered were in fact the main public relations argument used by the animal rights activists group, the International Fund for Animal Welfare (IFAW), to lead to a ban on the hunting of baby seals in Canada. According to Cox (1994, p. D1), the IFAW spent about five million dollars in the period 1988–1994 fighting the seal hunt.

> And it is these adorable liquid-eyed creatures that have always been the IFAW's most potent weapon. It was widespread revulsion at photos of Newfoundlanders clubbing baby seals in the British press, starting in 1968, that led to a European ban on seal-fur products in 1983 and ultimately to a Canadian government ban on the hunting of baby seals in 1988. [p. D8]

One can see how this type of photograph pulls to the viewers need for an elemental need to help. The seal pups, with their big liquid eyes, are being clubbed. The picture appeals to the urge to protect the pups, as though they were helpless human babies. This resemblance is noted by Cox (p. D1):

> The moan of the wind is broken only by the piteous wail of dozens of newborn seals out here on the ice ridges in the Gulf of St. Lawrence. Their distress is understandable. Just a few hours ago, all they knew was the warmth and security of their mothers' wombs. Now the bewhiskered whitecoats with liquid black eyes are flopping helplessly on frigid ice in -30 degree temperatures, their howls ignored by their mothers who are dozing in the sunshine The cubs sound uncannily like human babies.

The picture of hunters clubbing these babies to death is extraordinarily powerful.

A summary of developments subsequent to the publicization of pictures of the seal slaughter is given by Cox (p. D2):

1968 Photos of the slaughter appear in London's *Daily Mirror*, sparking worldwide concern. Canadian Brian Davies forms the International Fund for Animal Welfare.

1976 Greenpeace Foundation joins the protest and invites celebrities to get involved.

1977 Canada introduces quotas. In the first year it allows the taking of 160,000 seals, 152,000 of them pups.

1983 Europe, representing 75 per cent of the export market, bans the importation of any products made from Canadian seal pups.

1985 A Canadian royal commission says public opinion will not allow a seal-pup hunt event though it concludes the pups are killed humanely.

1988 The federal government bans the killing of baby seals but allows a land-based hunt for adults.

In recent years, especially with the declining of fishing resources, which some attribute to the abundance of seals, there has been a shifting of public opinion more toward tolerance of limited hunting of adult seals. To counter these developments, the IFAW argued in 1994 that the seals were being killed so their penises could be exported to Asia to be used as aphrodisiacs. The IFAW spent one hundred thousand dollars on an ad that appeared in leading newspapers featuring a picture of a dried-up seal penis with the text: "How do you get away with exporting seal penises to China? Leave the seal attached" (Cox, p. D2).

As a public relations campaign using the *argumentum ad misericordiam* to advocate its cause, this sort of argumentation by the IFAW seems to have all the Hollywood theatrics that Walter the hard-nosed logician finds objectionable in appeals to pity. But even though critics dispute the truth of the premise that hunters are killing seals for their penises, this *ad misericordiam* argument should not be classified as fallacious per se.

However, in deliberations on the practical issue of whether the government should ban the hunting of seals or not, the discussion should be argued out using practical reasoning that takes the consequences of banning versus not banning into account. And of course, this question is very controversial. The opposed viewpoint, spoken for particularly by those who have made their living by hunting or fishing, stresses the prudence of a balanced ecology. According to this viewpoint, a ban on the harvesting of any single animal will lead to imbalances in the animal population that will disrupt the ecology, and in general have bad consequences.

It is not for us to try to resolve this dispute, but only to note the terrific impact that the *ad misericordiam* argument has had in the argumentation on the issue. One thing to notice is that the appeal to pity typically has a tremendous immediate impact as an argument, causing an audience to temporarily throw all other considerations aside. But its impact tends to be short-term, as other relevant factors once again are considered.

Used over and over again, the appeal to pity tends to lose its impact. After repeated exposure, it seems that people become more resistant to appeals to pity. This has been observed, for example, in public attitudes towards the homeless on the streets in large cities. According to Bragg (1944, p. A11), while the homeless tended to inspire sympathy a few years ago, now people look the other way, or even react to begging with hostility. It seems that now there are so many homeless people evident in urban areas, that people have become "numbed" or "weary." Several incidents (Bragg, p. A11) are cited where someone is pushed away or cursed when he tries to beg for money or cigarettes.

Perhaps it was the need to overcome the lessening impact of the appeal to pity produced by the pictures of baby seals being attacked that led the public relations people advising the animal rights activists to introduce the penis removal argument as a new part of their argumentation tactics.

Cases like this one raise the interesting question of why the *ad misericordiam* is such a powerful and effective method of argument in so many contexts, like persuading juries, and when used in public relations. This is not a logical question of normatively evaluating the *argumentum ad misericordiam*, as it is an empirical and psychological question that can be tested by experiment.

Even so, from the structural and normative point of view of our analysis of this type of argument, it is possible to formulate a hypothesis.

4. EFFECTIVENESS OF
AD MISERICORDIAM ARGUMENTS

An important question in the pragmatic analysis of any type of argument is that of effectiveness. How does the argument work as an instrument that is commonly and effectively used to gain acceptance for a conclusion or course of action? With respect to the *ad misericordiam*, there are two aspects to how the argument works as a method of gaining acceptance.

The first aspect is the appeal to compassion or pity for a situation that the respondent of the appeal will recognize as a bad situation, so that by empathy, the respondent will respond: "Here is another sentient being who is suffering." Thus the appeal, to be successful, must elicit feelings of sympathy, and possibly also, feelings of guilt, that people should allow such suffering to occur, and not relieve it.

As noted in the baby seals case, what people will feel sympathy for varies a lot, depending on how people feel about an issue at the moment. The freshness of the appeal, as noted in section 3, is important here. And of course, empathy is all-important here.

The second aspect has to do with practical reasoning. The second premise says, in effect, here is an easy way you can solve this problem—by doing such-and-such, the proposed solution, you can stop the suffering, and feel good that you can put an end to the guilt.

This analysis applies to the typical kinds of charitable appeal, for causes like disaster relief, and so forth. These cases are generally instances of some kind of deliberation, where a specific action is recommended as a solution to the problem. What is advocated is that if the respondent acts in the manner recommended, the suffering will be relieved.

Thus for such an appeal to be effective, two requirements must be met. First, the appeal must successfully make the respondent feel empathy for another individual who appears to be suffering. And second, some solution or course of action must be offered that will be convincing to the respondent as a way to relieve the suffering.

There is also a third aspect to the *ad misericordiam* argument that makes this type of argument much more effective—the solution must be a relatively easy and painless solution. For if the solution is perceived as too difficult, the appeal is not likely to be successful.

In the case of charitable appeals, this factor is realized, for the proposed line of action is relatively easy and painless—simply donate some money, by sending it to the address indicated, or giving it to the charitable organization. All the hard work part of it is taken out, because the organization is already in place, and (purportedly anyway) has the means to alleviate the suffering, or to do something about it.

In the baby seals case, the action recommended is for respondents to take part in the democratic process, and to thereby pass a law that bans the hunting of seals. Such an action is made relatively easy for most voters in a democratic system.

In this case, however, the question of side effects of the proposed action would be raised as one of the critical questions applicable to the case. Wouldn't respondents raise this question?

The answer is that the policy of banning seal hunting would be very costly to those who earn their living from seal hunting, and also possibly to those who earn a living from fishing. But these individuals are in a minority. In a democracy, for most respondents, the action seems painless.

So the conditions under which such an appeal can fail are, broadly, of three kinds. One is if the respondent does not feel compassion for the individual's situation as portrayed in the message. For example, this situation occurred in attitudes about the homeless, which gradually began to change over the years, so that there was an erosion of compassion. The second condition of failure occurs where the respondent does not believe, or doubts that the recommended action will in fact do much to relieve the suffering. The third condition occurs where the recommended action is too difficult for the respondent. For example, if the respondent has no money to spare, or if donating to the charity would pose a hardship for him, then the *ad misericordiam* appeal is less likely to be successful.

This analysis can also be applied to many of the other cases of appeals to feelings we have studied. In the Nayirah case, the appeal was used as a justification to go to war. But connected with the effective use of the appeal in this case was the assumption that by means of an invasion of Kuwait, we could stop these abuses. In the student's plea type of case, especially when the plea was put in the form of an argument from consequences—for example, "If you don't give me an *A*, I won't get into law school, and my parents will be devastated"—the proposal is that if you do give me an *A*, these unfortunate consequences will not occur.

However, these three conditions of effectiveness of the use of the *ad misericordiam* argument do not explain (by themselves, anyway) why and how such arguments are used fallaciously.

It is well to emphasize again that the primary goal of our project has been to evaluate cases of the *argumentum ad misericordiam* normatively—that is, from a logical point of view. But studying the reasons for its effectiveness is, to some extent, useful in understanding how this type of argument works as a fallacy.

5. COMPARING CASES

Comparing the Nayirah case to the baby seals case, on the question of whether there is an *ad misericordiam* fallacy present, is interesting. Probably most people react with the opinion that there is no *ad misericordiam* fallacy in the baby seals case, because there is legitimate controversy here. The people who are opposed to the point of view tend to see the use of the appeal to pity by their opponents as unreasonable or fallacious. But most of us recognize that there is controversy here, and that two points of view are possible. Consequently, we infer that if the activists want to use appeal to pity to advocate their point of view on seal hunting, as they see the issue, then that is all right for them. We don't have to be persuaded by the appeal, but we don't have to find it fallacious either.

In the Nayirah case, by way of contrast, the appeal to pity was based on a claim that appears to be false, judging by the weight of evidence turned up in subsequent investigations. Moreover, it appears that this claim was known to be false by the public relations firm that staged the whole event. At least, this was the allegation made by several news media reports, based on their investigations of the case. If this interpretation of the case is warranted, then there does seem to be a good basis for saying that an *ad misericordiam* fallacy was committed here. A significant part of the basis for this judgment is the "staged" aspect of the whole appeal, as indicated in chapter 5, section 7.

On the other hand, however, the appeal to pity in the use of the photographs of cuddly seal pups being beaten to death was also very much part of a well-funded and orchestrated public relations campaign, as indicated in the description of this case. So what's the key difference, if any, between the two cases that makes us seem to want to say that the *ad misericordiam* argument is fallacious in the one case but not the other?

The fallacy resides not just in the appeal to pity or compassion grafted onto the argument from need for help, contrary to the tradition of many of the textbooks. For example, in cases 1.18 and 1.19, classified as instances of the *ad misericordiam* fallacy in the textbook treatment, there is an appeal to pity used in conjunction with the argument from need for help. In case 1.18, the beggar emphasizes his appeal for money by prominently displaying his blind eyes. In case 1.19, the ad pleads for an apartment for a "veteran with sick infant." But in neither case should we justify the argument as an instance of the *ad misericordiam* fallacy. If these people voluntarily take an advocacy stance of pleading for money or help to relieve their problem, then that is not a fallacy, for there is nothing deceptive or logically incorrect about their use of argumentation from need for help.

Fearnside and Holther (1959, p. 21), as noted in conjunction with case 1.20, describe the *ad misericordiam* fallacy as *"taking advantage* of pathetic circumstances." They are on to something important here. If the beggar displays his rags or deformities in a way that is staged (see chapter 5, section 7), or "prearranged for show," as Fearnside and Holther put it, this is an important kind of evidence for his committing a fallacy in this use of argument from need for help. This staging aspect can be evidence for use of a deceptive tactic of twisting the argument from need for help around to an inappropriate purpose, or a different purpose from the ostensible one.

But the staging aspect is not itself sufficient for a fallacy to have been committed. How the staging is carried out as an argumentation tactic used in a context of dialogue also seems to be significant. The appeal to pity in the Nayirah case was brought forward before a Senate subcommittee, and ultimately before the U.S. public, through the media in an argument from distress that exploited *kairos*, or the timely moment in the debate, to influence the deliberations at just the right moment to tilt the balance of considerations toward the decision to make war.[3] In this case, there was a decision made on the basis of an appeal to pity, that presumably would have been made differently if the true facts had been made known at the time. The baby seals appeal to pity also exploited public sympathy in a timely way that influenced government deliberations, but the impact here was not so abrupt. We are free to be persuaded by the appeal or not, and reactions to it continue to exhibit controversial argumentation on both sides.

The bottom line has to be, however, that in the Nayirah case, once Nayirah's identity and the involvement of Hill and Knowlton were made known, it became apparent to many that the appeal to pity was based on misinformation that was an essential part of the argument from distress used by the public relations campaign to influence the Senate vote. It follows that if we are to say that the *ad misericordiam* argument in the Nayirah case is fallacious, our grounds for *enstatis* must partly include the disproof of a false premise (*anairesis*). That is, it must include the subsequent finding that the incubator babies story was essentially a false or unproven (and doubtful) account.

6. FURTHER COMMENTS ON CASES

One problem with arguments based on empathy is that the person to whom the appeal is directed generally makes the assumption that the person he is asked to have empathy with is a reasonable person who is similar to himself in relevant respects. In fact, people are more likely to have empathy for other people they think or assume are like themselves, or are closer to being in the same distressful situation. Recent research reported in *Newsweek* (Salholz, Beachy, and Rosenberg 1992, p. 23) indicated, for example, that people with less income, who are closer to knowing what it feels like to lose a job or home, are more likely than the wealthy to contribute to the homeless or jobless during hard times.

But in some cases, these assumptions of similarity based on empathy can simply be mistaken, as noted in chapter 3. For example, a juror in a child abuse case might have sympathy for a defendant who is shedding tears, and who appears to be suffering great remorse for his crime—see case 3.3. But what if the pedophile is a psychopath who has learned to mimic these feelings like a brilliant actor, but has no remorse at all for his crimes of rape and murder? The nature of the false premise in this kind of *ad misericordiam* argument is well indicated by the fable of Babrius on the viper that kills the man who tries to help it (case 3.4).

However, there is a basic difference between these two cases. In case 3.4, the snake is (presumably) not feigning distress. It is the kindly person who thinks he is helping the snake who himself decides to interpret the situation this way, and this blunder, or inappropriate assumption of empathy, is the outcome—the conclusion that the person ill-advisedly acts upon. This is more like a blunder or imprudent conclusion derived by practical reason on the basis of an unjustified reading of the situation. It is a projection of empathy onto another party, where the other party is an object that is not an appropriate entity for the projection. The results, predictably enough, turn out badly.

Case 3.3 is different, because the psychopath is staging the display as a clever and persistent tactic to try to exploit the sympathy of the jury. Here there is a dialogue exchange of a kind that could properly be considered fallacious.

The baby seals case is between these two cases in that an animal is used as the basis of the appeal to sympathy. These animals look somewhat misleadingly like human babies, but even so, they could be appropriate to feel pity for, as cuddly creatures that are in distress and need help. And while there is a staged, public relations argumentation tactic in this case, it could be nonfallacious as advocacy argumentation for the animal rights cause.

Why then is the case of the psychopath in court different? Here there are a number of factors that come into play. One is that, like the Nayirah case, there is a combination of a false premise used in conjunction with a staged tactic of appeal to pity. But we have to be careful in this case, because, although a witness is not supposed to lie in court, the attorneys are free on both sides to present testimony that would be persuasive to a jury, in order to make a strong argument (according to the adversarial framework of the legal system). While it does have many of the characteristics of the *ad misericordiam* fallacy, from a more narrowly legal point of view of its use in the context of a trial, it might be better described as a bad or weak argument, based on deceptive testimony, that a jury should not be inclined to accept as persuasive (but may in fact accept). This takes us back to the question of evaluating the argument in the context of the trial, as a legal argument, to be judged by legal standards of evidence, versus evaluating the argument from a broader logical perspective of whether it is correct or not from a normative point of view appropriate for informal logic. From this latter standpoint of a critical discussion, or perhaps a deliberation type of dialogue, the argument could be judged as fallacious.

This takes us to an evaluation of the *ad misericordiam* argument in the Menendez case. What are we to conclude here? Is the appeal to pity fallacious, or are there any defects that it has different kinds of failures?

What many of us find objectionable about the defense argument is that it stretches the imperfect self-defense plea, a somewhat tenuous line of defense to begin with, to what appears to be preposterous lengths. Indeed, the remarks of Abramson indicate that she is really attacking the whole notion of personal responsibility and substituting a new social science criterion for judging behavior, blaming everything on the defendant's environment, so that the whole idea of punishment for crime is thrown out the window. This represents an ethical point of view that certainly has been advocated strongly by many persons in recent times. Is it a basis for calling her argument fallacious?

The evaluation proposed here is that this argument is controversial, and open to dispute—and as well, it goes against the basic idea of personal responsibility, *mens rea*, or the "guilty mind," that is central to the criminal law—but it is not fallacious.

In this case, the appeal to pity was relevant, once the self-defense plea was allowed. But was there ever enough evidence that the self-defense plea should have been allowed? The second trial in 1996 indicated that there was not. But in 1994, the "abuse excuse" was riding high on a crest of public popularity, pushed forward by advocacy groups who were pressing vocally for reforms of the legal system. To exclude the "abuse excuse" at that time would have subjected the court to considerable public pressure by advocacy groups, especially given the media coverage of the trial.

The problem in this case was that once the self-defense plea was allowed, Leslie Abramson exploited this opening by staging a dramatic appeal to pity to the media and the public, as well as to the jury. The victims of the shooting were not present to be able to present their side of the story. So the appeal to pity was inappropriately, and even ludicrously, one-sided. Since the crime occurred, and the alleged abuses, within the confines of the family, with no other witnesses, Lyle and Erik were free to present their version of the story, and it could not be contradicted or falsified by any surviving witnesses. Was this a fair trial? It does not seem so. Was it a fallacy?

In this kind of case, it needs to be remembered that the appeal to pity can be countered by the banishment of pity argument, in two ways: (1) by presenting a counter-appeal to pity for the plight of the dead victims of the crime, and (2) by arguing that the accused perpetrators did not themselves show pity, and therefore do not deserve our pity now.

Of course, the defense argument was very much a staged tactic of appealing to the feelings of the jury, and it turned out to be relatively successful in achieving this objective. But that does not make it a fallacy. The fact that the judge allowed the extensive appeal to pity to be argued by the defense attorneys, even if he had misgivings about it, indicate that the *ad misericordiam* was seen to be within the legal framework of evidence.

It seems then that not much has changed since ancient times, concerning the use of the *ad misericordiam* argument in courts.[4] It will continue to be used and tolerated, often in a questionable way that exploits its powerful impact on a jury. Its use by an attorney may raise questions about that person's conscience as a private citizen, or professional ethics as a lawyer. And its admission by a judge, according to the rules of a legal system, may reflect badly on that judge, or even on the legal system as a whole (at any given time). Yet the argument should not be judged fallacious, in a particular case where it is used within the framework of rules appropriate for the dialogue.

In an adversarial legal system, it is the attorney's job to use the strongest possible arguments to advocate the client's interests, within the framework of the legal system. If the judge will allow the "abuse excuse," according to the trial rules at any given time, and the jury will be persuaded by it, then, according to the adversary system, the defense attorney can use this argument. It is up to the prosecution to challenge or refute that argument. If the legal system allows such arguments, then even if a clever attorney blows the argument all out of proportion, playing on pity in a ludicrously illogical theatrical display *ad misericordiam*, it is not getting to the real nature of the problem to say that the attorney has argued fallaciously. The problem is in a legal system that tolerates or even encourages such practices. By way of contrast, let us go on to look at a fallacious use of the argument.

7. THE STUDENT'S PLEA CASE ANALYZED

In the student's plea type of case, there is no single *ad misericordiam* fallacy that is common to every case. Various cases exhibit different types of arguments, and different types of failures in these arguments. In case 4.12, where the student cried and said he would not be headman in his village, this argument from negative consequences does not appear to be relevant in the case (as far as the information given indicates). In other cases as well, like 1.13, 1.14, and 4.1, the argument from negative consequences does not really appear to be relevant to the conversation that is supposed to be taking place either.

However, a subtlety noticed in chapter 1, section 5, is that the appeal to pitiable circumstances does have a kind of practical relevance. For example, the student may have had some illness or personal problem that could be part of an explanation why he could not write an assignment, or did not do very well. And this could be part of a legitimate plea to have his special circumstances taken into account, or to get a deferred exam. As noted in chapter 1, the relevance of this sort of argument from distress should not be totally discounted in advance, or evaluated as irrelevant in every case of this type. As Runkle (1978) noted in conjunction with case 1.16, an appeal to pity can be relevant in some cases of the student's plea type.

So failure of relevance is not the only explanation of the *ad misericordiam* argument's fallaciousness. In the context of excuses, as noted in chapter 1, section 6, appeals to compassion can be relevant and appropriate as arguments.

A deeper analysis of the *ad misericordiam* as it occurs in the student's plea type of case involved the observation that, in some of these cases, there is a kind of shift from one type of conversation to another, so that the argument from consequences (or argument from distress, or argument from need for help) is twisted around to a different purpose. The phenomenon characteristic of this situation, studied extensively in Walton and Krabbe (1995), is called a *dialectical shift*—that is, the argument in a given case was originally supposed to be part of one type of dialogue, but then came to be used as a part of a different type of dialogue.[5] The application of this notion to the student's plea type of case was already made in Walton (1992a, p. 262), where the *ad misericordiam* appeal for a higher grade (so the student would be able to get into law school) is cited as being used to "shift the dialogue from a discussion of whether any of the test answers merit a higher grade on the examination from consequences concerning failure to gain entry to law school" (p. 262). The *ad misericordiam* was diagnosed as fallacious in this case because the conversation was shifted away from the kind of deliberation the professor and student are supposed to be engaged in. This is a tactic used by the student to try to twist the deliberation around so that the professor is making the decision on a basis other than the one that is proper—that is, his judgment by professional standards of the worth of the student's answers on a test, as expressed in his grading evaluation.

This kind of problem is also evident in case 1.9, where the student's mother cites the financial difficulties of the family, reminding the professor that he has always been a good friend of the family. The implicit plea for special consideration is unethical, and an invitation to entrapment. So there is an ethical violation, in this case, by someone asking for special concessions on the basis of a personal (family) relationship.

But over and above the ethical problem posed by this case, there is also a logical fallacy involved, because the argument from need for help is being twisted around to a different purpose, in a context where this appeal is an obstruction to the kind of deliberation that the professor is properly supposed to be engaged in. The inappropriate appeal to sympathy puts the professor on the spot, making him appear impolite or unhelpful when he is forced to back off from it.

The student's plea case, in at least some of its instances, does then turn out to be a very good example of the fallacious type of case of *ad misericordiam* argument. Other cases examined above have some of the characteristic signs of the *ad misericordiam* fallacy, but the student's plea case combines all (or the right mixture, excluding irrelevance) in the right way to make it a clear instance of the fallacy.

Another case, interestingly, also has all these characteristics as well. This case is, in some ways, even clearer, and provides a kind of model of what is fallacious in the *ad misericordiam* argument (when it is fallacious). This was the Thackeray case, presented above in chapter 2, section 2.

8. THE THACKERAY CASE

The argument from need for help is based on a kind of practical reasoning.[6] *S*'s argument, in this case, has the form: "I need help, because I am poor, etc., therefore you should publish my poem." The implicit premise is: "Publishing my poem is a way to help me." And in fact, possibly this premise could even turn out to be true, in the given case.

Where then is the fallacy in this *ad misericordiam* argument? To see the basis of the fallacy, you have to look more closely at the context of the dialogue in which the two parties are taking part. He is the editor of a journal, who has the job of selecting material for publication based on certain criteria. Both participants know this, and she sends the poem to his journal so that a judgment can be made to print it or not, based on the criteria for that journal, which may even be stated by the journal, in some cases, as an editorial policy.

However, the editor is also a private citizen, a person who will naturally feel an obligation, or at least a pull to respond to cries for help, from someone who appears to be in distress. This is a fundamental kind of human relationship, and an appeal based on it can be emotionally strong.

So the editor is caught in a conflict between two forces. On the one hand, he is an editor, who has the job of judging submissions to his magazine by certain criteria. On the other hand, he is a private person who is responsive to cries for help from persons in distress.

When the pleader argues "This is a way to help me," she puts the editor on the spot. From the point of view of his job as editor, this is not a good way to help her, if he thinks the poem is not worth publishing, according to the given editorial standards. In fact, if he does so, he would be derelict in his duty as editor, and could rightly be criticized for making a bad editorial decision.

In this case, we have to begin by asking what kind of dialogue the parties are supposed to be engaged in. The answer is that it is a kind of editor-contributor dialogue, where one party submits a piece for publication, and the other party has the obligation of arriving at a decision for acceptance/rejection based on deliberation in relation to goals set by the criteria formulated by the editorial policy of the journal. In this context, the plea "This is a way to help me" is a piece of bad practical reasoning. Although printing the poem regardless of its quality may somehow help the pleader (or then again, it may not), this question is really beside the point. The real question is whether the poem will contribute to the goals of the magazine (in the judgment of the editor), and whether, all things considered, printing this poem would be the best way to contribute to these goals.

Presumably, printing the poem just out of pity, or out of a misguided motive to help the pleader in the way she proposes, would not contribute to the goals of the magazine, and would not constitute the editor's doing his job properly, in his deliberations on what to print and what not to. As a piece of practical reasoning, the plea for help, viewed in its proper context of dialogue, is a failure, a very bad sequence of practical reasoning. The action proposed (or solicited) simply does not mesh properly with the goals that are appropriate for the type of dialogue the two participants are supposed to be engaged in.

This case is closely related to the student's plea case. Once we see how practical reasoning is involved, it also becomes clear how the appeal is an argument from consequences. The student pleader argues: "If you don't give me an *A* grade, bad consequences will happen to me." Therefore, the plea goes: "You should give me an *A* grade, and then these bad consequences won't happen." There is also an implicature to the effect: "If the bad consequences happen, it will be your fault." The appeal to argumentation from consequences is very much a part of the practical reasoning framework.

Similarly to the Thackeray case, you have to consider the initial type of dialogue the participants were supposed to be engaged in. The teacher is supposed to grade the student's assignment, based on merit, according to academic criteria. But if he gives in to the student's plea, basing his decision on the appeal to pity posed by the citing of bad consequences, he arrives at his judgment via the wrong criteria. It may well be true that there will be bad consequences for the student of his receiving a lower grade. The premise may be true, but the practical reasoning is deficient or incorrect. For the teacher's goal should not be simply to avert these bad consequences, or to help the student by any means, but to grade the student's work according to certain criteria appropriate for their relationship as teacher and student of this particular course, in the given institutional setting.

Comparison of these two cases gives us a good account of the ingredients, and how they are combined, in the *ad misericordiam* fallacy.

9. SUMMARY OF THE METHOD

Throughout our case studies of the various aspects of the *argumentum ad misericordiam*, a method of dealing critically with this type of argument has come to be adopted. Clarifying the main steps of this method, we can see that it has three distinct stages involving different tasks—identification, analysis, and evaluation.

At the identification stage, it is useful to make a finer discrimination among the different types of *ad misericordiam* arguments, and ask: Is it an appeal to pity, an appeal to compassion, an appeal to sympathy, or an appeal to mercy? In some cases, it is hard to tell, exactly, and in the end it may not matter too much anyway. However, in many cases, the difference may have significant implications for how the argument is to be analyzed and evaluated. As we saw in chapter 2, the concept of pity has especially sensitive negative implications.

In the traditional treatment of the textbooks, *argumentum ad misericordiam* is translated as *appeal to pity*, and the word *pity* has a negative connotation for most people, implying being sorry for someone who is in a bad or painful situation, or even implying an attitude of condescension toward that person. On September 7, 1993, a radio report on the Jerry Lewis Telethon for muscular dystrophy said "critics allege he uses pity to raise money."[7] Kemp (1981) argued that by using "Jerry's kids" as a "pity appeal," the Telethon exploits the "appealing and huggable child" as a fund-raising tactic. According to Kemp, this "playing to pity" reinforces the prejudice that the handicapped are pathetic and helpless. This general attitude may suggest that the appeal to pity can be classified generally as an inappropriate or fallacious type of argument. That is, in fact, the traditional approach of the logic textbooks.[8]

However, if you define this type of argumentation using a more positive sounding label, like "appeal to sympathy," or "appeal to compassion," it is much less likely to be perceived as being generally or always fallacious. And, as we have seen, many cases of arguments that should be classified as appeals to feeling under the category of the *argumentum ad misericordiam* are nonfallacious. Considered in the context of conversation in which they were put forward, many such arguments are quite reasonable appeals to emotion, used to shift a weight of presumption to one side in a balance-of-considerations argument, in order to support a course of action being advocated.

This approach is supported in Walton (1992a, 1992c, 1995), where it is contended that they can be used properly in a context of dialogue as arguments to gain assent by the other party by shifting a weight of presumption toward the arguer's side and away from the side of the other party in the dispute. Uses of appeals to feeling, justified on an evolutionary basis as useful components in practical reasoning in chapter 4, section 9, can have the function of steering an argument toward a conclusion, even if the argument is not conclusive. They may be open to questions, or even to defeat, at some later stage in the sequence of reasoning in a dialogue.

So even at this initial identification stage, it is important not to jump the gun and declare the argument fallacious just because it is an *ad misericordiam*, because such appeals to pity are objectionable per se on ethical grounds alone. Resisting this hasty leap ahead in the sequence, it is better to hold off with evaluation, and proceed to the analysis stage.

At the analysis stage it is important to collect the evidence furnished by the text and context of discourse in the given case, and dig out the underlying argument—the premises and conclusions. Characteristically, the appeal to feeling in a typical *ad misericordiam* argument is grafted onto an argument from need for help, or argumentation from consequences. What needs to be done at this stage is to identify the premises and conclusions of this argument, determine what type of argument it is, and analyze how it is being used for some purpose in the context as a sequence of practical reasoning. Here, the larger picture of evidence should be assembled, taking into account the other consequences of the proposed course of action in relation to the goals the participants in deliberation presumably are working with.

At the analysis stage, it is important to recognize that the argument from distress or need for help may not be literally being used to solicit efforts to help the individuals alleged to be in distress. For example, in the Nayirah case, the babies allegedly pulled from the incubators were presumably beyond help, at the time Nayirah's tearful plea was made before the Senate subcommittee hearings. Clearly the argument was being turned to a different use.

At the evaluation stage, the tendency to dichotomize all the cases into the two categories of being correct or fallacious should be resisted. Already in Walton (1992c, p. 140), a more fine-grained approach to evaluation of cases of the *argumentum ad misericordiam* had been proposed. They are divided into five categories: (1) reasonable, (2) weak, but not fallacious, (3) irrelevant, (4) not enough information given, and (5) fallacious. Thus the project of evaluating given cases of the *argumentum ad misericordiam* is something more of a case-by-case type of argument, requiring careful preliminary analysis of the evidence given by the text of discourse in a case, than the traditional approach of the textbooks suggested.

As part of the evaluation process, we should check the argument for relevance, but be very careful not to make the error of assuming that instances of the *ad misericordiam* can be evaluated as fallacies only on grounds of failure of relevance. Appeals to pity are in fact quite often, and even generally, failures of relevance in a critical discussion or in an inquiry. But they can quite often be relevant in a deliberation type of dialogue. Our case studies have now positively verified Hamblin's hesitantly expressed conjecture (1970, p. 43) that "where action is concerned, it is not so clear that pity and other emotions are irrelevant." Hence it is important for evaluation purposes to try to determine what type of dialogue the argument is supposed to be being used as a part of. This will very much influence our evaluation of whether it may rightly be judged to be fallacious or not, in a given case.

Indeed, the cases in which the *ad misericordiam* was judged in this book to be fallacious are precisely those in which, on the surface, it appears that the argument is being put forward as a legitimate contribution to one type of dialogue, while under the surface, it is used as a deceptive tactic to contribute to a goal of a different type of dialogue. These cases tended to be ones where what is called a *dialectical shift* (Walton and Krabbe 1995) has occurred—that is, the argument in a given case was originally supposed to be part of a particular type of conversation (type of dialogue), but then as it proceeded, it came to be used as though it was part of a different type of dialogue. The fallacy involved a twisting around of the argument from need for help to serve a concealed or illicit purpose in the exchange, one that had the effect of tending to prevent or frustrate the other party from legitimately fulfilling his function in the type of dialogue that was really supposed to be taking place.

10. REVISING THE TEXTBOOKS

As Hamblin (1970) has indicated generally, the textbook treatments of fallacies have tended for a long time to be superficial, disorganized, and contradictory. In general, the area of fallacies has not been a subject of serious research—curiously, for it is fundamental to philosophy as a field, and to the academic enterprise of critical thinking generally.

However, now that a serious attempt to analyze the *ad misericordiam* fallacy has been undertaken, the textbooks will need to take this research into account.

If our analysis is correct, there are several leading assumptions in the textbook treatments of the *ad misericordiam* fallacy that need to be corrected. The first one is the idea that we can generally take it for granted that appeals to pity are fallacious. As noted in chapter 6, more care is needed not to make the logical leap from an ethical condemnation of pity to a conclusion that every appeal to pity in argument is fallacious. Awareness is needed of the gradation of negative connotations of the terms *pity, compassion*, and *sympathy*.

Also, we need to define *argumentum ad misericordiam* more clearly and less ambiguously. Does it mean *pity, compassion, sympathy, mercy*, or all of the above, or some subset of the above? Also, the key words—*pity, compassion*, and the like—need to be clearly defined. My recommendation is to offer the definitions given in chapter 3, using the system of nomenclature in Figure 3.1.

Another problem that needs to be cleared up in the textbook treatments is that they need to make the forms of arguments used more specific—for example, the argument from need to help, and the argument from distress. A proposal to solve this problem has been given in chapter 4.

Another idea that needs to be given up is the one that *ad misericordiam* is a fallacy only because it is a failure of relevance. The student's plea case, the Nayirah case, and other cases we have studied, show that this is not so. Sometimes the problem is one of irrelevance of the argument in a context of dialogue. But in even more cases the fallacy is a twisting around of the argument so it is used to put inappropriate pressure on a respondent, as revealed by a profile of dialogue.

Finally, the textbooks need to be aware that the job of evaluating cases of the use of the *ad misericordiam* is pragmatic, in the sense that the argument needs to be judged in relation to how it was used in context of dialogue. Part of the job is the assessment of how the requirements of the argumentation were met or not in the given case. But the other part of the job is how the argument was presented so that it is open to appropriate critical questioning. And generally, our assessment of an *argumentum ad misericordiam* in any given case needs to take into account the type of dialogue in which the argument was supposed to be used.

Notes

CHAPTER ONE

1. The *ad misericordiam* is treated as a distinct fallacy, in its own right, in roughly somewhat more than half of the logic textbooks that cover fallacies. In some textbooks, it gets only a line or two, while in a few it gets a couple of pages. Around half a page is very typical though, and this is its length of treatment in the two currently most popular introductory logic textbooks, Copi and Cohen (1990) and Hurley (1991).

2. The textbooks searched included all those (that could be identified as containing material on fallacies) at the University of Winnipeg Library, the University of Manitoba Library, and in the author's personal collection of logic textbooks (both historical and current). Most, but not all, that had something on *ad misericordiam* are mentioned in this chapter.

3. See the references to these individual works in Hamblin's bibliography.

4. *On Sophistical Refutations*, 166 b 23 and 167 a 20–35.

5. In Plato, there is a strong contrast drawn between the rational part of the soul and the spirited or appetitive parts, which are the places for the emotions.

6. The same remark applies to case 1.1.

7. See, for example, Copi (1982, pp. 103–4).

CHAPTER TWO

1. See below, section 2.

2. Hamblin (1970, pp. 159–61).

3. These questions of terminology and classification for different types of appeals to feeling are taken up in chapter 3.

4. See chapter 4, section 2.

5. This will turn out to be an important factor in the analysis of the *ad misericordiam* fallacy given in chapter 5, especially section 8, and chapter 6.

6. A translation of Gorgias's *Apology of Palamedes* is given in Seeskin (1987, pp. 155–61).

7. *On Sophistical Refutations*, 167 a 22–167 a 36.

8. See chapter 3, section 6, on the definition of sympathy.

9. Ibid.

10. This may not be too surprising, as Seneca made no systematic attempt to classify or analyze fallacies, in the way that Aristotle did.

11. The transition from Greek to Latin would therefore seem to be highly significant.

CHAPTER THREE

1. At least, this had been true in the past. Due to medical advances, there are now much better rates of survival for adults with muscular dystrophy.

2. These figures are disputed, however, by Bill Bolte, "Jerry's Got to Be Kidding," *Utne Reader*, March/April, 1993, 103–4:

> The annual Jerry Lewis Muscular Dystrophy Association Telethon raises more than $40 million dollars, while the MDA brings in a total of more than $100 million each year. Yet according to the MDA's 1991 annual report, only one MDA dollar in six goes to research awards, grants, and fellowships. Another sixth of MDA revenues goes to services purchased for the disabled. The remainder of donations go to overhead, including more than $31 million in salaries (MDA's executive director, Robert Ross, makes $284,808 and recently received a $30,000 increase), fringe benefits, and payroll taxes. Almost $9 million goes for "non-medical contract services and professional fees."

3. This could be called the us-them attitude that seems to be characteristic of pity appeals.

4. See Steven A. Holmes, "House Approves Bill Establishing Broad Rights for Disabled People," *New York Times*, May 23, 1990, p. A1 and A18.

5. Kurt F. Liedecker.

6. *De Clementia.*

7. Brinton (1993).

8. This aspect will turn out to be particularly important when I come to defining *sympathy* and contrasting it with pity, below.

9. Wispé (1986, p. 316).

10. Walton (1985).

11. Walton (1992b).

12. Walton (1990).

13. Walton (1989).

14. Walton (1992c).

15. Hamblin (1970, p. 162).

CHAPTER FOUR

1. Walton (1992a).

2. This case was reconstructed from notes from the author's experience of being on a university committee.

3. This aspect will later turn out to be of some importance—see section 7 below.

4. See section 5 below.

5. Walton (1989, chap. 7).

6. Van Eemeren and Grootendorst (1992).

7. Walton (1992c, chap. 2).

8. Lascher (1994).

9. May of 1994.

10. Walton (1992a, pp. 270–73).

11. Walton (1994).

CHAPTER FIVE

1. The author would like to thank Victor Wilkes for assistance in collecting data on the Nayirah case. Thanks are also due to Alan Brinton and

Michael Gilbert for critical comments and suggestions that proved to be very helpful.

2. As shown in chapter 2, Seneca thought that the wise person should not pity, but simply give help. Spinoza also claimed that pity involves some pain, as well as good, and is therefore to be overcome in a life dictated by reason (Runes 1984, p. 286).

3. This point is controversial, in the study of fallacies, however, as will be noted in section 10. Just because appeal to pity is generally taken in a negative way, as having connotations of some lapse or inappropriateness, it does not follow that appealing to pity is fallacious. To say that a fallacy has been committed is a special type of criticism implying a systematic type of fault in the structure of an argument. Thus not all lapses or improprieties are fallacies.

4. Walton (1992a, pp. 112–16).

5. Walton (1992a, pp. 265–73).

6. See also Walton (1992c) for discussions. Unfortunately, this slogan has often been interpreted in a misleading and unfavorable way that suggests a type of psychologism that has been criticized (Hamblin 1970; Walton 1992a; van Eemeren and Grootendorst 1992).

7. This question was suggested by Michael Gilbert.

8. As Alan Brinton noted (in correspondence), the concept of the tie-breaker or defining moment so important to the analysis of this case is related to the classical rhetorical notions of *kairos* (the timely) and *to prepon* (the fitting or proper). This case illustrates the importance of these notions for informal logic. Poulakos (1994), who discusses these notions of rhetorical timeliness in the Greek sophists, calls *kairoi* "opportune rhetorical moments" that an arguer can create or "capitalize on."

CHAPTER SIX

1. Walton (1995).

2. Walton (1992a).

3. Walton (1995).

4. See chapter 2, section 5.

5. Walton (1992c).

6. See chapter 2, section 6.

CHAPTER SEVEN

1. Walton (1975).

2. Ibid.

3. See chapter 5, section 6.

4. See chapter 2, section 3.

5. See also Walton (1992d).

6. See chapter 4, especially section 2.

7. See chapter 3, section 1.

8. See chapter 1.

Bibliography

Adler, Jonathan. "Reasonableness, Bias, and the Untapped Power of Procedure." *Synthese*, 94, 1993, 105–25.

Alford, C. Fred. "Greek Tragedy and Civilization: The Cultivation of Pity." *Political Research Quarterly*, 46, 1993, 259–90.

Alter, Jonathan. "Killing as a Cry for Help." *Newsweek*, November 20, 1993, 103–4.

Amnesty International. "Stop the Cries of Torture" [letter with enclosures], no date, signed "Paul Bentley," sent to author in 1994.

———. "Stop the Cries of Torture" [letter with enclosures], no date, signed "Roger Clark," sent to author in 1996.

Aquinas, Thomas. *Summa Contra Gentiles*, in *Basic Writings of Saint Thomas Aquinas*, vol. 2, ed. Anton C. Pegis. New York: Random House, 1945.

Ardal, Pal S. *Passion and Value in Hume's Treatise*. Edinburgh: Edinburgh University Press, 1966.

Aristotle. *Nicomachean Ethics (Ethica Nicomachea)*, trans. W. D. Ross, in *The Works of Aristotle*, ed. W. D. Ross. Oxford: Oxford University Press, 1915.

———. *On Sophistical Refutations*. Loeb Classical Library, trans. D. J. Furley, Cambridge, Mass.: Harvard University Press, 1928.

———. *Rhetoric*. Trans. John H. Freese, Loeb Library, Cambridge, Mass.: Harvard University Press, 1937.

Associated Press. "Supplementary Material from the New York Times News Service," *New York Times*, Sept. 5, 1978, p. 69.

Audi, Robert. *Practical Reasoning*. London: Routledge, 1989.

Austin, J. L. "A Plea for Excuses." *Proceedings of the Aristotelian Society*, 57, 1956–57, 1–30.

Azvedo, David. "Destroying the Sympathy Element in a Malpractice Trial." *Medical Economics*, 67, 1990, 102–8.

Baier, Annette C. *A Progress of Sentiments*. Cambridge, Mass.: Harvard University Press, 1991.

Barker, Stephen F. *The Elements of Logic*. New York: McGraw-Hill, 1965.

Barth, E. M., and Krabbe, E. C. W. *From Axiom to Dialogue: A Philosophical Study of Logics and Argumentation*. Berlin: Walter De Gruyter, 1982.

Basore, John W., trans. *Seneca: Moral Essays*, vol. 1, Loeb Classical Library. Cambridge, Mass.: Harvard University Press, 1928.

Bellet, Paul S., and Moloney, Michael J. "The Importance of Empathy as an Interviewing Skill in Medicine." *Journal of the American Medical Association*, 266, 1991, 1831–32.

Ben-Ze'ev, Aaron. "Envy and Pity." *International Philosophical Quarterly*, 33, 1993, 3–19.

Billinkoff, Arlene. "Pressure Forces Government to Reverse Stand on Burning." *Winnipeg Free Press*, October 17, 1992, A7.

Blyth, John W. *A Modern Introduction to Logic*. Boston: Houghton Mifflin, 1957.

Bonevac, Daniel. *The Art and Science of Logic*. Mountain View, Calif.: Mayfield Publishing Co., 1990.

Bragg, Rick. "U.S. Hearts Harden Against Homeless." (New York Times Service), *The Globe and Mail*, February 28, 1994, A11.

Brinton, Alan. "Pathos and the Appeal to Emotion: An Aristotelian Analysis." *History of Philosophy Quarterly*, 5, 1988, 207–19.

———. "A Plea for *Argumentum ad Misericordiam*." *Philosophia*, 23, 1994, 25–44.

Byerly, Henry C. *A Primer of Logic*. New York: Harper and Row, 1973.

Callahan, Sidney. "The Role of Emotion in Ethical Decisionmaking." *Hastings Center Report*, 18, 1988, 9–14.

Canadian Press. "Man's Behavior, 'Idiotic,' but Homeowner Must Pay." *The Globe and Mail*, February 2, 1994, A2.

Capaldi, Nicholas. *Hume's Place in Moral Philosophy*. New York: Peter Lang, 1992.

Carney, James D., and Scheer, Richard K. *Fundamentals of Logic*. New York: Macmillan, 1964.

Castell, Alburey. *A College Logic*. New York: Macmillan, 1935.

Cederblom, Jerry, and Paulsen, David W. *Critical Reasoning*. Belmont, Calif.: Wadsworth, 1982.

Chismar, Douglas. "Empathy and Sympathy: The Important Difference." *The Journal of Value Inquiry*, 22, 1988, 257–66.

Church, George J. "Sons and Murderers." *Time*, October 4, 1993, 68–69.

Cicero (Marcus T. Cicero). *Brutus*. Trans. G. L. Hendrickson, Loeb Classical Library. Cambridge, Mass.: Harvard University Press, 1952.

——— . *Pro Flacco*. Trans. Louis E. Lord, Loeb Classical Library. Cambridge, Mass.: Harvard University Press, 1947.

Clark, Romane, and Welsh, Paul. *Introduction to Logic*. Princeton, N.J.: J. van Nostrand, 1962.

Clarke, D. S. Jr. *Practical Inferences*. London: Routledge, 1985.

Clarke, Richard F. *Logic*. London: Longmans Green, 1921.

Clinton, William Jefferson. Address Before Joint Session of Congress, "Health Security for All Americans." Office of the Press Secretary [transcript], September 22, 1993, 12 pages.

Cooper, Craig. "Supplication in Greek Oratory." Unpublished paper, 1994.

Copi, Irving M. *Introduction to Logic*, 2nd ed. New York: Macmillan, 1961 [6th ed., 1982; 8th ed., with Carl Cohen, 1990; 9th ed., 1994].

Cox, Kevin. "The Seal Hunt: Guns and Roses." *The Globe and Mail*. March 12, 1994, D1–D2.

Creighton, James Edwin. *An Introductory Logic*. New York: Macmillan, 1929.

Crossley, David J., and Wilson, Peter A. *How to Argue: An Introduction to Logical Thinking*. New York: Random House, 1979.

Cuff, John Haslett. "Avoiding the Hard Questions." *The Globe and Mail*, March 14, 1996, A12.

Damer, T. Edward. *Attacking Faulty Reasoning*. Belmont, Calif.: Wadsworth, 1980.

Damasio, Antonio R. *Descartes' Error: Emotion, Reason, and the Human Brain*. New York: Grosset /Putnam, 1994.

Darwall, Stephen L. "Hutcheson, Francis." *Encyclopedia of Ethics*, vol. 2, ed. Lawrence C. Becker and Charlotte B. Becker. New York: Garland, 580–82.

Degnan, Ronan E. "Evidence." *Encyclopaedia Britannica*, 15th ed., vol. 8, 1973, 905–16.

Del Valle, Christina. "Some of Jerry's Kids are Mad at the Old Man." *Business Week*, Sept. 14, 1992, p. 36.

Engel, S. Morris. *With Good Reason: An Introduction to Informal Fallacies*. New York: St. Martin's Press, 1982.

Facts on File. *1992 Index*, vol. 52, #2669. January 16, 1992, 31–32.

Fearnside, W. Ward. *About Thinking*. Englewood Cliffs, N.J.: Prentice-Hall, 1980.

Fearnside, W. Ward, and Holther, William B. *Fallacy: The Counterfeit of Argument*. Englewood Cliffs, N.J.: Prentice-Hall, 1959.

Fletcher, Agnes. "Piss on Pity." *New Statesman*, July 24, 1992, p. 22.

Freeman, James B. *Thinking Logically*. Englewood Cliffs, N.J.: Prentice-Hall, 1988.

Frye, Albert M., and Levi, Albert W. *Rational Belief: An Introduction to Logic*. New York: Greenwood Press, 1969.

Gill, Carol. "Telethon Trick." *Mainstream*, 17 (August), 1993, 27–31.

Glare, P. G. W. ed. *Oxford Latin Dictionary*. Oxford: Clarendon Press, 1982.

Green, Michael. "Nietzsche on Pity and Ressentiment." *International Studies in Philosophy*, 24, 1992, 63–70.

Grice, H. Paul. "Logic and Conversation." *The Logic of Grammar*. Ed. Donald Davidson and Gilbert Harman. Encino, Calif.: Dickenson, 1975, 64–75.

Hamblin, Charles L. *Fallacies*. London: Methuen, 1970 [reprinted by Vale Press, Newport News, Virginia, 1986 and 1993].

Hands, A. R. *Charities and Social Aid in Greece and Rome*. Ithaca: Cornell University Press, 1968.

Harrison, Frank R. *Logic and Rational Thought*. St. Paul: West Publishing Co., 1992.

Hart, H. L. A. *Punishment and Responsibility: Essays in the Philosophy of Law*. Oxford: Clarendon Press, 1968.

Hess, Henry. "Even Experts Hoodwinked." *The Globe and Mail*, March 19, 1994, A4.

Hume, David. *A Treatise of Human Nature* (1888), ed. L. A. Selby-Bigge. Oxford: Clarendon Press, 1965.

Hurley, Patrick J. *A Concise Introduction to Logic*, 4th ed. Belmont: Calif.: Wadsworth, 1991.

Inwood, Brad. *Ethics and Human Action in Early Stoicism*. Oxford: Clarendon Press, 1985.

Johnson, Mary. "Jerry's Kids." *The Nation*, Sept. 14, 1992, 232–33.

Joseph, H. W. B. *An Introduction to Logic*. 2nd ed. Oxford: Clarendon Press, 1916 [first edition, 1906].

Kahane, Howard. *Logic and Philosophy*. Belmont, Calif.: Wadsworth, 1969.

Kaminsky, Jack, and Kaminsky, Alice. *Logic: A Philosophical Introduction*. Reading, Mass.: Addison-Wesley, 1974.

Kaplan, David A., and Foote, Donna. "The Menendez Brothers Run Out of Excuses." *Newsweek*, April 1, 1996, 64.

Kemp, Evan, Jr. "Aiding the Disabled: No Pity Please." *New York Times*, Sept. 3, 1981, A19.

Kilgore, William J. *An Introductory Logic*. New York: Holt, Rinehart and Winston, 1968.

Knoll, Erwin. "Too Far Ahead." *The Progressive*, 56, April 1992, 4.

Koring, Paul. "For Whom the Aid Flows." *The Globe and Mail*, Dec. 21, 1993, A1.

Kozy, John, Jr., *Understanding Natural Deduction*. Encino, Calif.: Dickenson, 1974.

Kraye, Jill. "Moral Philosophy." *The Cambridge History of Renaissance Philosophy*, ed. Charles B. Schmitt. Cambridge: Cambridge University Press, 1988, 301–86.

Kreyche, Robert J. *Logic for Undergraduates*. New York: Holt, Rinehart and Winston, 1970.

Lambert, Karel, and Ulrich, William. *The Nature of Argument*. New York: Macmillan, 1980.

Lascher, Edward L. "Assessing Legislative Deliberation." Faculty Research Working Paper Series, John F. Kennedy School of Government, Harvard University, 1994.

Leo, John. "Spicing up the (Ho-Hum) Truth." *U.S. News and World Report*, March 8, 1993, 24.

———. "Watching as the Jury Turns." *U.S. News and World Report*, February 14, 1994.

Lewis, Jerry. "If I Had Muscular Dystrophy." *Parade*, September 2, 1990, 4–5.

Lewis, Charlton T., and Short, Charles, eds. *A Latin Dictionary*. Oxford: Clarendon Press, 1907.

Lewis, Thomas. "Identifying Rhetoric in the *Apology*: Does Socrates Use the Appeal for Pity." *Interpretation*, 21, 1993, 105–14.

Lindgren, J. Ralph. "Smith, Adam." *Encyclopedia of Ethics*, vol. 2, ed. Lawrence C. Becker and Charlotte B. Becker. New York: Garland Publishing, 1992, 1160–63.

Little, Winston W., Wilson, W. Harold, and Moore, W. Edgar. *Applied Logic*. Boston: Houghton Mifflin, 1955.

Locke, John. *An Essay Concerning Human Understanding* (1690), ed. John W. Yolton. London: Dent, 1961.

Lofberg, John O. *Sycophancy in Athens*. Chicago: Ares, 1976.

MacArthur, John R. *Second Front: Censorship and Propaganda in the Gulf War*. New York: Hill and Wang, 1992.

MacKenzie, Colin. "White House Welcomes Exiled Kuwaiti Leader," *The Globe and Mail*, September 29, 1990, A10.

Mackenzie, J. D. "The Dialectics of Logic," *Logique et Analyse*, 24, 1981, 159–77.

Manicas, Peter T., and Kruger, Arthur N. *Essentials of Logic*. New York: American Book Company, 1968.

Marjoribanks, Edward. *The Life of Sir Edward Marshall Hall*. London: Victor Gollancz, 1929.

Marks, Isaac. "Feeling the Way Forward," *The Times Higher Education Supplement*. January 14, 1994, p. 19.

Matas, Robert T. "A Taxing Problem for Revenue Canada," *The Globe and Mail*. December 2, 1994, A11.

Mercer, Philip. *Sympathy and Ethics.* Oxford: Clarendon Press, 1972.

Michalos, Alex C. *Principles of Logic.* Englewood Cliffs, N.J.: Prentice-Hall, 1969.

———. *Improving Your Reasoning.* Englewood Cliffs, N.J.: Prentice-Hall, 1970.

Milam, Lorenzo W. "Jerry's Kids: That's Us," *Mainstream,* August 1993, 23–25.

Mooney, Edward F. "Sympathy." *The Encyclopedia of Ethics,* vol. 2, ed. Lawrence C. Becker and Charlotte B. Becker. New York and London: Garland, 1992, 1222–25.

Moore, W. Edgar. *Creative and Critical Thinking.* Boston: Houghton Mifflin, 1967.

Munson, Ronald. *The Way of Words.* Boston: Houghton Mifflin, 1976.

Mydans, Seth. "Stories of Sexual Abuse Transform Murder Trial." *New York Times,* September 12, 1993a, 30.

———. "Focus of Trial Shifts to a Tape." *New York Times,* November 7, 1993b, 34.

———. "Killers as Victims: Defending the Menendez Brothers." *New York Times,* November 19, 1993c, A30.

———. "After 5 Months of Drama, Brothers' Trials Near End." *New York Times,* December 12, 1993d, 26.

———. "In Brothers' Lurid Trial, One Woman Dominates." *New York Times,* December 20, 1993.

New York Times National. "Jerry Lewis Criticized Over Telethon's Approach." *The New York Times National,* Sept. 6, 1992, p. 39.

Nussbaum, Martha. *Love's Knowledge: Essays on Philosophy and Literature.* New York: Oxford University Press, 1990.

Perry, Ben Edwin, trans. and ed. *Babrius and Phaedrus.* Cambridge, Mass.: Harvard University Press, 1925.

Peters, F. E. *Greek Historical Terms.* New York: New York University Press, 1967.

Piper, Adrian S. "Impartiality, Compassion, and Modal Imagination." *Ethics,* 1991, 726–57.

Plato. *Apology,* in *The Trial and Death of Socrates,* trans. G. M. A. Grube. Indianapolis: Hackett, 1975.

Post, Edward. *Aristotle on Fallacies or the Sophistici Elenchi*. London: Macmillan, 1866. Reprinted by Garland Publishing, New York, 1987.

Poulakos, John. "The Logic of Greek Sophistry," in Douglas Walton and Alan Brinton (eds.), *Readings on the History of Informal Logic*. To appear, 1994.

Quintilian (M. F. Quintilianus). *Institutio Oratoria*. Loeb Classical Library, trans. H. E. Butler. London: William Heinemann, 1916.

Rainbolt, George W. "Mercy: An Independent, Imperfect Virtue." *American Philosophical Quarterly*, 27, 1990, 169–73.

Rainold, John. *John Rainold's Oxford Lectures on Aristotle's Rhetoric* [1587], ed. and trans. Lawrence D. Green. Newark: University of Delaware Press, 1986.

Register-Dispatch, Beckley, West Virginia (editorial). "In the Business of Subsidizing Stupidity?" *The Globe and Mail*, November 11, 1993, A21.

Reinhold, Robert. "Real Life Produces Plot Fit for Movie." *New York Times*, March 14, 1990, A20.

Rescher, Nicholas. *Introduction to Logic*. New York: St. Martin's Press, 1964.

———. *Unselfishness*. Pittsburgh: University of Pittsburgh Press, 1975.

Reuters News Agency. "Patients Killed, Kuwaitis Say." *The Globe and Mail*, September 7, 1990, A14.

———. "Iraqi Atrocities Cited by Amnesty." *The Globe and Mail*, December 19, 1990a, A1–A2.

Rossetti, Livio. "The Rhetoric of Socrates." *Philosophy and Rhetoric*, 22, 1989, 225–38.

Rowse, Arthur E. "Flacking for the Emir." *The Progressive*, 55, 1991, 20–22.

———. "How to Build Support for War." *Columbia Journalism Review*, 31, 1992, 28–29.

Rowse, Ted. "Kuwaitgate." *The Washington Monthly*, 24, September, 1992a, 16–18.

Runes, Dagobert D. *Dictionary of Philosophy*. Totowa, N.J.: Rowman and Allanheld, 1984.

Runkle, Gerald. *Good Thinking: An Introduction to Logic*. New York: Holt, Rinehart and Winston, 1978.

Salholz, Eloise, Beachy, Lucille, and Rosenberg, Debra. "The Empathy Factor." *Newsweek*, January 13, 1992, 23.

Scheler, Max. *The Nature of Sympathy*. Trans. Peter Heath. London: Routledge and Kegan Paul, 1954.

Schopenhauer, Arthur. *The World as Will and Idea* (1818). Trans. R. B. Haldane and J. Kemp. Garden City, N.Y.: Doubleday, 1961.

Seeskin, Kenneth. *Dialogue and Discovery*. Albany: State University of New York Press, 1987.

Seneca, Lucius Annaeus. (55–56 A.D.). *On Mercy*, in *Seneca: Moral Essays*, vol. 1. Trans. John W. Basore. Loeb Classical Library, Cambridge, Mass.: Harvard University Press, 1928.

Shapiro, Joseph P. "Disabling Jerry's Kids." *U.S. News and World Report*, Sept. 14, 1992, 39–40.

——— . *No Pity: How the Disability Rights Movement is Changing America*. New York: Times Books, 1993.

Shepard, Scott. "Atrocities Ravage Kuwait as Time is Running Out." Cox News Service, *Winnipeg Free Press*, October 11, 1990, pp. 1 and 4.

Simpson, J. A., and Weiner, E. S. C. *The Oxford English Dictionary*, vol. 1, 2nd ed. Oxford: Clarendon Press, 1989.

60 Minutes. January 19, 1992. *CBS News Transcript*, vol. 24, no. 18, "Nayirah," pp. 7–12.

Smith, Adam. *The Theory of Moral Sentiments* (1759), in *British Moralists*, ed. L. A. Selby-Bigge. New York: Bobbs-Merrill, 1964.

Smith, Holly M. "Excuses." *Encyclopedia of Ethics*, vol. 1. Ed. Lawrence C. Becker and Charlotte B. Becker. New York: Garland, 1992, pp. 344–46.

Snow, Nancy E. "Compassion." *American Philosophical Quarterly*, 28, 1991, 195–205.

Special to the *New York Times*. "Hubert Humphrey Among Nine Honored for Public Service," June 28, 1978, A16.

——— . September 1, 1993, A17.

Soccio, Douglas J., and Barry, Vincent E. *Practical Logic*. Fort Worth: Harcourt Brace Jovanovich, 1992.

Spinoza, Benedict de. *Ethics* (1675). Ed. James Gutman. New York: Hafner Publishing Co., 1949.

Stanford, W. B. *Greek Tragedy and the Emotions.* London: Routledge and
    Kegan Paul, 1983.

Stevens, Edward B. "Some Attic Commonplaces of Pity." *American Journal
    of Philology,* 65, 1944, 1–25.

Striker, Gisela. "Stoicism," vol. 2, *Encyclopedia of Ethics.* Ed. Lawrence C.
    Becker and Charlotte B. Becker. New York and London: Garland
    Publishing, 1992, 1208–13.

Thackeray, William Makepeace. "Thorns in the Cushion." *The Cornhill
    Magazine,* vol. 2, July to December, 1860, 122–28.

Toulmin, Stephen, Rieke, Richard, and Janik, Allan. *An Introduction to
    Reasoning.* New York: Macmillan, 1979.

van Eemeren, Frans H., and Grootendorst, Rob. "Fallacies in Pragma-dialec-
    tical Perspective." *Argumentation,* 1, 1987, 283–301.

——— . *Argumentation, Communication and Fallacies.* Hillsdale, N.J.:
    Erlbaum, 1992.

Vernon, Thomas S., and Nissen, Lowell. A. *Reflective Thinking: The
    Fundamentals of Logic.* Belmont, Calif.: Wadsworth, 1968.

Vicksburg (Miss.) Evening Post. (Editorial, Dec. 5, 1993). "Making a Mugger
    a Millionaire." *The Globe and Mail,* Dec. 21, 1993, A19.

Waller, Bruce N. *Critical Thinking.* Englewood Cliffs, N.J.: Prentice-Hall,
    1988.

Walton, Douglas N. "Philosophical Perspectives on the Insanity Defense."
    The Human Context, 7, 1975, 546–60.

——— . *Arguer's Position.* Westport, Conn.: Greenwood Press, 1985.

——— . *Informal Logic.* Cambridge: Cambridge University Press, 1989.

——— . *Question-Reply Argumentation.* New York: Greenwood Press, 1989.

——— . *Begging the Question.* New York: Greenwood Press, 1990a.

——— . *Practical Reasoning.* Savage, Md.: Rowman and Littlefield, 1990b.

——— . "Bias, Critical Doubt, and Fallacies." *Argumentation and Advocacy,*
    28, 1991, 1–22.

——— . *The Place of Emotion in Argument.* University Park: Pennsylvania
    State University Press, 1992a.

——— . *Slippery Slope Arguments.* Oxford: Clarendon Press, 1992b.

———— . *Plausible Argument in Everyday Conversation.* Albany: State University of New York Press, 1992c.

———— . "Types of Dialogue, Dialectical Shifts and Fallacies," in *Argumentation Illuminated.* Ed. Frans H. van Eemeren, Rob Grootendorst, J. Anthony Blair, and Charles A. Willard. Amsterdam: SICSAT, 1992, 133–47.

———— . *A Pragmatic Theory of Fallacy.* Tuscaloosa: University of Alabama Press, 1995.

Walton, Douglas N., and Krabbe, Erik C. W. *Commitment in Dialogue.* Albany: State University of New York Press, 1995.

Ward, Olivia. "Kuwaitis Tell U.N. of Iraqi Atrocities." *The Toronto Star,* November 28, 1990, p. A2.

Watts, Isaac. *Logick.* London: John Clark and Richard Hett, 1725.

Weddle, Perry. *Argument: A Guide to Critical Thinking.* New York: McGraw-Hill, 1978.

Werkmeister, W. H. *An Introduction to Critical Thinking.* Lincoln, Nebr.: Johnson Publishing Co., 1948.

Whately, Richard. *Elements of Logic.* London: Longmans Green, 1870.

Wispé, Lauren. "The Distinction Between Sympathy and Empathy." *Journal of Personality and Social Psychology,* 50, 1986, 314–21.

Yanal, Robert J. *Basic Logic.* St. Paul: West Publishing Co., 1988.

Zeller, Edward. *Outlines of the History of Greek Philosophy.* New York: Longmans, Green & Co., 1901.

Zuckerman, Morton B. "The Blind Eye of Television." *U.S. News and World Report,* January 18, 1993, 84.

Index